BREAK

THE

CASTE

A NOTE ABOUT THIS BOOK

This book was completed in the summer of 2020 as George Gerharz watched with hope as the world reacted and took action in response to the brutal murder of George Floyd. This book focuses on the caste of class but acknowledges the caste of race and the horrible legacy of enslaving Africans and their descendants. Gerharz's last edits were complete in July, 2020 and he died of mesothelioma in August, 2020. The few edits made since then were minor.

-Editors

ACKNOWLEDGEMENTS

Special thanks to Larry McDonald, Jerry Gilbert and Joe Schlangen for their review of early drafts and to Joe for his careful review of the final document. Their input was extremely helpful.

-George Gerharz

Designed by Kevin Stone

www.gcpress.com

BREAK

THE

CASTE

INEQUALITY, IMMOBILITY, AND POVERTY IN AMERICA
AND HOW WE CAN CHANGE IT

GEORGE GERHARZ

TABLE OF CONTENTS

PREFACE

America has not achieved its goal of opportunity for all. I know that "equal" opportunity for all is not, nor will it ever be, a reality. All do not start from the same place, biologically or socially. A person with severely diminished intellectual abilities will not be an A student. A person born in a very poor neighborhood does not have the advantages as one growing up in an affluent suburb.

P.J. O'Rourke noted:

> Yes, it's upsetting that some people have so much while other people have so little. It isn't fair. But I accept this unfairness. Indeed, I treasure it.
>
> That's because I have a 13-year-old daughter. And that's all I hear, "That's not fair, " she says. " That's not fair! That's not fair!" And one day I snapped, and I said, "Honey, you're cute, that's not fair. Your family is pretty well off, that's not fair. You were born in America, that's not fair. Darling, you had better get down on your knees and pray that things don't start getting fair for you."[1]

I share to a large degree Mr. O'Rourke's analysis of life in contemporary America but do not accept the current situation nor pray to maintain it. Opportunity can be expanded; inequality decreased, social and economic mobility enhanced, and poverty reduced.

The data and my experience led me to two assumptions evident throughout this book: social change must occur and individuals must assume responsibility for their own lives. Social patterns in America contribute to inequality, immobility and poverty. At the same time, regardless of social structures, individuals must assume responsibility for their lives and their future. An either-or approach is inadequate. Individuals live and operate in a social order, an order that shapes and molds their behavior, but they must operate responsibly in this order.

Using this approach entails examining information in a wide range of academic fields, e.g. psychology, sociology, political science, economics, and history. No single academic discipline can provide all the data and the answers. Data and theoretical frameworks from all are included here and are referenced. To the extent possible, the sources used are those that can be easily accessed by the reader.

Throughout I have tried to follow the dicta of Bamergee and Dufflo:[2]

- **Don't be seduced by the obvious**
- **Be skeptical of promised miracles, the simplistic "silver bullets"**
- **Accept the complexity of major issues**
- **Be honest about what is known, what is still unknown, and what may never be known.**

Notes

(1) P. J. O'Rourke: Fairness, Idealism and Other Atrocities, La Times, May 4, 2008 http://articles.latimes.com/2008/may/04/opinion/op-orourke4

(2) Abhijit Bamerjee and Esther Duflo, Good Economics for Hard times, New York: Simon and Schuster, 2019.

INTRODUCTION

Income and wealth inequality, social mobility, and poverty are fundamental societal issues. Especially during the past twenty years, these topics and their interrelationships have been, and continue to be, foci of major policy discussions and disagreements. Some see the current patterns of inequality, mobility, and poverty (IMP) as givens; others see a need for changes in these patterns. Americans as a whole are supportive of greater equality and economic mobility for all—especially upward mobility—and decreasing poverty. This book seeks to identify ways to achieve these aspirations.

The persistent patterns that affect inequalities, mobility rates, and poverty (IMP) are embedded in America's social order. What causes these patterns? Some place primary responsibility on individual attitudes and actions. Others identify structural barriers that make individual advancement difficult, if not impossible. These two positions are often placed in opposition to each other. A brief overview of these two positions helps frame the discussion that follows.

Those who focus on individual actions and behaviors trace IMP back to individuals and what they do. They see the failure of individuals to adhere to core American values such as protecting marriage, industriousness, honesty and religiosity, and individuals' failure to apply themselves as the fundamental cause of inequality, lack of mobility, and poverty. Those with stronger values who apply themselves succeed. All individuals can work their way out of poverty, obtain additional income, and climb the economic ladder. They cite numerous examples of individuals who grew up in poverty and disadvantaged circumstance, improved their situations, and became successful. Single mothers support and raise a family while going to college. Individuals start businesses with little or no money and their companies are now included in the Fortune 500.

Those who identify social structures as the major causes of IMP point out that patterns of inequality, mobility, and poverty are caused by social structures or barriers that inhibit individuals from achievement. Persistent patterns are found throughout America. These patterns negatively impact an individual's ability to succeed.

In truth, both social structures and personal behavior are important. Individuals live in a particular social order. Personal actions take place in a social context of families, local communities, and the broader society. Individuals live and act in a social context. The social order of a given society has a significant impact on the inequalities among the society's members, if and how individuals move up and down the social order, and if and what kinds of poverty exist in that society. This social context can be supportive, neutral, or damaging in reducing inequality, increasing mobility, and reducing poverty. At the same time, every individual has to assume responsibility for success. This book seeks to identify those changes in America's social order that can reduce IMP and, at the same time, points out the critical need for individual responsibility.

The overall premise of this book is that IMP in America is due to persistent patterns within America's social order. The first section (Part I. A) begins with a review of the basic concepts of human needs and the necessity of a social order to meet these needs. Power, the basis of social order, is then reviewed. How power maintains the social order, transmitting the order to members of society through socialization, and forming the identities of the members of particular societies concludes this review. The intent of this section is to provide a basic understanding of the central elements underlying America's social order.

With a basic understanding of social order, the core and unique elements of America's social order are then reviewed. (Part I B.) The ideological, economic, political, military/police, and the voluntary/religious sectors of America's social order and their powers are addressed separately and their joint impact discussed. Multiple powers operate in each of these sectors. Individually and jointly, they maintain America's existing social order.

After establishing the social order context of IMP in America, America's inequality, mobility, and poverty patterns are separately presented as part of America's social order. (Part II) The analysis for each begins with a review of perceptions, an often-neglected but important source of information—especially if changes are to be proposed. The current status of IMP is described, with special attention to the period 1970 to 2020. The various forms of inequality in America are reviewed, ranging from income and wealth inequality to other forms of unequal status. Mobility is reviewed, including identification of the different forms of mobility, and, for some Americans, the lack of mobility. Poverty is examined, with special attention to various types of poverty. After reviewing each separately, their connections are discussed.

After the discussion of IMP, causes are identified with an eye to identifying possible solutions. Major causes of IMP are identified and grouped in to five key categories: wealth concentration, ascribed status (race, sex, citizenship), skill gaps, lack of responsibility, and luck. Each of the causes and its elements is discussed individually. In conclusion, their interrelationship is considered.

Using identified causes as a framework, a variety of changes are proposed. (Part III) Prior to proposing specific changes, a brief introduction explores social change. Broad general goals are offered: enhanced fairness, opportunity, merit and personal responsibility.

General change strategies are offered:

- Decrease concentration of income and wealth
- Decrease discrimination
- Equalize skill/educational levels
- Increase individual responsibility

In each of these strategic areas, a number of specific changes are suggested. The book ends with some concluding comments that summarize these findings and recommendations. (Part IV)

PART I: HUMAN NEEDS AND SOCIAL ORDER

- **Social:** *Humans need to love and be loved. People need to feel a sense of belonging and connection, a sense of acceptance, and affiliation with others (for example, membership in families, community groups, and churches).*

- **Esteem/Recognition:** *Humans need to be appreciated, respected, and recognized for their competence and personal qualities.*

- **Self-Actualization/Achievement:** *Humans need a positive sense of self through developing and using their talents, potentials, and capabilities.*

- **Cognitive:** *Humans need to explore, discover, gain knowledge and understanding, and know the true and the good.*

- **Procreative:** *Human society needs humans to reproduce for society to continue.*

Extensive research provides almost no support for organizing these needs into a hierarchy where, for example, physiological needs must be met before security needs are met, before social needs are met, and so on. Human needs are present at all times and all need to be met in varying degrees.[2]

A look at these basic human needs in the context of life in America provides more concrete detail.

PHYSIOLOGICAL NEEDS

Throughout the US, various types of food are available and can be obtained in multiple ways, including through grocery stores, restaurants, and food pantries. Shelter in the US, in addition to the physical structure of a house or apartment, includes utilities for light, heating, and the operation of home appliances, such as refrigerators, clothes washers and dryers, and air conditioners. A variety of types of dwelling are available for individuals, families, or households. Residents can rent or own the dwelling in which they live. Water is provided in most cases through a public or private water company. Linked to water provision is waste disposal, usually through a sewage system. While air is available throughout the world, the air quality in the US is monitored and actions are taken to address harmful air quality conditions.

SAFETY AND SECURITY

Within the home, security is offered by adult family members. It is assumed that parents provide safety and security for their children. If parents fail to provide safety and security for their children, a system of child protection is in place to take over from parents and assure the children's safety and security.

Outside of the family, US security systems address the whole range of external and internal threats. Armed forces protect the country from threats and incursion by other countries. The armed forces are supported by a number of "intelligence" agencies that monitor and inform of potential threats. Our borders are patrolled by federal officers who have the power to stop those who seek to enter, and to apprehend and expel those that enter illegally. Internal to the country a wide variety of investigative and policing jurisdictions are organized to protect people and property. Sworn officers are authorized to stop those who are attempting to take property inappropriately or cause harm to individuals. A judicial system takes action to punish those who commit crimes against persons or property.

SOCIAL NEEDS

Americans meet their social needs by connecting to others in a wide variety of ways. The family and its members are starting points for social interaction, but many other groups can meet an individual's social needs. The workplace is a common place of social interaction. Other organizations offer options ranging from neighborhood places to convene, such as bars and parks, to more organized groups that focus on a wide range of social needs and/or political purposes. Most Americans join churches. Many local organizations are part of state or national groups, extending an individual's set of relationships in these groups to national or even international scope.

ESTEEM/RECOGNITION

A person gains self-esteem and recognition from and within their various groups. Individuals are recognized and appreciated. In groups, individuals can see themselves as valued and contributing. In the workplace, in clubs, and in churches, individuals receive recognition and take pride in doing a good job, participating in community events, donating to a church, or helping elect a candidate. They are able to see themselves as good, special, or important. They feel worthwhile.

SELF-ACTUALIZATION/ACHIEVEMENT

As part of a group or as an individual, Americans see themselves as having been successful in a variety of arenas. They have been able to reach goals that they have set for themselves: for example, being a good father, a skilled welder, an effective teacher, a valued volunteer. They have made something of themselves.

COGNITIVE

Americans fulfill their need to understand using a wide range of verbal, written, and electronic information sources. Information ranges from the most specific to the most general, from practical to abstract, religious, and metaphysical. Individuals can take advantage of this wealth of available information to fulfill their need to know and understand.

PROCREATIVE

America needs to continue its society. All of the needs noted above need to be sustained for the members of a society, especially as they age. New children are needed to take on a variety of roles to meet the wide range of human needs, desires, and goals of American citizens and residents.

To meet needs and achieve goals, individuals follow broad sets of rules and expectations. These rules and expectations provide required or desired ways of acting at the family level and in other communities. Each individual takes up her or his position to maintain and create a social order. For example, children obey parents, cross the street at the corner, don't take other people's property, don't hurt others. Adults earn money, pay bills, and nurture their children, caring for their children's health and safety and promoting their development. This order does not occur all the time, but it happens in most cases and when it does not, deviance is recognized and, most often, corrective action is.

The wide array of human needs and goals is met by various groups and in various ways. Different groups meet different needs. The larger society in its entirety enables individuals to meet the full range of their human needs and achieve goals. The continuation of a society depends on its ability to continually meet the needs for the vast majority of its citizens. A society has an ideology. It proclaims values and promotes symbols to foster belonging, create aspirations, and provide a sense of pride and self-worth. A society has an economy that not only provides for the basic needs noted above but also can meet other needs, for example, esteem and self-actualization. A society establishes customs, laws and rules to be followed and puts mechanisms in place to direct actions.

The social order meets the needs of the individuals belonging to it.

Notes

(1) This general discussion on human needs and goals relies upon and summarizes a number of discussions of human needs including:

Fallatah, Rodwan Hashim Mohammed, and Jawad Syed. "A Critical Review of Maslow's Hierarchy of Needs." SpringerLink. Palgrave Macmillan, Cham, January 1, 1970. https://link.springer.com/chapter/10.1007/978-3-319-67741-5_2.

Pandan, Written by Deomar, 2020 Updated October 19, and First published 7 years ago. "6 Types of Human Needs." COSMONS, October 19, 2020. https://cosmons.com/spirituality/spirituality-and-health/maslow-hierarchy-needs/.

"Hierarchy of Needs: The Five Levels of Maslow's Hierarchy of Needs." Awaken, February 7, 2021. http://www.awaken.com/2015/12/hierarchy-of-needs-the-five-levels-of-maslows-hierarchy-of-needs/.

Some approach the issue of human needs from the perspective of human goals. See for example:

Chulef, Ada & Read, Stephen & Walsh, David. (2001). A Hierarchical Taxonomy of Human Goals. Motivation and Emotion. 25. 191-232. 10.1023/A:1012225223418.

"List of Common Human Goals." LessWrong. Accessed February 7, 2021. https://www.lesswrong.com/posts/ZJJH45J6eF2JCSQhW/list-of-common-human-goals.

"News Flash." Common Goals For All Humans. Accessed February 7, 2021. https://www.rc.org/publication/ftg/readings/pt58_29_hj.

(2) See for example, op. cit., Critical Review of Maslow's Hierarchy of Needs

SOCIAL ORDER AND SOCIAL POWERS WORKING TO MAINTAIN ORDER

A community without power is chaos. Chaos is not merely the absence of power but the absence of political power and political rights is merely the absence of order. —Mehdi Shokri [1]

A social order is required for people to continously live together. Social order is:

the way in which the various components of society—social structures and institutions, social relations, social interactions and behavior, and cultural features such as norms, beliefs, and values—work together to maintain the status quo. [2]

Patterns of human interaction are conserved, maintained, and enforced.

"Social order is not a given but historically developed ideas, beliefs, and patterns of conduct and of feeling which each culture has evolved as the guides to human conduct and the management of group activities." [3]

Laws and numerous other factors maintain social order. (4) Social order provides groups of people with consistent rules for interaction that allow them to live together on a continuous basis and meet their human needs. Examples from everyday life illustrate the presence and importance of social order.

When we walk out of our homes, we see cars roll by on streets which federal, state, or local governments have laid out and constructed in patterns. In the US, cars drive on the right side of the street, following the "rules of the road." The cars have license plates required by the state. The gas that fuels the cars comes from pumps that have been inspected according to standards by set by the state.

We say hello to neighbors. They have property that is theirs that we cannot claim or even enter unless invited in. At the same time, these neighbors cannot take my property. If I tell them to leave my home, they must do so. It is expected that the neighbors will not harm us. If they attempt to do so we can call police who will come in their uniforms and marked vehicles, enforce the law, and protect us, using the powers established by law. A portion of our taxes are used to support the police.

A variety of powers are operating to maintain this order. Without these powers there would be no roads, no rules of the road, no assurance of the car's safety, engines fouled by "bad gas," people coming in and out of my house, no public recourse for my safety, no one to call on when the established rules are broken.

At root, social power is an ability to achieve something. For example, police have police powers, spelled out in a variety of laws and regulations. The traffic stop, the pulling over of an intoxicated driver, and the apprehension of a fugitive are all manifestations of this power. Their power gives police the ability to act and acceptance of their actions. The laws have power over us. We know and feel that the rules must be followed and if not followed, the consequences must be accepted.

Social order does not just happen. It is the result of powers working in and through societies and their components. Social powers work to meet the human needs of its members in an orderly fashion. These powers are established and maintained through a variety of socialization processes that create and maintain identities that operate in the social order. (Identity and socialization and how power shapes them is discussed in detail below.)

SOCIAL ORDER AND SOCIAL POWERS WORKING TO MAINTAIN ORDER

Social powers are continually at work to maintain social order. In simplest form:

Social power is the capacity to influence others.[5]

The University of Hawaii's "The Fundamental Nature of Power" adds:

> "... the essence of social power should be parallel: *social power is a capacity to produce effects through another self.* [6]

Power can be exerted because individuals need things they cannot obtain on their own. Other humans are required so individuals can meet needs and achieve goals. Social power is found in relationships between people.

Social power in itself is neither good nor evil.[7] Having power is neither good nor evil. Exercising power, however, can result in good or evil actions. The determination of whether power is good or evil is based upon both intent and the outcome of its use. As Richard Stuart Dixon states in Quora:

> "Power" is morally neutral. To "have power" in a given situation simply means to have enough deployable resources to influence outcomes in that situation. The exercise of power is not morally neutral because it requires, either consciously or unconsciously, a process of evaluation, choice, and deployment. Power is neither good nor bad, but the exercise of power results in varying proportions of helpfulness (good) and harmfulness (bad). (8)

By being born into and belonging to a society, an individual cedes power to society in numerous areas of her or his life, often not consciously, especially in her or his early years. (9) The individual accepts the implied tradeoff (again probably not consciously) believing society able to meet the individual's needs.[10]

The exercise of power is influence or control. Influence in most cases is not physical, although threat of actual physical force and use of force can occur. (Some would say that influence by force alone is not really social influence since it occurs without going through the person's identity or self.) Most often power and influence work through the self and its multiple identities to direct behaviors in ways that maintain the society.[11]

In social relationships, power comes into play when a person cannot control the outcome by himself or herself and must rely on another for a desired result. The individual is subject to the power of someone who can affect the outcome. A worker wants a job and wages so an employer has power. A student wants a good grade and teachers determine grades, so the teacher has power. Someone needs $1,000 and someone who can provide money has power. Social power exists only if something that is desired can only be provided by another.

Patterns of power relationships at home, in school, at work, and in the broader community are established. Individuals play roles in these patterns and follow these patterns' rules. These patterns are what are often called social structures. These social structures reflect the power that is embedded in them. It is the argument of this book that current power structures are major causes of inequality, limited social mobility, and poverty in America and in turn inequality, limited social mobility, and poverty patterns influence the social order.

To briefly summarize:

- **Social power is the ability to influence the behavior of other people.**
- **Social power is neither good nor evil in itself.**
- **Social power can be implicit or explicit, conscious or unconscious.**
- **Social power is exercised within relationships and sets up patterns of order, creating and maintaining a social order in groups.**

Power is embedded in a society. It is part and parcel of the social order. It operates to create and maintain order in society. But power is usually not absolute and is often subject to change. Those who do not like the current order for the most part are persons who want another social order.

BASES OF POWERS

Before discussing the process by which the powers of a society are deployed to socialize its members and form their identities, some of the major bases of power are briefly reviewed. A common typology of power is that offered by Bertram Raven. [12]

- Reward
- Coercive
- Legitimate
- Referent
- Expertise
- Information

Reward power is the ability to provide positive rewards to another; for example, to give a raise. Coercive power is the ability to provide sanctions or punishments, such as firing or demoting. Legitimate power is the ability to influence because of position that a person holds and arises from social norms. A boss has legitimate power by virtue of her position. Referent power arises from the identification with another, e.g., admiration of a co-worker's interpersonal skills. Expertise power is based on a person's expertise, such as skill in a particular job. Informational power is based on a person having needed knowledge; for example, someone who "knows the ropes" at the plant has informational power. Identifiable bases of power often operate in conjunction. For example, a boss who is esteemed can also have great knowledge and can reward or punish subordinates.

A common distinction is often made as to whether power is available because of a person's position or their personal characteristics.

Positional Power

- Legitimate (because of the position held, not personal characteristics)
- Reward (monetary reward, praise)
- Coercive (threats and punishments)
- Informational (access to and control of the dissemination of information)

Personal

- Expert (respect or admiration)
- Referent (relationships and identification, being liked
  Johnathan H. Turner identifies four sources of political power: [13]
- Coercion (force or the threat of force; military and police)
- Administrative structure (the apparatus to implement and monitor activities)

SOCIALIZATION INTO A SOCIAL ORDER[1]

In the previous chapter, the social order and its driving force, power, were discussed. Individuals and groups with power indoctrinate a society's members on the operation of its social order, "inculcating ideas, attitudes, cognitive strategies, or a professional methodology."[2] Those who socialize have greater power in a social order than those socialized. Socializers use their power to indoctrinate individuals to act according to a society's rule of order.[3] Socialization forms identities that support and maintain a social order. (More on identities in the section below.)

Socialization prepares, and continually supports, individuals to continue the social order in which they are formed. In general, socialization is:

the process beginning during childhood by which individuals acquire the values, habits, and attitudes of a society [4]

Socialization transmits culture, norms, laws, and behaviors. Socialization works through human interaction. Frequently a distinction is made between primary socialization and secondary socialization:

- **Primary socialization** occurs when a child learns the attitudes, values and actions appropriate to individuals as members of a particular culture. This is mainly influenced by the immediate family and friends.

- **Secondary socialization** is the process of learning what behaviors as appropriate as members of the larger society. It is the behavioral patterns reinforced or altered by socializing agents of society such as schools and workplaces. [5]

Socialization shapes the individual's behavior, thinking, goals, and identities. Socialization is a messy process. It starts immediately after birth and continues throughout life. [6] The various contexts in which an individual finds themself have a major impact on the socialization process.[7] Socializing individuals and institutions are multiple. Commonly, the agents of childhood socialization are identified as family, peers (including physical neighborhood), schools, religion, government, and mass media.[8] In addition to these childhood socializers, the workplace and voluntary associations are major socializing agents later in life.

There is no single source of socialization. Different types of relationships with individuals from diverse backgrounds who possess differing amounts of influence occur at different times of a person's life. These relationships, operating in multiple contexts, are all elements of the socialization process. All these socializing forces have received significant attention and detailed analysis. What is offered below is a brief summary of each socializing agent and how it operates.

PARENTS/FAMILY

While socialization occurs throughout one's life, most recognize and accept the major importance of childhood socialization. Humans are most impressionable early in life.[9] A child's brain is extremely malleable and early impressions register more deeply.[10] The family is structured to provide this early socialization and have primary influence.

What constitutes a family is determined by the social order in which families exist. Each society establishes rules for procreation and the raising of children and how the adults in the family will relate (for example, through monogamy or polygamy). However, the basic function of the family remains consistent:

The primary function of the family is to ensure the continuation of society, both biologically through procreation, and socially through socialization.[11]

SOCIALIZATION INTO A SOCIAL ORDER

The Vanier Institute identifies these as the central elements of family socialization in America:[12]

- Physical maintenance and care of group members
- Addition of new members through procreation or adoption
- Socialization of children
- Social control of members
- Production, consumption, distribution of goods and services
- Affective nurturance—love

Early in life children are totally dependent on adults to meet their range of needs: (See section on needs for more detail)

- Physiological
- Safety and Security
- Social Needs
- Esteem/Recognition
- Self-Actualization/Achievement
- Cognitive

The family socializes children through power possessed by adults. Previously the various types of power were outlined:[13]

- Reward
- Coercive
- Legitimate
- Referent
- Expertise
- Information

During a child's earliest years, the parent holds overwhelming power. Parents reward and punish children. The parent's acts and words are accepted as legitimate. The parent serves as a model of behavior and source of acceptance. The parent is the one with abilities and skills. The parent is the primary source of knowledge.

In America the family has responsibility for the care, nurture, and development of children. Parents are delegated to transfer the rules, norms, and customary ways of acting in a society. Laws, regulations, and customs set boundaries on how parents may act. For example, if a child is harmed by the parent, child abuse laws and regulations come into play and authorities may intervene in a family. Broad power is given to the family, but society is able to act to set limits on this power if norms of society as reflected in the law are violated.

SCHOOLS

Most also recognize schools as a critical part of the socialization process. By law most children are required to go to school through high school age. The multiplicity of the socialization activities carried out by the schools in modern, developed societies is summarized by Jullie Flavia as "essential functions": [14]:

1. Knowledge of basic intellectual skills such as reading, writing, verbal expression, quantitative and other cognitive abilities. Education teaches language as well as how people communicate with each other according to positions in society.
2. Cultural achievements of one's society. Opportunities to acquire social and vocational abilities which are necessary in order to make one a social, useful and economically productive member of the society.
3. Gender roles as perceived as suitable roles by the society. Educational systems socialize students to become gendered members of society, to play meaningful roles in the complex network of independent positions.
4. Education helps in shaping values and attitudes to the needs of the contemporary society. Education widens the mental horizons of pupils and teaches them new ways of looking at themselves and their society.
5. Education offers young people opportunities for intellectual, emotional and social growth. Thus education can be influential in promoting new values and stimulating adaptation to changing conditions.
6. Informally and especially through social clubs, the school enables the child to learn a number of other social roles and skills which are also important for his/her overall development as a member of society. For example, education teaches the laws, traditions and norms of the community, the rights that individuals will enjoy and the responsibilities that they will undertake.

7. Education teaches how one is to behave toward his/her playmates and adults.
8. Education teaches how to share things and ideas.
9. Education teaches how to compete responsibly.
10. Schooling teaches how to cooperate.
11. Schooling instills the community's pattern of respect, thus how to relate to others well and obey rules.
12. Schooling enables one to internalize the culture of one's society.
13. Education leads toward tolerant and humanitarian attitudes. For example, college graduates are expected to be more tolerant than high school graduates in their attitudes toward ethnic and racial groups.
14. Education will train useful citizens who will obediently conform to society's norms, and will accept the role and status that society will confer upon them when they have finished their schooling.

The socialization powers of the schools are multiple. Schools provide new information and thinking skills. Schools are structured processes, instilling following structured processes in students. Adults, primarily teachers, are the controlling and powerful force. All grades and progressions are determined by the teacher. The teacher also has a major impact on how a student sees themself: special or ordinary, good or bad, average or smart. Required behaviors are set forth. Successful students reproduce the required behaviors. The student is recognized for accomplishments in areas such as academics, sports, or music. Boy and girl roles are established. Racial groupings are recognized.

Alongside parents, schools are a major force of socialization. Schools can offer perspectives on life and goals other than those of parents. New inputs are provided into the formation of one's identity but these other perspectives are consistent with America's social order.

PEERS AND NEIGHBORHOOD

Other early socialization is provided by peers. Before, during, and after school, one's peers, often of the same or similar age and sex, become part of the socialization process. Peers operate individually and as groups of friends and associates to shape one's identity.

he individual moves from the home to the larger community. Individuals from outside of the family share their knowledge, information, ideas, values, and customs with each other. New possibilities, opportunities, and goals emerge as young people relate to one another. New social relationships and attachments that shape the individual are formed.

WORKPLACE

As individuals grow older, they enter the workforce. They bring skills and values from early socialization to the workplace. A person applies and competes for a job without having control over the hiring process. Once employed, the boss guides the person, and arranges the employee's time and activities. The boss provides rewards: money, promotion, better responsibilities or working conditions. The boss can also be a source of recognition and esteem. The boss can also provide sanctions: work probation, demotion, and ultimately dismissal. The power of the boss controls and further shapes the employee's identity.

ADULT ASSOCIATIONS

In addition to family, school, and work, most adults also become involved in voluntary associations. People gather in a variety of groups to carry out social and community betterment activities such as trade associations, trade unions, learned societies, professional associations, and charitable groups. Individuals commit their time and talents to specific shared purposes. Within these relationships ideas and values similar to those of others are conveyed and strengthened or perhaps even altered.

CHURCHES/RELIGION

Churches are voluntary organizations but, in the US, can be considered as a special case. The vast majority of Americans are church members. Churches are unique in that they can be, and often are, a part of socialization from the time of childhood throughout life. Churches seek to engage children at an early age so that their membership continues throughout life. Churches are also unique in that they appeal to a source of power other than the family or state to guide actions: the power of God.

MEDIA

Media in various forms also are part of the socialization process in the US. At the present time, TV and, especially, the internet, present a wide range of information on life and values. The media's images and words offer a wide range of ideas with visual and emotional content that can shape an individual's perceptions and desires.

CONCLUDING COMMENTS

Socializing agents work, often simultaneously, to shape and form individuals in the US. They enable individuals to understand how the social order of the US works. Socialization works through the powers exercised by socializing agents. Socializing agents have great power, but this power is not absolute. Because of socialization's complexity and limited power of each socializing agent, in addition to individual differences, socialization does not present a homogeneous outcome. Instead, socialization results in the production of a general common pattern with many variants.

With these caveats in mind, the result of socialization, identities, are reviewed in the next section.

Notes

(1) What follows is a summary overview of the socialization process in America. Each of the socializing agents noted below has been examined in detail by numerous academics, policy makers and religious leaders. Also, it should be noted that the mechanisms, e.g. the psychological mechanisms, by which socialization occurs are not addressed in this discussion.

(2) Socialization, Definitions https://www.definitions.net/definition/indoctrination

(3) Eleanor E. Maccoby, The Role of Parents in the Socialization of Children: An Historical Overview Developmental Psychology1992, Vol. 28, No. 6,1006-1017, https://pdfs.semanticscholar.org/353b/824 813759e7330e71281e2dd660604884244.pdf

(4) Socialization, Mirriam Webster https://www.merriam-webster.com/dictionary/socialization

(5) Socialization Through the Life Span, Lumen Learning, https://courses.lumenlearning.com/boundless-sociology/chapter/socialization-throughout-the-life-span/

(6) Agents of Socialization, Lumen Learning https://courses.lumenlearning.com/sociology/chapter/agents-of-socialization/

(7) See for example, Rand Conger and Shannon J. Dogan, Social Class and Socialization in Families

Handbook of socialization: Theory and research (pp. 433-460). New York, NY, US: Guilford Press November 15, 2015 https://psycnet.apa.org/record/2006-23344-017 and Edward Zigler, Social Class and the Socialization Process, Research Article, Yale University 1971 https://journals.sagepub.com/doi/10.3102/00346543040001087

(8) Agents of Socialization, op. cit.

(9) A variety of sources provide evidence of the importance of childhood socialization. For a summary see for example, https://www.learningrx.com/4-cognitive-stages-for-child-development-faq.htm. This summary points out come major time periods of development:

    1. Sensorimotor Stage: Birth through about 2 years. During this stage, children learn about the world through their senses and the manipulation of objects.
    2. Preoperational Stage: Ages 2 through 7. During this stage, children develop memory and imagination. They are also able to understand things symbolically, and to understand the ideas of past and future.
    3. Concrete Operational Stage: Ages 7 through 11. During this stage, children become more aware of external events, as well as feelings other than their own. They become less egocentric, and begin to understand that not everyone shares their thoughts, beliefs, or feelings.
    4. Formal Operational Stage: Ages 11 and older. During this stage, children are able to use logic to solve problems, view the world around them, and plan for the future.

Various ways to explaining these stages and the developments have been developed, a common one being that of Erick Erickson. See, for example, Saul Mcleod, Erik Erikson's Stages of Psychological Development, 2018 http://cdd.unm.edu/%5C/ecln/PSN/common/pdfs/Psychodynamic_erickson.pdf

(10) Extensive research is available on brain development and great significance of early childhood socialization. See for example, Stages of child development Piaget, CDC https://www.cdc.gov/ncbddd/childdevelopment/early-brain-development.html

(11) Family, Lumen Learning https://courses.lumenlearning.com/boundless-sociology/chapter/family/
At the same time, it needs to be recognized that there are many types of families with children: Nuclear (two parent), single parent, step parent and grandparent are common but many other alternatives exist. In general, we use parent here as the individuals who exercise primary care giving, especially in a child's earliest years. Family Types, Better Help, https://www.betterhelp.com/advice/family/there-are-6-different-family-types-and-each-one-has-a-unique-family-dynamic/

(12) Definition of Family, Vanier Institute https://vanierinstitute.ca/definition-family/ Others have developed lists of functions of the family that are similar to that of the Vanier Institute See for example, Functions of the Family, Oscar Education, https://oscareducation.blogspot.com/2013/06/functions-of-family.html and "7 Important Functions of Family," 1698 Words http://www.yourarticlelibrary.com/family/7-important-functions-of-family-1698-words/6171

(13) See Power Section Above

(14) Julllie Flavia, How the school performs the function of socialization https://www.kenyaplex.com/resources/5742-how-the-school-performs-the-function-of-socialization.aspx

SOCIAL IDENTITY FORMATION

IDENTITIES

Through the complex processes of socialization, an individual's self takes on identities. Here an overview of identity as part of social order is presented (without going into detail regarding identity's psychological and social-psychological dynamics).

Identity is a concept that most people, to some degree, recognize. Yet the term "identity" and related terms such as "self" are used in a variety of ways. The discussion here uses the following definitions.

- Self: our awareness of being a distinct person that appears at a young age; the self embodies all of one's identities. [1]

- Identity: one of many ways in which an individual sees themself and/or presents themself in social situations, embodying the individual's unique qualities, value, beliefs, and personality. [1a]

- Identities: the various ways an individual can see or present themself in social situations.

- Core identities: the most stable identities that an individual falls back on and which reflect fundamental values of the individual.

- Social situation: a relational context that elicits different identities.

- Social Power: the ability of an individual in a social situation to influence or control another's behavior.

One's identities are formed and taken up in relationships with others. Different identities can emerge as a person participates in various social interactions, for example, in the family, at work, or at church. Identities can have a variety of importance; some are very important, others less so. In addition, identities can have differing degrees of salience in different situations. A specific identity can be used in a given situation, regardless of its importance. For example, a member of the Elks may act as being an Elk even though being an Elk may not be one's most important identity.[2]

Among one's many identities are those identified as social identities.

> "...social identity" refers specifically to those aspects of a person that are defined in terms of his or her group memberships. Although most people are members of many different groups, only some of those groups are meaningful in terms of how we define ourselves. In these cases, our self-definition is shared with other people who also claim that categorical membership, for example, as a woman, as a Muslim, as a marathon runner, or as a Democrat.[3]

A personalized example helps one to understand identities and their formation. Your parents, as parents, assume responsibility for your development. Parents provide food, water, and shelter. They also provide safety; they protect. They offer you affection and connect you to others in the family, to relatives, and to other community members. They reward you for good behavior, show you recognition. They give you the possibility of growth and a sense of self. They teach you about things and how to do things. They relate to you and you relate to them. You take on the identity of 'child'.

Parents can do this because they have the ability and power to meet your basic needs. They reward you if you act appropriately (as they deem your acts to be appropriate). They also threaten and punish if you do not act in the ways they define as appropriate. Parents are the experts in your life, the leaders. They provide you information. And if you like them, they hold referent power. Parents are acting toward you in ways that they have been taught to behave and ways that they think will help you to succeed in society. They provide you with an understanding of society and how it works, the roles and order and powers in society. They teach you to accept the powers of society and how those powers order society. You have a social identity as 'child' that is a result of their socialization of you.

When you leave home, you find yourself with others who follow or do not follow the rules and roles of your home. While these others are different than you, they have the same needs. You begin to relate to them for rewards: esteem, respect, being themselves. They share similar rewards, punishments and sources of esteem and respect. You establish social identities in relation to your peers.

You go to school and there is a system of rewards and punishments for specific actions. You want the respect of teachers and other students. In school, the teacher has the power of position. The teacher hands out rewards (good grades) and punishment (stay after school or in at recess or fail the course). Teachers are the experts in what you are learning. They are the learned ones. You take on the 'student' role.

Along the way you are part of a number of other groups—perhaps Scouts, the school band, or athletic teams. These groups have their own rules and their own rewards and punishments. They have their experts, those with the needed knowledge. You belong, you are accepted, you expand your knowledge and sense of self. You learn an identity and expected behaviors and become part of the group.

On to work. The same needs are being met by your acquiescence to those in power at work. On the positive side a boss can reward you, providing a salary to meet your basic and other needs. The boss can provide positive evaluations and tell you how important you are (esteem) to the organization. You follow the rules (belonging) and you get along with your fellow workers (belonging). You learn more about the business and your particular job (knowledge) and feel that you are doing well (actualization). Or on the negative side, a boss can punish you. You can lose your job. A boss can provide negative evaluations and tell your how you are failing (no esteem), tell you how you do not fit in (don't belong) and you don't get along with your fellow employees. You are not learning and you are not really actualizing yourself. Either way you have taken on a work identity.

The parent, teachers, the club leaders, and the boss are given positional power that they exercise over you. They have power because of the system in which they operate. The parent, the teacher, the club leader, and the boss all work within the fabric of a broader society that is structured to meet the needs of all who are members of this society.

In the broader society there are ideological rules, economic rules, political rules, military/police rules and voluntary association/religion rules. Parents follow these rules, as do teachers, group leaders, and bosses. At a minimum the socializers act within the rules, follow the law, and provide perspectives that fall within a broad societal purview. A variety of identities of an individual are formed as part of the social order.

One of each American's self's identities is that of being an American and living the American way of life. For most, this identity is of high importance. Numerous surveys point out that Americans see themselves as Americans and identify themselves as Americans.[4] Numerous surveys illustrate that Americans have somewhat differing perceptions of America. For example, an Atlantic article summarizing a number of surveys notes:

> Nearly two-thirds of the white working class say American culture has gotten worse since the 1950s. Sixty-eight percent say the U.S. is in danger of losing its identity, and 62 percent say America's growing number of immigrants threaten the country's culture. [5]

However, at some level, all Americans have a collective identity as Americans. They share values and norms that allow them to align with other Americans and distinguish themselves from those in other societies.[6] One views things as getting better—or worse— in America because of one's identity as an American.

These American identities, shaped by socialization, incorporate the ideology, economy, and politics of America. America's social order through the exercise of power is transmitted to all Americans and found in their identities.

SOCIAL IDENTITY FORMATION

SUMMARY

In this overview some fundamental concepts were offered. Societies are organized to meet the broad range of human needs. Social order is absolutely essential for these human needs to be met. Various social powers operate to maintain and permeate this order. Social power works through the ongoing processes of socialization, processes that begin at birth and continue throughout life. The socialization process results in the formation of identities. Social order is not extrinsic to individuals but is embodied in them, in their identities.

With this broad understanding as a framework, the social order of the US can be reviewed.

Notes

(1) Sense of Identify, Psychological Dictionary, https://psychologydictionary.org/sense-of-identity/

(1a) Identity, Wikipedia https://en.wikipedia.org/wiki/Identity

(2) See for example, Philip S. Brenner, Richard T. Serpe, and Sheldon Stryker, The Causal Ordering of Prominence and Salience in Identity Theory: An Empirical Examination, HHS Public Access, July 1, 2014, https://www.ncbi.nlm.nih.gov/pmc/articles/PMC4896744/ As R.C. Morris notes, When people are given a behavioral choice between their two most important role-identities they did not always choose the identity that they identified as most important to their self-concept. R.C. Morris, Identity Salience and Identity Importance Identity Theory, https://www.researchgate.net/publication/287896435_Identity_Salience_and_Identity_Importance_in_Identity_Theory)

(3) Kathy Deaux, Social Identity Encyclopedia of Women and Gender, Volumes One and Two Copyright © 2001, Cambridge: Academic Press 2001,York, https://pdfs.semanticscholar.org/97b3/929263667bf754777da7a94260ecbad9f625.pdf

(4) National Opinion Research Center. The American Identity: Points of Pride, Conflicting Views, and a Distinct Culture, http://apnorc.org/projects/Pages/HTML%20Reports/points-of-pride-conflicting-views-and-a-distinct-culture.aspx

(5) Emma Green, Atlantic Monthly, May 9, 2017, https://www.theatlantic.com/politics/archive/2017/05/white-working-class-trump-cultural-anxiety/525771/

(6) Marilynn Brewer and Wendi Gardner. "Who is the "We" Levels of Collective Identity and Self Representation? Journal of Personality and Social Psychology 71(1):83-93 · July 1996, https://www.researchgate.net/publication/232469632_Who_Is_This_We_Levels_of_Collective_Identity_and_Self_Representations

AMERICA'S SOCIAL ORDER

OVERVIEW

Social order and how it is embodied and enforced through socialization and formation of identities was summarized in the previous section. In this section, detail on America's social order is presented.

In presenting America's social order, a framework offered by Michael Mann is used. (1) Mann identifies four sources of power, to which a fifth is added here: Voluntary/Religious. The categories of power used here are:

- Ideological
- Economic
- Political
- Military/Police
- Voluntary/Religious

These "sources" are better perhaps better described as realms of power. These realms are of major significance in any large society. They do not function independently; they mutually support and reinforce one another. Members of a society need to share a common set of values and norms (ideology). They need to have their material needs met (economic). They need to follow common rules to get along with one another (political). They need protection and security to maintain organized social relationships. (military/police). In the United States, they join with others in a voluntary fashion for a variety of purposes, including and especially religious purposes. (voluntary/religious)

In each of these realms, individuals and organizations possess and deploy resources to influence the behavior of others. As noted above, Jonathan H. Turner identifies three sources or bases of power that can be deployed in these realms: [2]

- Coercion (force or the threat of force; military and police)
- Authority (the apparatus to implement and monitor activities)
- Persuasion (ability to make others think actions or decisions are correct)

In each of these realms there are individuals or groups that have power. Their power flows from four sources:

- Punishment
- Reward
- Administrative Structures
- Symbols

Those with power have the ability to punish: to fire someone or give someone a lousy job, and to remove a person completely from the group (society) through incarceration. Those in power can provide raises and promotions. Those in power use symbols, such as titles, clothes, and ideology to influence how individuals behave. Those with power deploy an administrative apparatus to make sure that their desired outcomes are attained. All of these sources have an emotional component that reinforces the cognitive dimension.[3]

Each source of power is exercised individually, but also works with the other sources to maintain the social order. While distinguishable, realms of power operate together, as a whole. However, individual sources of power have differing degrees of influence in specific areas of human need. For example, the economy meets physiological needs; the need for esteem and recognition is supported by ideology and religion; the police and the military are the sources of power that meet safety and security needs.

With this understanding each of the realms of power will be reviewed before addressing their interrelationship.

Notes

(1) Mann, Michael. The Sources of Social Power. New York, NY: Cambridge University Press, 2012.

(2) Turner J.H. (2001) Sociological Theory Today. In: Turner J.H. (eds) Handbook of Sociological Theory. Handbooks of Sociology and Social Research. Springer, Boston, MA . https://doi.org/10.1007/0-387-36274-6_1

(3) "Up to this point, the focus has been on the rational element of sources that provide power. Symbols, however, hint at the emotional, the feeling part of power." Harding, Jennifer, and E. Deidre Pribram. "The Power of Feeling: Locating Emotions in Culture." European Journal of Cultural Studies 5, no. 4 (November 2002): 407–26. https://doi.org/10.1177/1364942002005004294.

IDEOLOGY: PERVASIVE AMERICAN BELIEFS AND VALUES

A society's ideology, its core beliefs and values, are both the cause and effect of its political, economic, military/police, and voluntary social orders. Together and separately, these major social powers establish America's social order. An examination of America's ideology serves as a jumping-off point.

It must be noted from the beginning that Americans' beliefs are not monolithic. A great deal of diversity exists. Recognizing this diversity, it is still possible to identify common beliefs and values held by almost all Americans.

A basic definition of America's ideology helps to guide the discussion:[1]

> Ideology is a comprehensive set of normative beliefs, conscious and unconscious ideas, that an individual, group, or society has that provides a set of values and feelings that Americans do not often realize are there.

The first part of the definition focuses on the cognitive components of ideology: beliefs and values. This cognitive dimension can be both conscious and unconscious. One can "have" an ideology without being fully aware of or able to articulate it. The second portion of the definition brings to the fore the emotional elements of ideology. One not only thinks but also feels an ideology, as evidenced by a number of social symbols that take on meaning in a society, such as flags and anthems, and elicit emotions. [2]

The American ideology is fundamental to American life and identity.[3] It sets forth ideals that are unquestioned assumptions. Alexis de Tocqueville noted: "The majority has staked out a formidable fence around thought. Inside these limits a writer is free, but woe betide him if he dares to stray beyond them." Americans are far more ideological than is often assumed.

America shares much of its ideology with other Western (European) nations.[4]

> Western democracy is characterized by elections between multiple distinct political parties, a separation of powers into different branches of government, the rule of law in everyday life as part of an open society, a market economy with private property, and the equal protection of human rights, civil rights, civil liberties and political freedoms for all people.[5]

While sharing these basic Western ideals, America has its unique understanding and application of these ideals. For example, in America there are two major parties, three branches of government, a set of federal, state, and local laws to govern conduct, a private capitalist system (more on this later in the discussion of economic order), and a detailed exposition on various rights. This pattern, while incorporating shared Western ideals, is unique to America.

There is broad consensus on basic American values. All of these values are often summarized as the "American Dream":

> The dream of a land in which life should be better, richer, and fuller for every man with opportunities for each according to his abilities and achievement ... a dream of social order in which each man and each woman shall be able to attain to the fullest stature of which they are innately capable, and be recognized by others for what they are, regardless of the fortuitous circumstances of birth or position.[6]

The dream has been spelled out by numerous authors who identify many common ideological elements. [7]

IDEOLOGY: PERVASIVE AMERICAN BELIEFS AND VALUES

- America is a great country
- Individual Freedom: speech, arms, press, religion
- Privacy
- Choice
- Private property
- Individualism
- Self-Reliance
- Achievement
- Competition
- Hard Work
- Merit
- Pragmatism
- Better Future
- Material Wealth
- Equality of Opportunity
- Rule of Law
- Fairness
- Voluntarism
- "Religiosity"

These basic elements are interrelated and form a whole. The following groupings are used as a framework to provide more detail.

- America is a great country.
- Individual freedom: privacy, choice, private property
- Individualism, self-reliance, competition hard work, merit
- Better future, material wealth
- Equal opportunity, fairness, rule of law
- Voluntarism
- "Religiosity"

AMERICA IS A GREAT COUNTRY

Americans believe that they live in a good country—some would say great. They love the life, liberty, and pursuit of happiness that America promises and are willing to defend it from others. At the same time, they believe it can be even better.

BREAK THE CASTE

INDIVIDUAL FREEDOM: PRIVACY, CHOICE, PRIVATE PROPERTY, RELIGION

In America, the individual is preeminent. An individual can say what they wish. The individual is free to do what they want as long it is within the limits of law (see more below). The individual is entitled to privacy. There should be no intrusion or surveillance of one's personal life. Individuals can make choices regarding their life and its direction. No one can tell them what to do, what to buy, where to go, what to do, or where to work. Individuals can own things. No one has the right to take what they own (such as their homes, cars, guns, stocks). The primacy of private property is not unique to America, but it is of amplified value in the US when linked to the other basic values in the US: individualism, privacy, competition

INDIVIDUALISM, SELF-RELIANCE, COMPETITION HARD WORK, MERIT

Individualism establishes the individual as preeminent. The individual's rights are more important than the group's rights. Individuals are responsible for themselves and the outcomes of their lives. They must be self-reliant. They must achieve their goals by hard work and deserve what they have. In America competition is critical. Individuals compete with others to achieve what they want as they and all Americans seek the American Dream.

BETTER FUTURE, MATERIAL WEALTH

Individuals who apply themselves will have a better future for themselves and their children. A fundamental measure of a better future is more income and wealth. Success is defined by having more material things, things which can be (and often are) used as a measure of success.

EQUAL OPPORTUNITY, FAIRNESS, RULE OF LAW

While individuals are responsible for their own lives, they should operate on a "level playing field." All should have an equal opportunity for success. The competition of the individual for success should be fair. No one should be given an advantage. All must operate within the context of the law. Laws should protect all so that some do not take advantage of others.

IDEOLOGY: PERVASIVE AMERICAN BELIEFS AND VALUES

VOLUNTARISM

Individuals can choose to join with whomever they wish. No one is required to join a political party or a particular religion. People are able and are encouraged to gather together to pursue goals which can best be accomplished by a group, such as election of representatives, assisting the disadvantaged, promoting ideas, or preserving art.

"RELIGIOSITY"

America is "one nation under God," but an individual's religion is a personal choice. Religion is separate from government. No person, and especially no government, can force a person to believe in a certain way or to join a particular church, synagogue, mosque, or any other religious congregation. While a particular belief is not mandated, belief in a higher power is part of American life. [8]

Almost no person would say that America is no good. No one would say that all individuals should not be respected, or be coerced, or not be entitled to their privacy. No one would deny that all should have opportunities. No one would say that individuals should not work hard. No one would say that individuals should not compete. No one would say that things should stay the same or get worse. No one would say that they would not like a nice house and a good car. And almost all would say that there is a god—although not all would be churchgoers or agree on "who" God is. These are the elements of American ideology.

These basic tenets are the American "Overton Window," the parameters of discourse, how to think about things, and action.[9] Discussions about policies or programs must not contradict these beliefs. American political differences in our society are about how to achieve these ideals.

This American ideology is a critical part of every American's identity.

Notes

(1) Social 10 (5), Quizlet, https://quizlet.com/ca/276661616/social-10-5-flash-cards/ and Sabucedo, J. M., Durán, M., Alzate, M., & Barreto, I. (2011). Emotions, ideology and collective political action. *Universitas Psychologies*10(1), 27-34, http://www.scielo.org.co/scielo.php?script=sci_arttext&pid=S1657-92672011000100003

(2) Maurice Cranston, Ideology, Encyclopedia Britannica, https://www.britannica.com/topic/ideology-society#ref12154

(3) Dominic Tierney, Why Are Americans So Ideologically United, The Atlantic, August 23, 2011, https://www.theatlantic.com/national/archive/2011/08/why-are-americans-so-ideologically-united/243951/

(4) Helena Rosenblatt, Liberal Democracy is in crisis. But…Do We know what it is?, The Guardian, May 27, 2018 https://www.theguardian.com/commentisfree/2018/may/27/liberal-democracy-history-us-politics

(5) Liberal Democracy, Wikipedia, https://en.wikipedia.org/wiki/Liberal_democracy

(6) The American Dream, first published by Little, Brown and Company, 1931) https://www.loc.gov/teachers/classroommaterials/lessons/american-dream/students/thedream.html

(7) See for example, America's Beliefs and Values: Chapter 3 thru b, https://www.slideshare.net/laphat/american-beliefs-and-values-chapter-3-thuy-b, Six Basic American Cultural Values, Vintage American Ways, https://vintageamericanways.com/american-values/, Core Cultural Values, Study Library, https://www.hasdk12.org/cms/lib3/PA01001366/Centricity/Domain/854/American%20Core%20Beliefs.pdf, Key American Values, University of Missouri, Saint Louis, http://www.umsl.edu/~intelstu/Admitted%20Students/Visitor%20Handbook/keyvalues.html, Konto Usuniete, What Are Americans Basic Values and Beliefs, American Studies, http://www.goldenline.pl/grupy/Uczelnie_studia_studenci_absolwenci/american-studies/what-are-the-basic-american-values-and-beliefs,901536/ , What Are American Values, USA Hello, https://usahello.org/resources/american-values/

(8) There are indeed some who are not religious and some have talked about America being a secular society. Religion remains important in America: Secularization, Emory University http://sociology.emory.edu/home/documents/profiles-documents/lechner-secularization.pdf
While much has been made of the decreasing church attendance when we look at individuals' beliefs about a God, we find that over 90% believe in a higher power of some sort. See, for example, When Americans Say They Believe in God, What Do They Mean?, PEW, 2018, http://www.pewforum.org/2018/04/25/when-americans-say-they-believe-in-god-what-do-they-mean/ Full Report

(9) Overton Window, Wikipedia, https://en.wikipedia.org/wiki/Overton_window provide the following definition: "The Overton window is the range of policies politically acceptable to the mainstream population at a given time. It is also known as the window of discourse. "

AMERICA'S ECONOMY AS PART OF A WORLD ECONOMY

America's economy today is part of a global world economy. This global economy influences America's economy and, in turn, is influenced by America's economy as the world becomes more organized into a single economic system. While national economies have always been involved in trade, the scope and degree of international economic participation has expanded significantly, especially in the last 30 years. The economies of the world are now intertwined.

While a complete description of this intertwined, global economic reality is beyond the scope of this book, some of its major elements are identified here. Globalization overall is both a set of ideas and a variety of trades and transactions. A major element of globalization is the growing role of finance, including both the growth of financial institutions and new ways to move money more swiftly and securely between nations. Technology involves a variety of developments in production, transportation, manufacturing and information exchange. Globalization is supported by a variety of international regulations, agreements, and institutions, such as trade agreements and tariffs, that enable and determine how the movement of money, goods, and services will move between countries. An overriding ideology supports and justifies globalization. A discussion of these elements provides an essential context for understanding America's economic order as part of the world economy.

GLOBALIZATION

Globalization is a world view that the exchange of ideas and goods should be world-wide.

> Market globalism advocates promise a consumerist, neoliberal, free-market world. This ideology is held by many powerful individuals, who claim it transmits democracy and benefits everyone. However, it also reinforces inequality, and can be politically motivated.[1]

This world view is supported by a variety of concrete processes.[2] The oft-cited International Monetary Fund's (IMF) description of globalization identifies globalization's basic elements:

> Economic "globalization" is a historical process, the result of human innovation and technological progress. It refers to the increasing integration of economies around the world, particularly through the movement of goods, services, and capital across borders. The term sometimes also refers to the movement of people (labor) and knowledge (technology) across international borders. There are also broader cultural, political, and environmental dimensions of globalization.[3]

Trade and transactions, capital and investment movements, migration and movement of people, and world-wide dissemination of knowledge occur through globalization. Trade and business transactions take place world-wide. Capital flows to a variety of nations to support trades and transactions. People move more-or-less easily from place to place. Information is easily available and is accessible to more and more people in more and more nations. While all of these elements have existed in some form for many years, what is different between previous forms of economies and how globalization currently operates is the *degree of presence and the sophistication* of these elements.

World trade grew from $2 trillion in 1980 to nearly $18 trillion in 2011 and has remained in the range of $15.7 to $18 trillion since then. World trade accounts for 19% of the world's total $79.3 trillion output of goods and services (Gross World Product). In 2017 the dollar value of merchandise exports rose by 11 per cent to $17.73 trillion, while commercial services exports increased by 8 per cent to $5.2 trillion.[4]

In 1960 the percentage of the US Gross Domestic Product (GDP) due to world trade was 5%.[5] By 1990, exported goods and services were 9.3% of the US economy. This percentage continued to grow, reaching approximately 13.5% of US GDP in 2013-2014, dropping slightly to under 12% in 2016. [6]

FINANCIALIZATION

A widely cited definition of the term 'financialization' is that provided by Epstein: [7]

> ...for us financialization means the increasing role of financial motives, financial markets, financial actors and financial institutions in the operation of the domestic and international economies.

Money has always been important; financialization has made money even more important. In a financialized world, financial markets denominate other sectors of the economy.

> Financialization is a pattern of accumulation in which profit-making occurs increasingly through financial channels rather than through trade and commodity production.[8]

With financialization, values are increasingly reduced to money or to things that can translate into money, such as derivatives. In simplest terms, a derivative is:

A security whose price is dependent upon or derived from one or more underlying assets. The derivative itself is merely a contract between two or more parties. Its value is determined by fluctuations in the underlying asset. The most common underlying assets include stocks, bonds, commodities, currencies, interest rates and market indexes. Most derivatives are characterized by high leverage.[9]

Derivatives are often leveraged, adding of debt to an asset to create a total value that includes both asset and debt.[10]

The standard of world payment has changed over time. In the financialized world of today, the US dollar serves as the standard of value for exchange. World exchange occurs primarily through financial instruments or derivatives based on the US dollar.[11]

Both power and profit increasingly are found in the financial sector. Money is increasingly diverted from goods and services. Profit-making occurs increasingly through financial transactions rather than through trade and commodity production.[12] Malcolm Sawyer notes while that much has been written about globalization and neoliberalism little attention has been given to financialization:

> Yet, financialization is now increasingly seen as the dominant force in this triad (neoliberalism, globalization, and financialization) The financialization of capitalism—the shift in gravity of economic activity from production (and even from much of the growing service sector) to finance—is thus one of the key issues of our time.[13]

As part and as an essential element of globalization, the size of global finance has grown. International banking can be traced back to the fourth century AD.[14] Since then the number of international banks and the number of home countries has greatly expanded. While London England was initially the location of international banks, international banks have expanded throughout the world.[15] Using the IMF 2014 figures and calculations, the financial services sector is estimated to comprise about 16.9% of the global economy, as measured in GDP.[16] Today, at least 1,300 countries have international banks and the size of these international banks has increased.[17] A Federal Reserve report details the crucial role that international finance plays.[18] The World Bank points out that International financialization goes hand-in-hand with globalization.[19] The importance and growth of the financial sector has been a major part of the globalization process.

TECHNOLOGY

The growth and sophistication of technologies has supported globalization and financialization.[20] Technology, broadly speaking, is the application of science to address problems.

> Technology is human knowledge which involves tools, materials, and systems. The application of technology typically results in products. If technology is well applied, it benefits humans, but the opposite is true, if used for malicious reasons.[21]

AMERICA'S ECONOMY AS PART OF A WORLD ECONOMY

Technology can be divided into a variety of categories. A common division is:

- Transportation
- Construction
- Communication
- Energy and power
- Chemical and biological
- Manufacturing

It is not possible within the scope of this book to provide a full review of each of these types of technology. What is offered here is a brief synopsis of each of these areas with attention to their relationship to a global economy.

The advances in transportation in the past 50 years have been significant. Air travel has exploded with more and more people traveling to more and more places with ease and at relatively low cost. Larger and safer transoceanic ships can move large amounts of goods between countries and at a cost lower than 20-30 years ago. Train transport, employing containerized shipping, can move an ever-wider variety of goods. Goods can be made in one location, put in cargo containers that are put on ships, shipped internationally, unloaded while still containerized and delivered to an end user thousands of miles away.

The internet and other forms of telecommunication have expanded the reach and speed of communication. Individuals can communicate almost instantly nationally and internationally, relying to a large degree on satellites. Financial transactions speedily occur. Using international banks, financial capital can be moved with ease. A variety of "secure" networks allow individuals to comfortably make a wide range of financial transactions from their homes.

The materials and equipment used to construct everything from roads, to houses, to ships, to skyscrapers have dramatically improved. Construction equipment can perform large and, in some cases, more intricate activities that speed the construction process. Improved building materials are not only more structurally sound but also enable speedier construction.

The sources of energy have expanded as more and more solar and wind power is used. At the same time, a number of improvements in energy efficiency have been made in everything from production lines to home heating.

Chemical and biological developments have exploded. Major discoveries in genetics and medicine have led to improved treatments for a wide range of health problems. Applications of biological and genetic discoveries have led to major improvements in agriculture and pharmacology.

Manufacturing processes have vastly improved. The Subcommittee for Advanced Manufacturing of the National Science and Technology Council provides a description of the major changes in manufacturing processes: [22]

> Advanced manufacturing is a family of activities that (a) depend on the use and coordination of information, automation, computation, software, sensing, and networking, and/or (b) make use of cutting-edge materials and emerging capabilities enabled by the physical and biological sciences, for example nanotechnology, chemistry, and biology. It involves both new ways to manufacture existing products, and the manufacture of new products emerging from new advanced technologies.

Concomitant with the changes in manufacturing has been increased automation as machines take on activities previously carried out by humans. Changes will continue to occur through the use of artificial intelligence.[23] Technology has pervaded all of economic life and supported globalization and financialization.

INTERNATIONAL REGULATIONS, AGREEMENTS, AND INSTITUTIONS

Financialization and globalization rely on numerous international rules and institutions.[24] Hurve Hannon of the Bank of International Settlements notes:[25]

> Services once provided in tightly regulated, domestically oriented and fragmented financial systems are increasingly performed in an open, competitive and global system. [25]

He goes on to note:

> ...policymakers have a key role to play in establishing a well-functioning legal, regulatory and financial reporting infrastructure.[26]

In his book, "What are the main global institutions? And how do they relate to international trade?" Richard Lynch provides an overview of the multiple institutions that have established rules that govern international trade including regulation of financial institutions.[27] He highlights the Basel III agreement that sets forward general guidelines of international finance and banking. He also details a number of international organizations which have set forth policies, used for most international banking. Global Strategy lists a number of institutions and regulations that guide financial activities including trade and tariffs.[28]

International institutions support the easy flow of money, goods, and services between countries. The World Bank and a variety of other legal and political institutions guide globalization. For example, the General Agreement on Tariffs and Trade (GATT:1947), the World Trade Organization (WTO), and North America Free Trade Agreement (NAFTA:1995/USMCA: 2019), to name a few, provide international and regional legal frameworks for the operation of globalization. [29] Some 4,000 to 4,800 Special Economic Zones (SEZs) now operate in countries throughout the world, offering a wide range of business supports including tax breaks, reductions of custom fees, and expedited movement of goods. International agreements and their enforcement are critical to assure that risks in carrying out international business activities are, at least to some degree, mitigated.[30]

A growing number of international corporations have been formed to carry out international business. As the United Nations Conference on Trade and Development 2018 report states:[31]

> Global estimates indicate that roughly 7,000 parent MNEs (multinational enterprises) were counted in 1970 while in 2000 this number jumped to 38,000. The most recent figure on the number of non-financial transnational corporations was 82,000 in 2008 (UNCTAD 2010). Another indication of the spread of MNEs are the 230,000 foreign affiliates (data for 2014 that represents an underestimate in that not all countries are included) counted in the OECD Activities of Multinational Enterprises (AMNE) data base.

Antras and Yeaple note:[32]

> More corporations have become multinational, i.e. own or control production of goods and services in two or more countries. There are an estimated 100,000 multinational corporations. The largest

of the multinationals account for a significant portion of the sales, employment, GDP, and profits.

Globalization has been supported by growth in the political, legal, financial and business institutions needed for its operation.

THE IDEOLOGY OF GLOBALIZATION, FINANCIALIZATION, AND TECHNOLOGY

Globalization, financialization, increased use of technology, and international institutions are, in turn, supported by an ideological framework, generally referred to as neoliberalism.

While some disagreement regarding details exists, this ideology can be described as a broad notion that encompasses a number of elements. For example, Wikipedia notes that:

> These ideas include economic liberalization policies such a privatization, austerity, free trade, and reductions in government spending in order to increase the role of the private sector in the economy and society.[33]

While these ideas have been around for a long time, many attribute the spread of this ideology, in large part, to Margaret Thatcher and Ronald Reagan in the 1980s. This ideology was supported by many economists, notably Fredrick Hayek, Milton Friedman, and James Buchanan.

As Malcolm Sawyer notes, this ideology is reflected in practical activities:[34]

> In the last thirty years, the economies of the world have undergone profound transformations. Some of the dimensions of this altered reality are clear: the role of government has diminished while that of markets has increased: economic transactions between countries have substantially risen; domestic and international financial transactions have grown by leaps and bounds…. In short, this changing landscape has been characterized by the rise of neoliberalism, globalization and financialization.' (Epstein, 2005: 3). This raises the obvious question of the relationship between neoliberalism and financialization (and a similar question for globalization and financialization).

He adds:

> Its [neoliberalism's] main features are the removal of barriers to free movement of goods, services, and especially capital, throughout the global economy; a withdrawal by the state from the role of guiding and regulating economic activity; privatization of state enterprises and public services; the slashing of state social programs; a shift to regressive forms of taxation; a shift from cooperation between capital and labor to a drive by capital, with aid from the state, to fully dominate labor; and the replacement of co-respective behavior among large corporations by unrestrained competition.[35]

Globalization, financialization, improved technology, and the institutions and ideology that support them create the environment of a world economic order in which America participates.

Notes

(1) Manfred Steger, Chapter 7. Ideologies of globalization: market globalism, justice globalism, religious globalisms, Globalism: A Short Introduction, 3rd Edition, Oxford University Press: New York, 2013, http://www.veryshortintroductions.com/view/10.1093/actrade/9780199662661.001.0001/actrade-9780199662661-chapter-7

(2) Manfred B Steger, Ideologies of Globalization, Journal of Political Ideologies, February 2005, http://socialsciences.people.hawaii.edu/publications_lib/JPI%20Ideologies%20of%20globalization%20%20final.pdf

3) Globalization, International Monetary Fund, 2008, https://www.imf.org/external/np/exr/ib/2008/053008.htm

(4) World Trade Statistical Review 2018, World Trade Organization, July 2018,, https://www.wto.org/english/res_e/statis_e/wts2018_e/wts2018_e.pdf ; see also Gross Domestic Product, Statistica, https://www.statista.com/statistics/268750/global-gross-domestic-product-gdp/ and Estaban Ortiz-Ospina, Diana Beltekian and Max Roser, Trade and Globalization, https://ourworldindata.org/trade-and-globalization#

(5) Exports of Goods and Services (% GDP) World Bank, https://data.worldbank.org/indicator/NE.EXP.GNFS.ZS

(6) US Exports as a Percentage of GDP https://www.statista.com/statistics/258779/us-exports-as-a-percentage-of-gdp/

(7) Epstein, G. 2005a. 'Introduction: Financialization and the World Economy.' In Epstein (2005b) http://eprints.whiterose.ac.uk/82350/3/Sawyer.pdf 1 Emeritus Professor of Economics, University of Leeds, UK. These notes are a write-up of remarks made at workshop on 'What is financialisation?' held at School of Oriental and African Studies, London, 23rd October 2013)

(8) Giovanni Arrighi, "Globalization in World-Systems Perspective". In R. Appelbaum and W. Robinson, eds., *Critical Globalization Studies*. New York and London: Routledge, 2005,

(9) Derivatives, Investopedia, https://www.investopedia.com/ask/answers/12/derivative.asp

(10) Firms that rely significantly or primarily on debt are called "high leveraged".

(11) Investopedia, How the U.S. Dollar Became the World's Reserve Currency https://www.investopedia.com/articles/forex-currencies/092316/how-us-dollar-became-worlds-reserve-currency.asp

(12) Malcolm Sawyer, What is Financialization? 2014, http://eprints.whiterose.ac.uk/82350/3/Sawyer.pdf

(13) Ibid p. 12

(14) What percentage of the global economy is comprised of the financial services sector? Investopedia, https://www.investopedia.com/ask/answers/030515/what-percentage-global-economy-comprised-financial-services-sector.asp

(15) Bankers without Borders, World Bank, 2017-2018, https://openknowledge.worldbank.org/handle/10986/28482 p. 22

(16) Local Banking Statistics, Bank of International Settlements, March 12, 2019,https://stats.bis.org/statx/toc/LBS.html

(17) José María Álvarez / Javier Pablo García / Olga Gouveia The globalisation of banking: How is regulation affecting global banks?, https://www.bbvaresearch.com/wp-content/uploads/2016/08/The-globalisation-of-banking.pdf

(18) Davin Chor and Kalina Manova, Trade during Good Times and Bad, https://www.stlouisfed.org/~/media/files/pdfs/publications/pub_assets/pdf/re/2012/a/re_jan_2012.pdf See also

(19) World Bank Group, op. cit.

(20) Esteban Ortiz-Ospina, Diana Beltekian and Max Roser, Trade and globalization, Our World in Data, revised, October 2018, https://ourworldindata.org/trade-and-globalization#

(21) Karenka Ramey, What is technology – meaning of technology and its use, Techueducation, December 12, 2013 https://www.useoftechnology.com/what-is-technology/

(22) President's Council of Advisors on Science and Technology, Report to the President on Ensuring American Leadership in Advanced Manufacturing. June 2011, https://www.whitehouse.gov/sites/default/files/microsites/ostp/pcast-advanced-manufacturing-june2011.pdf

(23) Louis Columbus, The Future of Manufacturing Technologies, Forbes, 2018, https://www.forbes.com/sites/louiscolumbus/2018/04/15/the-future-of-manufacturing-technologies-2018/#187ca5d72995

(24) Alvarez et alia, op. cit.

(25) Keynote address by Hervé Hannoun, Deputy General Manager of the BIS, at the 41st Conference of the SEACEN Governors Bandar Seri Begawan, Brunei Darussalam, 4 March 2006. Page 1.

(26) Ibid, p. 2

(27) Richard Lynch, What are the main global institutions? And how do they relate to international trade?, http://www.global-strategy.net/main-global-/

(28) Ibid. See also Nitisha, 4 Major International Economic Institutions, http://www. economicsdiscussion.net/international-economics/4-major-international-economic-institutions/4249 The institutions noted are the World Trade Organization, International Monetary Funds, United Nations Conference on Trade and Development (UNCTD) and a number of regional economic integration pacts. See also, Michael Tornz, International Finance, Stanford, https://web.stanford. edu/~tomz/pubs/Tomz2012a.pdf

(29) A new agreement on a replacement of NAFTA, the United States-Mexico-Canada Agreement (USMCA), has recently been ratified. While different in some respects from NAFTA it continues an international agreement between the United States, Mexico and Canada.

(30) World Investment Report 2018, https://unctad.org/en/PublicationsLibrary/wir2018_en.pdf, see also How Special Enterprise Zones Are Quietly Advancing Freedom, https://fee.org/articles/how-special-economic-zones-are-quietly- advancing-freedom/

(31) Activities of Multinational Enterprises, Organization for Economic Development, 2019, https:// www.oecd.org/industry/ind/MNEs-in-the-global-economy-policy-note.pdf

(32) Pol Antràs and Stephen R. Yeaple Multinational Firms and the Structure of International Trade, https://scholar.harvard.edu/files/antras/files/antras_yeaple_pre_print_3.pdf

(33) Neoliberalism, Wikipedia https://en.wikipedia.org/wiki/Neoliberalism

(35) Malcolm Sawyer, What is Financialization?, http://eprints.whiterose.ac.uk/82350/3/Sawyer. pdf p. 12

(36) Ibid. p. 13

AMERICA'S ECONOMIC NARRATIVE

America's economy operates in the context of the global economy, yet is unique. While part of the global economy, America's economy reflects America's ideology, emphasizing in particular:

- Individual Freedom
- Self-Reliance
- Pragmatism
- Achievement
- Competition
- Hard Work
- Better Future
- Material Wealth

Private property is a core condition for the US economy. Money is the means of economic transactions. Private property establishes ownership, along with the basic rules of exchange. Money is the vehicle by which property exchanges most commonly occur.

American capitalism is not a "pure" capitalism. While individuals and companies make basic economic decisions and seek profits, government plays a significant role in the operation of America's "mixed" economy.

BREAK THE CASTE

Today, corporations conduct the vast bulk of economic activity and financial institutions play a dominant role in the US economy.

In the sections below, private property, money, capitalism, corporations, and, in particular, financial corporations are discussed in more detail. Governmental roles in the operation of the economy are addressed in this section as well as in the section on political power below.

PRIVATE PROPERTY

America's economic system is based on private property, that is, the ability of individuals and groups to own property, including and especially, property that produces goods and services. Individuals own their own home and cars, but perhaps more importantly, individuals and groups can own commercial and intellectual property, such as equipment facilities or patents, that produce goods and services and generate profits.

Private property is an absolute condition of American capitalism. Persons, both individuals and groups of individuals, have to be able to own something in order to use it or trade it for private gain. Rules of ownership are established to assure exactly how individuals or groups own and/or can sell a house or a car or a share of stock. Equally important are the rules of exchange, the rules that parties follow in selling or trading what they own.

Since property is so critical and basic, a brief discussion of the very complex meaning of the legal concept of property is essential to understanding its significance. (Here we begin to see the strong interrelationship between law, politics, and the economy.) Property is more than the ownership of a thing. Property is legally a set of rights or powers over the thing owned. This 'bundle' of rights includes:[1]

1. Power to transfer: The ability to give the property to another
2. Immunity against taking: Others cannot take your property against your will
3. Right to exclude others: Ability to keep others from your property
4. Liberty to use: One can use property within general societal constraints
5 Immunity from damage: Others cannot cause harm to your property

One not only has ownership; one also has the ability to use the property and to prevent others from taking or ruining one's property, and the right to use property for gain. Governments establish rules and laws regarding property. [2]

MONEY

In discussing America's economy, one must also consider the basic medium of exchange: money.[3] In day-to-day life, money serves as a means of payment and store of value. If I have $100 (my store of value), I can pay $20 for food (means of payment) as well as have $80 for future use (store of value). However, money is more than the currency and coins one carries around and uses. It is also the amount that one has on deposit in accounts or what Radcliff calls "notes plus bank deposits." An even broader definition includes the degree of liquid assets promised by financial mediators. Money can be not only what one has on hand but what one can pledge to obtain.

The primary functions of money are: medium of exchange, a standard of value, a standard of deferred payments, and a reserve for bank credit.[4] In addition to the primary functions, money also has a number of "secondary" functions:[5]

- Basis of the Credit System: Money is the basis to determine the amount of credit that can be provided
- Measure of national income: A standard to assess national production
- Distribution of national income: Identifies standards used to reward activities

With money, all exchange can be reduced to a financial instrument or a derivative of a financial instrument.

Private property and money are necessities, the basics elements of capitalism, especially capitalism as it currently operates in the US.

CAPITALISM IN ITS "PURE" FORM

There is a common textbook understanding of capitalism and its concepts that serves as a helpful starting point and provides a context for further examination of American capitalism.

The **principal goal of capitalism** is individual profit. An individual uses their property for economic gain. Individuals, businesses, and corporations make choices to maximize profits. A business makes investments in order to increase profits. Goods or services are provided to others who will pay more for them than it costs to produce or provide them. Decisions are made to obtain or increase profits. One cannot require an individual business to hire any person or determine their pay. One can offer incentives to make it more profitable to hire a person but hiring is a decision based on whether the hire will result in more profits. Capitalism can result in more employment but employment is clearly not the primary goal. Profits are.

For example, American manufacturing productivity has significantly increased since 1979. During this same period manufacturing employment has significantly decreased, from 19 million to 11 million employees. Manufacturing businesses made decisions that they thought would result in additional profits. Technology investment, not hires, was determined to be the best decision to increase profits. During the 2009-2010 recession or downturn, many companies invested in technology as a first step to increase their profits. They did not hire more people.[6]

In capitalism, demand for a product guides economic decision making. Government does not determine what is made or sold. Individual businesses make these decisions based on customer demand for their goods and services and the ability of the businesses to provide the good or service at a profit. Businesses determine if the demand for goods and services is sufficient to make desired profits.

In capitalism, at least part of the profit is reinvested to produce more profits, which are in turn invested to make more profit and so on. Individuals and corporations do not consume the totality of the profits they generate. Some portion of the profit is retained to be invested to make even more profits. This investment can be in the business currently generating profits or in another business. Availability of some of the money generated from economic activity for generation of new profits is critical to the ongoing success of capitalism.

Capitalism has its winners and losers, sometimes called "creative destruction." Businesses and individuals take risks to obtain income and profits. Those who succeed are successful and profitable. Some, however, lose their money and time; and their businesses cease to exist. Capitalism accepts this as part of the process. If your business makes more money, profits increase; your personal finances, and usually status, improve. If you do not make money, you will ultimately go out of business.

Capitalism unleashes individual energy. Capitalism fosters initiative and assertiveness. It requires that the participants want to win. Capitalism is a competitive system. Individuals and groups act for their own benefit and profit. A business leader may make charitable contributions for the benefit of others but this contribution is not typically part of their business operations. Many capitalistic businesspeople can be concerned about other people not connected with their business and carry out charitable projects. But as businesspeople, as capitalists, they are concerned with their profits.

With winners and losers, new technologies, and changing consumer demand, **capitalism is dynamic and ever-changing.** Out with the old, in with the new is a never-ending element of capitalism. With continual innovation things do not stay the same. New players come into prominence; old brands die. A&P is gone; Wal-Mart is on the scene. Kodak film is no longer made; digital and phone photography is in. Oldsmobiles are no longer produced; the Toyota Corolla is the world's best-selling car. Lehman Brothers is gone but J.P. Morgan Chase continues on.

The basic elements of "pure" capitalism are clear:

- Private property
- Individual profit
- Markets driven by individual's choices
- Reinvestment to obtain more profits
- Release of individual energy
- Winner and losers
- Continual and dynamic change

CAPITALISM IN THE AMERICAN MIXED ECONOMY

The above is a common theoretical description of capitalism as an economic system, often called laissez faire:
An economic system where prices for goods and services are set freely by the forces of supply and demand and are allowed to reach their point of

equilibrium without intervention by government policy.[7]

In what is described as a "mixed economy," many economic decisions are made in the marketplace by individuals and groups, but the government also plays a role in the allocation and distribution of resources.

America's economy, like the economy of most developed nations, is a "mixed" one.

Perhaps the US has the greatest role for the private economy. While there are some constraints from government, private ownership and decisions about production dominate.[8]

[The US economy is] a largely market-based economy consisting of both private ownership of the means of production and government interventionism through macroeconomic fiscal and monetary policies.[9]

In America, the core elements of capitalism are modified and contextualized by a set of government laws and regulations, the implementation of these regulations, and often, equally important, interpretation and enforcement of these laws and regulations. Legislators, the president and state governors, and the courts provide the framework in which the economic system operates.

Government actions have been and continue to be taken for a wide variety of reasons including, for example, to correct market failures, reduce unemployment, provide social benefits, or encourage savings. To achieve what the government deems to be a benefit for the overall good of society it uses both incentives and punishments.[10] The "mixture" of business and government does not always remain the same. Economic, social, and political circumstances change. Based on circumstances, governmental executives, legislators, and courts take actions not only to preserve the economic system but also to seek improvement in the overall society and the lives of American citizens. From this point forward the word *capitalism* refers to the mixed, American form of capitalism.

CORPORATIONS

An enduring element of US capitalism has been the corporation. As early as 1790 corporations were formed. Since this time, more and more business activity in America has been carried out by corporations. In the second half of the 19th century many states established "general incorporation statutes." These statutes allowed groups of individuals to establish business entities that were independent of individuals, able to establish their own management structures, and distribute profits (or losses) as they wished.[11]

Generically speaking, any business entity that is recognized as distinct from the people who own it, that is, not a sole proprietorship or a partnership, is a corporation. The generic "corporate" label now includes a wide range of entities such as limited liability companies, real estate investment trusts, and venture capital organizations, in addition to those organizations that are specifically designated as "corporations." Today almost all corporations are incorporated in individual states that establish their own rules on requirements for incorporation in the individual state.

There are four defining characteristics of the modern corporation:[12]

- Separate legal personality of the corporation (access to tort and contract law in a manner similar to a person)
- Limited liability of the shareholders (a shareholder's personal liability is limited to the value of their shares in the corporation)
- Shares/Units of ownership (each of the individual shareholders owns a part of the corporation based on the number of shares held)
- Delegated management (the board of directors delegates day-to-day operational management of the company to executives responsible for day-to-day operations) [13]

In addition, to the individual protections, there are many other advantages of a corporation, including: [14]

- **Tax Advantages** - Corporations often gain tax advantages, such as the deductibility of health insurance premiums paid on behalf of an owner-employee; savings on self-employment taxes, as corporate income is not subject to Social Security, Workers Compensation, and Medicare taxes; and the deductibility of other expenses such as life insurance.
- **Establishing Credibility** - Incorporating may help a new business establish credibility with potential customers, employees, vendors and partners.
- **Unlimited Life** - A corporation's life is not dependent upon its owners. A corporation possesses the feature of unlimited life,

meaning if an owner dies or wishes to sell his or her interest, the corporation will continue to exist and do business.

- **Transferability of Ownership** - Ownership in a corporation is typically easily transferable. (However, there are restrictions on S corporation ownership.)
- **Raising Capital** - Capital can be raised more easily through the sale of stock. Additionally, many banks, when providing a small business loan, want the borrower to be an incorporated business.
- **Retirement plans** - Retirement funds and qualified retirement plans, such as a 401(k) plans, may be established more easily.

There are some potential disadvantages of incorporation such as:

- **Double Taxation**—C corporations are subject to double taxation of corporate profits when corporate income is distributed to the owners in the form of dividends. The double tax is created when tax is first paid at the corporate level. If corporate profit is then distributed to owners as dividends, the owners pay tax at the individual level on that income. The double tax can be avoided by electing S corporation tax status with the Internal Revenue Service.
- **Formation and Ongoing Expenses**—To form a corporation, articles of incorporation must be filed with the state and the applicable state filing fees paid. Many states impose ongoing fees on corporations, such as annual report and/or franchise tax fees. While these fees often are not very expensive for small businesses, formation of a corporation is more expensive than for a sole proprietorship or general partnership, both of which are not required to file formation documents with the state.
- **Corporate formalities**—Corporations are required to follow both initial and annual record-keeping tasks, such as holding and properly documenting initial and annual meetings of directors and shareholders, adopting and maintaining bylaws and issuing shares of stock to the owners. Sole proprietorships, general partnerships, and even LLCs do not incur the formalities imposed on corporations.

The advantages of incorporation far outweigh the disadvantages for most US business ventures, especially for larger businesses.

Although most corporations are state entities, the federal government has increasingly played a role in regulating important elements of corporate life. For example, the Securities Act of 1933 and the reporting requirements of the Securities Exchange Act of 1934 were put in place, in large part, due to the crash of the stock market in 1929.[15] The Securities and Exchange Commission was given the responsibility of regulating securities (types, conditions, standards for dividends, and other policies), disclosure of the actual conditions (accounting standards), and overall surveillance of the market. The goals of this legislation were to improve public confidence, avoid manipulation, and temper behavior with information and disclosure. Since then, additional national legislation regarding securities has been enacted.[16]

As Edward T. McCormick, Securities and Exchange Commissioner, and a strong proponent of capitalism, noted in his December 12, 1950 speech to the Calvin Bullock Forum:

> "The frequency with which corporations had historically been used to avoid contract obligations, defraud creditors, evade covenants and perform skullduggery generally, led people like Woodrow Wilson who was certainly no rabid radical, to condemn lawyers for letting loose on society this instrument for subversion of individual obligations......something had to be done to preserve the integrity of the investment in corporate securities and the proper relations between management and investors. Federal regulation in this field was inevitable." [17]

As the role of corporations in the economy has grown, so has their size. While corporations have grown in size, the total number of publicly traded corporations has decreased. A brief review of this growth in size, why it has occurred, and corporate growth mechanisms provides a fuller understanding of the emergence of larger corporations and their increased role in America's economy.

Andrew Flowers provides an overview:

> As big business gets bigger, the biggest businesses are growing even faster. The Fortune 100, or the 100 companies with the

highest revenue, have seen their proportion of nominal GDP rise from about 33 percent in 1994 to 46 percent in 2013. As a share of all Fortune 500 revenues, revenues for these top 100 companies were up to 63 percent in 2013 from 57 percent in 1994.

With a slew of mergers and acquisitions—like the Verizon-AOL deal—big businesses might be snapping up or joining with rivals, and that corporate consolidation may have led to a concentration of market power. That's the skeptical-of-business view. [18]

The Tax Foundation points out that public corporations earn 62% of total business revenue in the US while being only 5% of the business tax filers. The other 95% of businesses has 38% of total revenue.[19]

Corporations seek to grow in size to increase their profits. Growth in size can offer a number of ways to increase profits, such as economy of scale, market growth, outsourcing, bypassing protective mechanisms, limiting transportation costs, reducing labor costs. All of these benefits can result in more profits for the corporation and its shareholders.[20]

Growth in size is and has been accomplished by a number of different mechanisms, the major ones being investing current profits, obtaining new investors, mergers and acquisitions, and globalizing. Corporations can use their own profits to grow internally. They can also obtain new funding from other investors, such as venture capitalists or hedge funds, to invest in growth. Many successful companies make large research and development (R&D) investments that provide them the direction in seeking additional investment.

Mergers and Acquisitions (M&A) are increasingly employed to increase corporate size. Two companies agree to join together (merger) or one company acquires another (acquisition). The increases in M&As and the size of these M&As have been extensively documented. The Institute for Mergers, Acquisition, and Alliances notes: [21]

Since 1985, more than 325,000 mergers & acquisitions transactions have been announced with a known value of almost $34.9B USD. In 2017, a new record has been broken in terms of number of deals with 15,100 which is a 12.2% increase over 2016. The record of total value of deals took place in 2015 with $24.2B USD. The compound annual growth rate (CAGR) for the number of deals from 1985 to 2018 was 5.86% while the value grew at 5.32%.

Andres Brownstein and others update 2017 M&A information with 2018 data and place US M&A in global context.[22]

> As a whole, 2018 proved to be another strong year for M&A. Total deal volume reached almost $4.2 trillion globally, higher than the $3.7 trillion volume of 2017, but still less than the record of over $5 trillion set in 2015. Deals involving U.S. targets totaled over $1.7 trillion, compared to approximately $1.5 trillion in 2017. The number of large deals significantly increased in 2018, with 60 deals over $10 billion announced globally (compared to 46 deals in 2017). The technology sector saw the largest deal volume, followed by healthcare, oil and gas, and real estate. Private equity firms also had a banner year. As of late December, private equity buyout volume had reached almost $384 billion, the highest since the PE [private equity] boom before the financial crisis. Although hostile and unsolicited M&A remained prevalent, the volume of these deals fell globally both in absolute terms, from $575 billion in 2017 to $522 billion in 2018, and in terms of share of overall deal volume, from 15% in 2017 to less than 13% in 2018.

As the number of M&A activities have increased, so have the sizes of corporations involved in M&A.[23] A sense of the size is provided by Samuel Stebbins in AZCentral. Mr. Stebbins points out that all five of the largest M&As in 2018 exceeded $31 billion with the largest, Cigna's acquisition of Express Scripts Holding company, being $68.5 billion.[24] While mergers and acquisitions have occurred in all industries, M&A activities have been especially prevalent in the financial sector (See section on Finance below)

Many, if not most, larger corporations have become multinational or transnational corporations. Greer and Singh document this growth. [25]

> Over the past quarter century, there has been a virtual proliferation of transnationals. In 1970, there were some 7,000 parent TNCs [Transnational Corporations], while today that number has jumped to 38,000. 90% percent of them are based

in the industrialized world, which control over 207,000 foreign subsidiaries. Since the early 1990s, these subsidiaries' global sales have surpassed worldwide trade exports as the principal vehicle to deliver goods and services to foreign markets.

The large number of TNCs can be somewhat misleading, however, because the wealth of transnationals is concentrated among the top 100 firms which in 1992 had US $3.4 trillion in global assets, of which approximately US. $1.3 trillion was held outside their home countries. The top 100 TNCs also account for about one-third of the combined outward foreign direct investment (FDI) of their countries of origin. Since the mid-1980s, a large rise of TNC-led foreign direct investment has occurred. Between 1988 and 1993, worldwide FDI stock—a measure of the productive capacity of TNCs outside their home countries—grew from US$1.1 to US$2.1 trillion in estimated book value.

Cool Geography has updated the number of transnationals through 2018. Currently there are 64 parent international corporations with 660,000 subsidiaries.[26]
Mergers and acquisitions have contributed to a decrease in the number of publicly traded corporations.[27]

Lately, though, the universe of such (publicly traded) companies has been shrinking in the U.S. New businesses have been offering shares to the public at less than half the rate of the 1980s and 1990s. Mergers and acquisitions have eliminated hundreds more. About 3,600 firms were listed on U.S. stock exchanges at the end of 2017, down more than half from 1997.

In addition to mergers and acquisitions, a number of other factors account for the decrease in the number of publicly traded companies. Some public corporations have become pass-through or C corporations. In addition, fewer companies go public and therefore fewer initial public offerings occur, but M&As have had a major impact on the number of publicly traded companies.[28]
Along with growth in size, a number of organizations and individuals

have expressed concern with the growth of "crony capitalism." In simplest terms, crony capitalism is an economic system in which economic success depends upon political connections. Investopedia defines crony capitalism as:

> A society based on the close relationships between businessmen and the state. Instead of success being determined by the free market and the rule of law, the success of a business is dependent on the favoritism that is shown to by the ruling government in the form of tax breaks, government grants, and other incentives. [29]

The Heritage report, "Cronyism: Undermining Economic Freedom and Prosperity Around the World," provides a description of crony capitalism that focuses on its impacts:[30]

> "Yet in far too many cases the future Sam Waltons, Ray Krocs, and Bill Gateses of the world are trapped in a system dominated by cronyism and corruption, where those with special access to government favors or information and those who already enjoy monopoly power dictate pricing and conditions of service, often becomingly extravagantly rich in the process while denying millions of their countrymen that very same access."

Mr. Roberts, the report's author, notes that: "When the collective decisions of the marketplace are overridden by government regulations, price setting, and even direct control or state ownership of natural resources, then 'the system' is something quite distinct from free-market capitalism and truly does become an enemy of the 'little guy.'" For Mr. Roberts any "substitution of government decision making for the collective judgment of the marketplace" is a major problem and there is a long history of such intervention.

Mr. Roberts draws a strong correlation and causation between cronyism, corruption, and reduced economic performance. What is required are policies "that empower individuals, avoid discrimination and ensure open and fair competition for all." He concludes that: "Urgent action is needed to restore the even-handedness and fairness of government expenditures and to roll back and eliminate special interest funding." Brink Lindsey and Seven Teles make the same argument in their book, *The Captured Economy.*[31]

The source of crony capitalism is widely debated. As Investopedia notes:

> Socialists believe that crony capitalism is the inevitable result of pure capitalism. This belief is supported by their claims that people in power, whether business or government, look to stay in power and the only way to do this is to create networks between government and business that support each other. On the other hand, capitalists believe that crony capitalism arises from the need of socialist governments to control the state. This requires businesses to operate closely with the government to achieve the greatest success.[32]

The type of, degree of, and rationale for governmental influence is disputed but it is clear that political influence on business occurs and that government does play a role in the operation of the economic system.

FINANCIAL SECTOR

Among corporations, financial corporations are especially important. The US financial industry has grown in size as the US economy has grown. For example, in 2017: [33]

- The banking system had $17.4 trillion in assets and had a net income of $164.8 billion.
- Asset managers held $51 trillion in long term assets, including $28.2 trillion of retirement assets (pension funds).
- Insurance premiums written totaled $1.1 trillion.
- Venture capitalists invested $84 billion.
- Private equity invested more than $500 billion.

The percentage of US GDP now accounted for by finance is now $1.6 trillion, slightly over 8% of the $20.9 trillion US GDP. The Wall Street Journal provides a picture of finance's growth. Finance was 2.8% of GDP in 1950, 4.9% in 1980, 8.3% in 2006, and (in the Great Recession) 8.4% in 2014.[34]

Finance has always been profitable and accounted for more profit that its percentage of GDP. [35] In the 1940s and 50s the financial sector was 3% of GDP and accounted for 8-15% of total US profits. Beginning in the 1980s, due in part to deregulation, the finance sector doubled and it reached profit levels exceeding 30% of all US profits. Today, finance, which accounts for only about 8% of GDP, reaps about a third (33%) of all profits.[36]

Financial sector employment and wages has also increased. As of March 2019, there were approximately 8.6 million employed in financial services; 2 million in supervisory positions and 6.6 million in non-supervisory positions. Average weekly earnings were $35.50 per hour, slightly over $1,050 weekly.[37] In March of 2019, total US employment stood 156 million; average wages stood at $26.80 per hour, $955 weekly.[37] Employment in the financial and real estate occupations grew from 520,000 and 2% of total employment in 1910 to 8.1 million and 5.7% of total employment in 2015.[38] Today the financial sector employment represents 5% of total employment, much less than the 8% of GDP in generates.

Both the size and profitability of finance in America has grown significantly in the past 60 years.[39] Finance is a major part of the US economic order, provides employment to many, and makes a major contribution to profits in America.

Up to this point, the financial sector has been considered as a whole. This sector is, however, very complex. The Census Bureau's North American Industry Classification System identifies eighty-nine (89) types of financial institutions. The Census Bureau groups financial institutions into five major areas: Monetary Authorities-Central Bank; Credit Intermediation and Related Activities; Securities, Commodity Contracts and other Financial Investments and Related Activities; Insurance Carriers and Related Activities; and Funds Trusts and Other Financial Vehicles.[40]

With the exception of the Central Bank, many financial organizations carry out activities in multiple financial areas. For example, a bank that carries out credit intermediation activities may also offer financial planning activities; an insurance company provides insurance but may also offer retirement advice. The classification system might be better viewed as types of financial activities. For the purpose of this discussion, financial activities can be grouped generally into two major categories, banking and insurance.

BANKING

The basic idea of banking is straightforward: make money with money.

Banks obtain money from many sources. People invest in a bank and become owners or shareholders. Some banks (see below) also obtain money from others who are not shareholders, most notably their depositors. Banks increasingly also charge fees for services provided to customers. All of a bank's money is pooled and provided to customers who need or desire money for a variety of purposes. These bank customers (buyers of the bank's money) pay the banks more for the money provided to them than the bank's cost to obtain the money provided.

At first glance, this looks pretty easy. Gather up money cheaply and then sell it to others for more than it costs you to obtain the money. Why don't individuals do this rather than employ banks? The reasons are numerous and include:

- Most individuals don't have enough money to make it available to others in the amount the others want or need.
- Most individuals don't have enough friends with money who would give money to them to provide it to others.
- Most individuals don't have the knowledge of to whom to provide money to get the highest return on the money with the lowest (or at least a low) risk of the money not being paid back.
- Most individuals aren't able to take the risk of losing all of the money they provide to others.
- Most individuals want some assurance that if things go bad, they can get some or all of their money back.
- Individuals can't get government insurance to cover their lending loss.

All banks collect and distribute money, but not all banks are the same. Banks can be roughly divided into four types: commercial/retail banks, investment banks, bank holding companies and shadow banks. Each of these types of banks is different and requires separate discussion.

Most are familiar with commercial/retail banks. The vast majority of Americans have at least one bank account, such as a checking account, a savings account, certificates of deposit (CDs), or money market accounts. They deposit money in these accounts, use checks, withdraw money, and get paid interest for savings, CDs, and even sometimes checking accounts.

Retail banks have other common sources of revenue in addition to deposits. Bank's shareholders invest their money to make money, paying to establish the bank and give it initial resources to obtain a charter from the federal or a state government. In addition to depositors and investors, banks also often charge a number of fees, such as overdraft fees, fees on credit card transactions or late payment fees, fees for the use of ATMs, that serve as sources of revenue.

The retail bank pools all this money and identifies individuals and businesses willing to pay more for the money than what it costs banks to lend, resulting in profit. Banks provide these funds to those willing to pay the most for these funds while at the same time keeping in mind that they need to have the money paid back.

Banks balance the amount they can charge for money with the risk of losing this money. Retail banks used to invest primarily in mortgages and business loans to get their returns. Now they often pursue other types of investment, some of which are riskier. (In the past, bankers joked that their business was 3-6-3: pay interest at 3% on deposits, obtain 6% interest on loans made, and go play golf at 3:00 PM.)

Since the 1930s most commercial banks have insurance, usually federal insurance provided through the Federal Deposit Insurance Corporation (FDIC).[41] To get this insurance, banks need to meet FDIC requirements and follow FDIC rules, especially regarding the amount and types of investment in which the bank can engage and the amount of money that banks must keep on hand to be immediately available for their depositors. With FDIC insurance, the bank's depositors can be assured that even if the bank "goes under" (owes more than it has), depositors will be able to recover the money they deposited up to a certain amount, currently $250,000 per account.

Investment banks, unlike commercial banks, don't have individual depositors. These banks find, for example, corporations who want money (sellers). The banks identify institutions such as pension funds, mutual funds, and affluent individuals (buyers) who want to buy what sellers have. The investment banks then provide the seller with cash it needs. In addition to these sources, investment banks also obtain money from commercial/ retail banks that use bank funds obtained from various sources.

In addition to providing money, investment banks usually provide guidance to those who issue stocks or bonds and to those who wish to invest in stocks and bonds. They help to facilitate mergers and acquisitions and corporate reorganizations. They also broker trades for both institutions and private investors and are normally paid for these services.

Investment banks, generally speaking, take more risks than commercial/ retail banks. Investment banks in the US are subject to monitoring by the US Treasury and other government institutions. Recently regulation of investment banks included the provisos of the Financial Stability Act of 2010 (Dodd-Frank Bill).[42] Even with these changes, however, investment banks are able to take more risks and are less regulated than commercial/ retail banks, and recent legislative and regulatory changes to Dodd-Frank have reduced investment bank regulation.

Together US commercial and investment banks have about $17.1 trillion in assets and approximately the same amount in liabilities.[43] On a monthly basis banks currently (in 2020) provide from $1.3 to $1.4 trillion in loans. This amount is less than the $1.7 trillion in monthly loans in the last quarter of 2010.

Another type of banking organization is the bank holding company. Any company that has legal and structural control over a bank is called a bank holding company. Bank holding companies operate under a different set of rules than commercial and investment banks. Larger bank holding companies (300 shareholders or more) must register with the Securities and Exchange Commission (SEC) and are subject to SEC rules.

Being a bank holding company has many benefits. Perhaps the largest advantage is the ability to both borrow money from the Federal Reserve to meet temporary liquidity shortages caused by internal or external disruptions and to borrow needed money at very favorable rates. Being a bank holding company also, among other things, allows a company to assume debt of shareholders on a tax-free basis and more easily acquire other banks and non-bank entities.

During the 2007 to 2009 recession, many of the larger banking organizations, e.g. Goldman Sachs, Morgan Stanley, American Express, and CITI Group became bank holding companies seeing the advantage of easier access to money more beneficial than any banking regulations that were imposed.

From December 31, 1990 through December 31, 2016, bank holding companies' consolidated assets rose from about $5.5 trillion to $19.5 trillion in real terms—an increase of 256 percent, or an average of slightly over 5.2 percent per year. Real GDP grew 91 percent over the same time period.[44]

In addition to "traditional" banks, so-called shadow banks also play a major financial role. Shadow banking refers to financial transactions, entities, systems, activities and practices that occur outside the realm of government regulation. Money Reserve provides the following description:[45]

> Shadow banking is an intermediary form of borrowing that provides both credit and capital outside the constraints of the conventional banking system. It is unsupervised lending by hedge funds, money market funds, trading houses, and structured investment vehicles that side-steps regulatory oversight. Shadow banking arose both from the need for credit and the desire for convenience.

The former Chairperson of the Federal Reserve, Ben Bernanke, offered the following definition:[46]

> Shadow banking, as usually defined, comprises a diverse set of institutions and markets that, collectively, carry out traditional banking functions—but do so outside, or in ways only loosely linked to, the traditional system of regulated depository institutions. Examples of important components of the shadow banking system include securitization vehicles, asset-backed commercial paper [ABCP] conduits, money market funds, markets for repurchase agreements, investment banks, and mortgage companies.

Among the common shadow bank institutions are mortgage lenders, money market funds, insurance companies, hedge funds, private equity funds, payday lenders, unlisted derivatives, and other financial instruments. Some activities of regulated institutions are also considered part of the shadow bank system, for example, credit default swaps. [47]

The international Financial Stabilization Board (FSB) notes that the more vulnerable segments of shadow banking have been reduced.[48]

> Many of the most vulnerable parts of shadow banking activities that contributed to the crisis that spread throughout the global financial system, such as asset-backed commercial paper (ABCP) programmes, structured investment vehicles (SIVs), subprime residential mortgage-backed securities (RMBS), and

collateralized debt obligations (CDOs), are no longer conducted at the same scale. Others, such as money market funds (MMFs) and repurchase agreements (repos), have experienced a normalization from elevated pre-crisis levels, and additional policy measures are being implemented for them. The declines have been attributed to changing risk appetite, rejection of particular products and funding models, and effective policy measures.

Shadow banks, like investment banks, act as intermediaries between buyers and sellers. They make money by providing money or other forms of assets available to "borrowers." As a rule, shadow banks take on higher market, credit, and liquidity risks. In many cases they do not have capital requirements commensurate with those risks immediately available.

The Financial Stability Act of 2010 (Dodd-Frank Bill) did not impose any regulatory constraints on the shadow banking system. However, some new regulations by the Security and Exchange Commission in terms of financial requirements has set some limits on non-banking institutions and instruments.[49] In the aftermath of the 2008-2009 recession an international body, the Financial Stability Board (FSB), was established and the United States is a charter member of this group.[50] The FSB, currently with 28 national members, is not a regulatory body but a standard setting and monitoring organization that provides information to its member organizations regarding the size, activities, and vulnerability of the shadow banking system.[51]

Because shadow banks are not regulated, it is very difficult to determine precisely their total assets or the number of their transactions. A 2010 Federal Reserve Report placed shadow banking assets at $22 trillion in 2007.[52]

The gross measure of shadow bank liabilities grew to a size of nearly $22 trillion in June 2007. We also plot total traditional banking liabilities in comparison, which were around $14 trillion in 2007. The size of the shadow banking system has contracted substantially since the peak in 2007.

Especially since 2010, shadow banking has continued its growth. A report by Keefe, Bryyette & Wood, (KBW) indicates that non-bank lenders have almost $18 trillion in assets, more than that of all regulated banks ($16 trillion).[53] The Financial Stability Board says shadow banking assets posing risks to the financial system grew 7.6 percent to $45 trillion in 2016, the most recent year it assessed risk.[54]

A large portion of the financial system is now what is called the shadow banking system. Most see major benefits of the shadow banking system as fostering economic growth and development. At the same time, they are concerned about the major negative effects that could occur should the shadow banking system fail.

While the major types of banks have been described separately above, in reality, they form a single interrelated system. A commercial bank may invest its resources using an investment bank. An investment bank may go to a shadow bank to invest its funds. Funds that are deposited in a commercial bank can end up in a shadow bank investment.

Also, a company with a "bank" name may be all types of banks as well as a bank holding company. For example, one can walk into a building with a Wells Fargo or Citibank or Bank of America sign on the door. Within this "bank" is a place to deposit individual funds (commercial bank), to invest bank and other funds into a venture (investment bank), or to obtain a position in a hedge fund (shadow bank).

Banks are critical institutions in the financial industry. They collect and distribute money to those who wish to obtain it for a variety of purposes. Money is the "oil" the economy needs for its operation and growth and banks are a major source of money.

INSURANCE

The Insurance industry is another major component of the America's financial system. It contributes significantly to American's GDP and is a major source of funds for multiple and varied investments. Insurance companies pool resources collected from individuals and businesses through premiums, addressing the needs of individuals and corporations to reduce their risk or mitigate negative consequences. Using the premiums and fees collected, insurance companies are major investors in the economy.

For example, at the individual level, homeowner's insurance is purchased to cover potential damage to one's residence. Almost no one purchases home insurance because they want their house to burn down; they do so to mitigate the financial consequences if the fire should a fire occur. The same is true of health insurance. At the individual level, health insurance protects from the financial consequences of illness. A third party, the insurer, is paid premiums to take care of the costs that could result from a fire or major health problem. While the hope is that one will not need to use the insurance, individuals are financially protected to some degree if things go awry.[55]

Insurance is not limited to addressing the risk of individuals. Businesses also seek insurance for protections from a variety of risks such as damage to property, accidents to employees and customers, disruption of supply chains, and risk of war. Insurance can be sought and, in most cases, obtained for a wide range of risks that individuals or organizations can face. Wikipedia provides an extensive list of 12 insurance general categories and 92 different kinds of insurance.[56]

The National Association of Insurance Commissioners places insurance in five major categories: Property & Casualty, Life, Health, Fraternal Organization, and Title.[57] In each of these areas both individuals and organizations are insured. Fraternal Organization insurance is insurance provided to a variety of social service organizations to cover potential liability. Title insurance, a uniquely American insurance, "insures against financial loss from defects in title to real property and from the invalidity or unenforceability of mortgage loans."[58] Together Fraternal Organization and Title insurance constitute 1.1% of total premiums.[59]

Property and Casualty, Life, and Health are the major types of insurance and constitute the bulk of the $3.32 trillion of insurance industry premiums. Premiums in each of these insurance areas are as follows:[60]

American Insurance Industry Premiums: 2017

Type of Insurance	Amount ($ Billions)	Percent of Total
Property and Casualty	$640	27.5%
Life	$810	34.8%
Health	$847	36.4%
Other	$25	1.2%
Total	**$3,320**	**00%**

As noted above, insurance companies invest their funds to obtain profits. Property and Casualty (P/C), Life (L) and Health (H) invested $ $5.7 trillion in 2017. Total P/C cash and invested assets were $1.69 trillion in 2017, according to S&P Global Market Intelligence. L/H cash and invested assets totaled $4.07 trillion in 2017[61]

Insurance companies invest in a variety of areas of the economy. The largest investment area was bonds (58% of P/C assets and 73% of L/H assets). P/C also invests a large percentage, nearly 25%, in stocks. Almost 80% of total assets of the insurance industry are invested in stocks and bonds. However, insurance companies also invest in diverse financial ventures.[62] As a whole, insurance is responsible for 3.1% of the US GDP.[63]

The period from 2005 to 2015 was profitable for insurance companies. Profit came from investments and fees. Net income for the industry—not pretax—equaled $448 billion in those ten years.[64] Life insurers' overall profitability—as measured by ROE—remains below 2008-2009 crisis levels, but is slowly trending upwards from that period. "At the end of 2017, return on equity (ROE) was 11% for a sample of both North American and European life insurers. For Asia, key market players have not yet reported their 2017 ROE, but the preliminary result of 10% indicates more or less stable profitability since the financial crisis."[65] In 2016 total PC and L/H insurance profits were approximately $80.6 billion, down from nearly $100 billion in 2015.[66]

A total of 2.69 million employees are employed in the insurance industry, divided almost equally between employees of insurance carriers and insurance agencies and brokers.[67] Insurance industry employees represent approximately 29% of total employment in the financial industry (finance and insurance).[68] Hourly wages in the insurance industry average $36.02; weekly wages $1071.[69] In March 2019 total US employment stood at 156 million. Average hourly wages were $26.80; average weekly wages $955.[61]

The insurance industry is highly regulated, primarily through state insurance commissions. The 2010 Dodd-Frank Act did establish federal oversight through the Federal Insurance Office (FIO).[71] The FIO is not, however, a regulator. "The FIO is charged with monitoring all aspects of the insurance sector, including identifying activities within the sector that could potentially contribute to a systemic crisis to the broader financial system, the extent to which under-served communities have access to affordable insurance products, and the sector's regulation."[72] Actual regulation of the insurance industry is the responsibility of individual states. State responsibility for regulation is most often delegated to a state insurance commission. While there are differences between states, commissions in each state generally have four functions: assuring insurance organizations are financially stable, setting rates for various type of insurance, assuring contract compliance, and addressing complaints.[73] Commissions are given a range of powers that enable them to enforce their decisions.

Insurance is a major part of the credit mediation process. While playing a smaller role than the traditional and shadow banking sectors, insurance companies contribute a significant amount ($5 trillion) in debt and equity financing to the American economy. As the remainder of the financial sector, insurance companies attain profits that are not commensurate with its size.

Corporations, especially financial corporations, dominate and support American's economy.

Notes

(1) See for example, Bundle of Rights, Investopedia, https://www.investopedia.com/terms/b/bundle-of-rights.asp; Bundle of Rights (Property Rights) Law and Legal Definitions, US Legal, https://definitions.uslegal.com/b/bundle-of-rights-property-law/

(2) A variety of justifications are given for the possession and use of property. Governments establish the laws and rules of private property and the remedies and punishments for violation of these rights.

(3) Anatol Murad, The Nature of Money, Southern Economic Journal, 1943 DOI: 10.2307/1052544, https://www.jstor.org/stable/1052544

(4) Money: Nature, Definitions and Functions of Money, http://www.yourarticlelibrary.com/economics/money/money-nature-definitions-and-functions-of-money/10863 Sir John Hicks stated: "money is defined by its functions: anything is money which is used as money: ' money is what money does."

(5) Ibid.

(6) Heritage Report Technology Explains Drop in Manufacturing Jobs rates, https://www.heritage.org/jobs-and-labor/report/technology-explains-drop-manufacturing-jobs

(7) Laissez Faire, Wikipedia, https://en.wikipedia.org/wiki/Laissez-faire

(8) Types of Economic Systems, Shmoop, https://www.shmoop.com/economic-systems/types.html

(9) Capitalism, Wikipedia, https://en.wikipedia.org/wiki/Capitalism It should be recognized that capitalism is not an American invention and that Americans were not the first to employ corporations

discussed below. See for example, Venkatesh Rao, A Brief History of Capitalism 1600 to 2010, June 8, 2011 https://www.ribbonfarm.com/2011/06/08/a-brief-history-of-the-corporation-1600-to-2100/ For example in Europe, initially a corporation received permission from the king to carry out certain functions for which permission it provided some of its revenue to the king. In many of these cases the license from the king or other ruling authority carried with it a monopoly over a certain business.

(10) More detail on the governmental role in America is provided in the Political section below.

(11) What is Capitalism? Investopedia, https://www.investopedia.com/ask/answers/041515/what-history-corporations-america.asp

(12) Corporate Law: Fritch Law Office, http://www.fritchlaw.com/index.php/corporate-law and http://www.company-registration.in/characteristics-of-a-company.php

(13) If the corporation is a public company, the shares are traded on a stock exchange, such as the London Stock Exchange, New York Stock Exchange, Euronext in Paris or BM&F Bovespa in Sao Paulo.

(14) Susan Ward, Advantages and Disadvantages of Incorporation, The Balance, Updated, December 7, 2018, https://www.thebalancesmb.com/should-you-incorporate-your-small-business-2947252

(15) Securities Exchange Act of 1934, https://legcounsel.house.gov/Comps/Securities%20 Exchange%20Act%20Of%201934.pdfocial and The Laws That Govern the Securities Industry https://www.sec.gov/answers/about-lawsshtml.html

(16) Laws That Govern, op. cit.

(17) Edward T McCormick, Capitalism and the Modern Corporation, The Calvin Bullock Forum, December 12, 1950, http://www.sec.gov/news/speech/1950/121250mccormick.pdf
(18) Andrew Flowers Big Business is Getting Bigger, Fivethirtyeight, May 18, 2015, https://fivethirtyeight.com/features/big-business-is-getting-bigger/

(19) Andrew Lundeen Kyle Pomerleau, Corporations Make Up 5 Percent of Businesses but Earn 62 Percent of Revenue, Tax Foundation, November 25, 2014 https://taxfoundation.org/corporations-make-5-percent-businesses-earn-62-percent-revenues/

(20) Billie Nordmeyer MBA, MA, Reasons for Multinational Corporations, AZ Central, https://yourbusiness.azcentral.com/reasons-multinational-corporations-23250.html

(21) M & A in the United States, IMMA, https://imaa-institute.org/m-and-a-us-united-states/#:~:targetText=Announced%20M%26A%20in%20the%20United,of%20almost%2034'900%20 bil.&targetText=In%202012%2C%20a%20new%20record,a%2012.2%25%20increase%20over%202016.

(22) Andrew Brownstein, Steven Rosenblum and Victor Goldfeld, Wachtell, Lipton, Rosen & Katz, Mergers and Acquisitions—2019, January 15, 2019, Harvard Law School Forum on Corporate Governance and Financial Regulation, https://corpgov.law.harvard.edu/2019/01/15/mergers-and-acquisitions-2019/ See also M. Szmigiera, Mergers and Acquisitions-Statistics and Facts, Statistica, Oct 10, 2019, https://www.statista.com/topics/1146/mergers-and-acquisitions/#:~:targetText=The%20 value%20of%20global%20mergers,approximately%201.6%20trillion%20U.S.%20dollars. This source places the 2018 MA global total at $3.9 trillion and the US MA total at $1.6 trillion just slightly lower than the amounts identified by Brownstein and alii.

(23) Number of merger and acquisition transactions in the United States in 2019, by deal value, Statistica, https://www.statista.com/statistics/245977/number-of-munda-deals-in-the-united-states/

(46) Bernanke, Ben S (8 November 2013). "The Crisis as a Classic Financial Panic" At the Fourteenth Jacques Polak Annual Research Conference, Washington, D.C.: Board of Governors of the Federal Reserve System. Retrieved 8 March 2016.

(47) Shadow Banking, Investopedia, https://www.investopedia.com/terms/s/shadow-banking-system.asp

(48) Assessment of shadow banking activities, risks and the adequacy of post-crisis policy tools to address financial stability concerns, Financial Stability Board 2017, http://www.fsb.org/wp-content/uploads/P300617-1.pdf

(49) Tobias Adrian and Adam B Aschraft, Shadow Bank Regulation, Staff Report No. 559 April 2012 https://www.newyorkfed.org/medialibrary/media/research/staff_reports/sr559.pdf

(50) History of the FSB, Financial Stability Board, http://www.fsb.org/history-of-the-fsb/

(51) Report to the G20 Los Cabos Summit on Strengthening FSB Capacity, Resources and Governance 18-19 June 2012, Financial Stability Board, http://www.fsb.org/wp-content/uploads/r_120619c.pdf

(52) Zoltan Pozsar Tobias Adrian Adam Ashcraft and Hayley Boesky, Shadow Banking, Staff Report No. 458 July 2010 Revised February 2012, https://www.newyorkfed.org/medialibrary/media/research/staff_reports/sr458.pdf

(53) Larry Light, Shadow banking is growing fast -- is that a threat? March 9, 2017 https://www.cbsnews.com/news/shadow-banking-fast-growth-threat/

(54) Global Shadow Banking Monitoring Report, Financial Stability Board, https://embargo.fsb.org/wp-content/uploads/Global-Shadow-Banking-Monitoring-Report-2016-EMBARGO-1.pdfJun Luo Shadow Banking Bloomberg, September 24 2018, https://www.bloomberg.com/quicktake/shadow-banking, see also Shadow banking grows to more than $45tn assets globally Caroline Binham, Financial Times, March 5, 2018, https://www.ft.com/content/c45bf332-1e48-11e8-956a-43db76e69936,and M. Irani, Raymakal Iyer, Ralf R. Meisenzahl, and Jos´e-Luis Peydr´o, The Rise of Shadow Banking: Evidence from Capital Regulation Rustom Federal Reserve 2019, https://www.federalreserve.gov/econres/feds/files/2018039pap.pdf, and Statistical work on shadow banking: development of new datasets and indicators for shadow banking, Anna Maria Agresti and Rok Brence, European Central Bank, Brussels, Belgium, 18-19 May 2017 https://www.bis.org/ifc/publ/ifcb46p.pdf

(55 Life insurance is somewhat different in that it is focused not on protecting the one who dies but those whom the insured wishes to protect from the ill effects of her/his death.

(56) Types of Insurance, https://en.wikipedia.org/wiki/Category:Types_of_insurance

(57) National Association of Insurance Commissioners 2017 Report Card, https://www.naic.org/state_report_cards/report_card_fl.pdf

(58) Title Insurance, Wikipedia, https://en.wikipedia.org/wiki/Title_insurance
(59) National Association of Insurance Commissions 2017 report, op. cit.

(60) Facts + Statistics: Industry overview, Insurance information Institute, https://www.iii.org/fact-statistic/facts-statistics-industry-overview

(61) Ibid.

(62) A Firm Foundation: How Insurance Supports the Economy, Insurance Industry, https://www.iii.org/publications/a-firm-foundation-how-insurance-supports-the-economy

(63) Contribution To GDP Insurance Information Institute, https://www.iii.org/publications/a-firm-foundation-how-insurance-supports-the-economy/driving-economic-progress/contribution-to-gdp

(64) Chris Burand, Insurance Company Profitability, Insurance Journal, December 7, 2015, https://www.insurancejournal.com/magazines/mag-features/2015/12/07/390548.htm

(65) World insurance in 2017: solid, but mature life markets weigh on growth Swiss RE Institute https://www.swissre.com/dam/jcr:a160725c-d746-4140-961b-ea0d206e9574/sigma3_2018_en.pdf

(66) Facts + Statistics: Industry overview, Insurance information Institute, https://www.iii.org/fact-statistic/facts-statistics-industry-overview

(67) Association of Insurance Commissioners 2017 Report Card, https://www.naic.org/state_report_cards/report_card_fl.pdf; Note that others place the number of employees somewhat higher, e.g. Facts + Statistics: Industry overview, Insurance information Institute, https://www.iii.org/fact-statistic/facts-statistics-industry-overview places the number at 2.7 million.

(68) Insurance Carriers and Related Activities: NAICS 524 Industries at a Glance, Bureau of Labor Statistics, https://www.bls.gov/iag/tgs/iag524.htm

(69) Ibid.

(70) Data, Tables and Calculation by Subject, Bureau of Labor Statistics, http://data.bls.gov/timesseries/LNS12000000

(71) Federal Insurance Office, Department Treasury, https://home.treasury.gov/policy-issues/financial-markets-financial-institutions-and-fiscal-service/federal-insurance-office

(72) Federal Insurance Office (FIO) National Association of Insurance commissioners, https://www.naic.org/cipr_topics/topic_fio.htm

(73) Chris MacKechnie, What Are the Duties of An Insurance Commissioner? Career Trends, September 26, 2017, https://bizfluent.com/list-6742445-duties-insurance-commissioner-.html

AMERICA'S POLITICAL ORDER

America's ideology and economy support and, in turn, are supported by the America's political order. The central elements of the US political order are elected officials, rule of law, and individual rights. These basics are set forth in the US Constitution, America's fundamental governmental organizing document.

The goal of the American government, as stated in the Preamble of the Constitution, is: "Form a more perfect Union, establish Justice, insure domestic Tranquility, provide for the common defence, promote the general Welfare, and secure the Blessings of Liberty to ourselves and our Posterity." The government, guided by these goals, seeks to care for the good of all.

The US Constitution establishes that American citizens elect those who enact the laws by which Americans live. All federal lawmakers (Representatives and Senators) are elected by the citizens, elections that serve as the basis of the legitimacy of the laws those lawmakers establish. On behalf of the citizens who elect them, elected legislators enact laws that govern American society. An executive (President) is also elected and has authority to implement these laws. A judiciary is appointed by the President and approved by Congress to ensure the fair implementation of laws, including exacting penalties if laws are not followed.[1]

A similar governmental framework is found at the state level. Citizens of the state elect legislative representatives and governors; legislators enact laws, governors implement the laws, and a judicial system guarantees a fair application of the law.[2] Within states, citizens of local jurisdictions (including cities, towns, and counties) elect individuals to pass laws and implement laws. These various state and local jurisdictions also put in place a judiciary to assure equitable application of the laws.[3]

Constraints are placed on the type and extent of federal laws that can be enacted, most notably by the Bill of Rights, the first 10 amendments to the Constitution. The Bill of Rights identifies the number of rights reserved for the individual, such as freedom of speech, religion, and assembly; ability to keep and bear arms to maintain a militia, right to due process, right to a trial by jury. These "constitutional guarantees" protect the individual from US governments infringing upon or abrogating these rights.[4] A constitutional amendment is required to alter these rights. States are not able to abrogate the individual and other rights that are included in the Constitution.

A whole network of laws and regulations, as well as enforcement mechanisms for these laws, has been established by local, state, and federal governments.[5] This network of laws governs basic activities in life. Life would be chaotic without them. For example, laws establish rules of the road, assurance of the car's safety, gas that is not fouled, and direction of traffic flows. Laws identify who can enforce these laws, the rules of enforcement, and penalties if the law is broken. A person speeds; they are stopped by the police; they pay the ticket or go to court if they believe that the police officer was incorrect.

Because of laws, individuals are able to choose the type of car they want and the food that they wish to eat. No one else can dictate these choices. When individuals enter into transactions they do so according to the rule of purchase and trade, rules that are embodied in law. Individuals are promised equal opportunity not by businesses, but by government. Individual freedoms, legalized fairness, and opportunity are part and parcel of what government guarantees.

Governments meet essential human needs, elements of human life not provided by business. No business takes overall responsibility for the quality of the air, or the drinkability of the water, or the elimination of human waste (sewage). Businesses do not provide basic (public) education for all children, do not build roads that all can use, do not put out fires, and do not deploy police to ensure that laws are upheld. The protection of public health, disease prevention, and identifying epidemics is not a role that individual businesses perform.[6] Some of the major things provided by the public sector as noted in Wikipedia are.[7]

> Public services include public good and governmental services such as military, police, infrastructure (public roads, bridges, tunnels, water supply, sewers, electrical grids, telecommunications, etc.), public transit, public education, along with [public] health care and those working for the government itself, such as elected officials. The public sector might provide services that a non-payer cannot be excluded from (such as street lighting), services which benefit all of society rather than just the individual who uses the service.

The political, governmental sector is a source of employment for many people and as such becomes part of the overall economy. The federal government has approximately 2.6 million employees. Another 2.1 million are employed in military service.[8] Approximately 5.3 million are state employees. Slightly over 14 million are employed by local governments.[9] Together federal, state and local government employees total approximately 22 million.[10]

> A staggering 22.3 million people work for the U.S. governments [federal, state and local]—but that's not just politicians or their staffs. It includes public school teachers, police officers, post office workers and those working at your local DMV ...[11]

In addition to those directly hired by governments, millions more work for organizations that receive government contracts. At the federal level, in 2018 over $554 billion was contracted to businesses that provide goods and services. [12] and another $1.2 trillion was provided to contractors by state and local governments.[13] These contracts result in significant "indirect" government employment by those organizations receiving contracts.

In addition to providing a legal framework for the overall social order and employing many Americans, governments, especially the federal government, directly impact the economy through a number of laws and regulations. Of special significance are the government's monetary and fiscal policies

MONETARY AND FISCAL POLICY

By action of the Congress, the United States' monetary policy is determined by the Federal Reserve. Fiscal policy is determined by the Executive and Legislative branches of the federal government which establish tax policies and designate how taxes collected are to be spent for the public good.

The United States Federal Reserve, America's central bank, establishes and monitors monetary policy, such as the amount of money in circulation and the cost of this money.[14] The Federal Reserve (commonly called the Fed) was created in 1913 "to provide the nation with a safer, more flexible, and more stable monetary and financial system." The Federal Reserve is controlled by a Board of Governors appointed by the President and confirmed by the Senate. Board members have fourteen [14] year terms. The Chair and Vice Chair are appointed by the President and serve four-year terms. Congress has made multiple changes to the reserve system since 1913 but its basic role has been constant. [16]

- Conducting the nation's monetary policy by influencing money and credit conditions in the economy in pursuit of full employment and stable prices.
- Supervising and regulating banks and other important financial institutions to ensure the safety and soundness of the nation's banking and financial system and to protect the credit rights of consumers.
- Maintaining the stability of the financial system and containing systemic risk that may arise in financial markets.
- Providing certain financial services to the U.S. government, U.S. financial institutions, and foreign official institutions, and playing a major role in operating and overseeing the nation's payments systems.[14]

In simpler terms, the Federal Reserve establishes the nation's monetary policy, provides and maintains an effective payments system, and supervises and regulates banking operations.[16] The Federal Reserve has almost total control of money supply and implementation of bank regulations.

The Federal Reserve pursues two basic goals: control inflation and support employment. The primary tools which the Fed employs to achieve these purposes are control of the amount of money that is available and the cost of this money. Generally speaking, if a large supply of money is available at low cost, borrowing and investment are supported. On the other hand, if the money supply gets too large, inflation can occur since money begins to lose value. Historically, the Federal Reserve has sought to keep inflation at approximately 2% and unemployment at 6% or less.

At the federal, state, and local level government also plays a major role in the economy through fiscal policy.[17] "Fiscal policy is the means by which a government adjusts its spending levels and tax rates to monitor and influence a nation's economy."[18]

The fiscal policy of the nation can be stated simply as the collection of revenue through taxes and the expenditure of the revenue collected for specific governmental purposes. In recent years this policy role has been very controversial and often the result of heated debate. Many propose that the "ideal" budget is one in which revenue equals expenditures: the so-called 'balanced budget'. This idea has not been the practice in recent years and the controversy regarding balanced budgets continues.

The revenue/expenditure side of fiscal policy is a complex one. Policy decisions are made to determine what items will or will not be taxed and how the revenues collected through taxation will be expended. Tax breaks can be given to a variety of businesses and individuals based on legislators' determination that such breaks provide incentives that assist the overall economy or benefit individuals. For example, a deduction for mortgage interest can be put in place to both assist individual tax payers to buy a home and at the same time promote and support the home building industry.

At the federal level, expenditures are made for things that are determined to be for the overall good of society. Some are acted upon annually (discretionary expenditures); others have been determined to be more or less permanently in place (non-discretionary). Congress has the ability to determine which items are discretionary and which are not.[19] (More extensive discussion on taxation is presented in the Solutions section below.)

POLITICAL PARTIES

No review of the US political order would be complete without some discussion of the role of political parties. Political parties exert extensive power in the determination of those for whom citizens can vote. While others not in the major US parties can and do run for office, it is most often those nominated by the Republican or Democratic parties who receive the majority of votes, are elected, and who enact and implement laws. As Wikipedia summarizes:[20]

> The modern political party system in the U.S. is dominated by the Democratic Party and the Republican Party. These two parties have won every United States presidential election since 1852 and have controlled the United States Congress to some extent since at least 1856. There are numerous minor, or "third," parties. The Libertarian, Green, Reform, Independent and other parties have won elections throughout history at different levels, but the success of those parties is sparse.

The Republican and Democratic parties operate not only at the national level but at state and local levels. Based on a recent (2019) Gallup poll, 28% of Americans identify themselves as Republicans, 31% identify themselves as Democrats, and 39% identify themselves as Independents.[21]

Parties are able to organize the electorate to vote for their candidates. Major parties receive significant financial contributions to enable them to organize voters. For example, from January 1, 2015 to December 31, 2016, Democrats received slightly over $870 million in contributions, and Republicans approximately $706 million.[22] These figures do not include amounts spent by Political Action Committees (PACs) who obtain and expend money for specific candidates or issues. The Federal Election Commission notes:[23]

> Based on reports filed with the Commission from January 1, 2017 through March 31, 2018, 7,802 federal PACs reported total receipts of $1.9 billion, disbursements of $1.6 billion, debts of $16.1 million, and combined cash-on-hand of $881.5 million.

Most of PAC contributions are made to support the election of Democratic or Republican party candidates.

Given their significance in determining candidates for office and the value of their support for candidates, political parties play a significant role in the political process and political order of the United States. Both political parties and PACs are important voluntary organizations that individual and organizations join and support to achieve political purposes.[24]

America's political order and its powers are extensive and pervasive and exert major influences on America's social order.

Notes

(1) Federal judges are not elected but are appointed by the President and approved by Congress. While not elected, they are chosen by those who have been elected.

(2) The bases of state laws are state constitutions that must be consistent with the US Constitution. Counties (Parishes) and municipalities are in turn chartered by states and given authority to establish certain laws in their jurisdiction.

(3) In some jurisdictions some or all judges are elected to their position. Others follow the federal process: executive appointment and legislative approval.

(4) The only way that these rights could be taken away is through a constitutional amendment.

(5) Systems of enforcement are discussed in the military and police section below.

(6) In certain cases, governmental agencies pay businesses to provide water services but this is not the norm.

(7) Public Sector, Wikipedia, https://en.wikipedia.org/wiki/Public_sector. See also, What is the Public Sector, Privacy Sense, http://www.privacysense.net/terms/public-sector/

(8) Federal employees by State, The States and Localities, Governing, https://www.governing.com/gov-data/federal-employees-workforce-numbers-by-state.html#:~:targetText=The%20federal%20government%20currently%20employs,employees%2C%20excluding%20Postal%20Service%20workers.

(9) Lisa Jessie and Mary Tarleton, 2012 Census of Governments: Employment Summary Report, Bureau of the Census, March 6, 2014 https://www2.census.gov/govs/apes/2012_summary_report.pdf

(10) Ibid.

(11) Jennifer Callas, The Biggest Employers in the US, Money, April 27, 2017, http://money.com/money/4754123/biggest-us-companies/

(12) A Snapshot: Government-Wide Contracting, A 2018 Update, Government Accountability Office https://www.gao.gov/multimedia/GAO-17-244SP/infographic/summary This snapshot notes that "Federal Agency contracts for good and services account for about 40% of the government's discretionary spending." Daniel Snyder, Federal Contract Spending Trends: Fiver Years in Five Charts, Bloomberg Government, January 22, 2019 https://federalnewsnetwork.com/fiscal-2019-federal-contracting-playbook/2019/01/federal-contract-spending-trends-five-years-in-five-charts/ See also, Moshe Schwartz, Joseph F Sargent Jr., Christopher T. Mann, Defense Acquisitions: How and Where DOD Spends Its Contracting Dollars, July 2, 2018 https://fas.org/sgp/crs/natsec/R44010.pdf

(13) Sizing Up the $1.5 trillion State and Local Contracting, Go Win+OnVia, https://www.onvia.com/market-research/special-reports/sizing-15-trillion-state-local-contracting-market See also, State and Local Expenditures, Urban Institute: Cross Center Initiatives, 2011 to present, https://www.urban.org/policy-centers/cross-center-initiatives/state-and-local-finance-initiative/state-and-local-backgrounders/state-and-local-expenditures

(14) A more detailed description of monetary policy is as follows: Monetary policy is a set of economic policy that manages the size and growth rate of the money supply in an economy. It is a powerful tool to regulate macroeconomic variables such as inflation and unemployment. Monetary policies are implemented through different tools, including the adjustment of the interest rates, purchase or sale of government securities, and changing the amount of cash circulating in the economy. The central bank or a similar regulatory organization is responsible for formulating monetary policies. See What is Monetary Policy? Corporate Finance Institute, https://corporatefinanceinstitute.com/resources/knowledge/economics/monetary-policy/ and James Chen, What is the Federal Reserve System? Investopedia, July 30, 2019, https://www.investopedia.com/terms/f/fiscalpolicy.asp

(15) What is the Purpose of the Federal Reserve System, Board of Governors of the Federal Reserve, https://www.federalreserve.gov/faqs/about_12594.htm

(16) The Federal Reserve System, Federal Bank of Kansas City, Reserve System https://www.kansascityfed.org/aboutus/federalreservesystem#:~:targetText=The%20responsibilities%20of%20the%20Federal,unions%2C%20and%20savings%20and%20loans.

(17) It should be noted that all levels of government In America, federal, state and local have their fiscal policies, i.e. systems of levying taxes and making public expenditures.

(18) Leslie Kramer, What is Fiscal Policy?, Investopedia, Nov. 21 2019, https://www.investopedia.com/insights/what-is-fiscal-policy/

(19) Discretionary versus non-Discretionary Fiscal Policy, Brain Mass, https://brainmass.com/business/contingencies/discretionary-nondiscretionary-fiscal-policy-548826,

(20) Political Parties in the United States, Wikipedia, https://en.wikipedia.org/wiki/Political_parties_in_the_United_States#Second_Party_System:_1828%E2%80%931854

(21) Party affiliation, 2004 to the present (October 2019) Gallup, https://news.gallup.com/poll/15370/party-affiliation.aspx

(22) Statistical summary of 24-month campaign activity of the 2015-2016 election cycle, Federal Elections Commission, March 23, 2017, https://www.fec.gov/updates/statistical-summary-24-month-campaign-activity-2015-2016-election-cycle/

(23) Statistical Summary of 15-Month Campaign Activity of the 2017-2018 Election Cycle,

Federal Elections Commission, June 12, 2018 https://www.fec.gov/updates/statistical-summary-15-month-campaign-activity-2017-2018-election-cycle/#:~:targetText=Contributions%20by%20 PACs%20to%20presidential,million%20and%20%24207.3%20million%2C%20respectively.

(24) For additional information see the section on Voluntary Associations below.

AMERICA'S MILITARY/ POLICE ORDER

Both the US military and the multiple domestic police forces are significant sources of social power in America. Legitimized by ideology, political, and economic powers, military and police are empowered to carry out activities to maintain America's social order. Federal and state constitutions and laws, along with local laws, establish the realms where military and police carry out their activities. Both the military and the police are organized into large institutions with numerous individuals. They are supported by private security and a variety of other institutions, such as courts and prisons and jails, that assist them in their work.

Both military and police are sanctioned to exert physical force. Military power is authorized to protect borders and to take action, up to and including taking of life, to protect the US from those who seek to claim territory or appropriate possessions held by American citizens. Police have the power to physically restrain and, should the situation require it, shoot and even kill those who break the laws.

> The role of the police is to suppress civilian criminal activity, maintain public order and safety, and keep citizens safe from crime. The role of the military is to deter hostile invasions from other countries, and to engage in combat operations overseas to support a country's interests there.[1]

Police and military power include deterrence power, the instilling of fear of consequences in order to inhibit law-breaking, instilling fear that punishment will result if a violation occurs. (1a) While there are specific forms of deterrence that focus on particular behaviors of individuals, the form of deterrence as used here refers to the generalized form provided by military and police presence.[1b]

> The day-to-day work of individuals employed in law enforcement, corrections, and other parts of the criminal-justice system involves identifying, capturing, prosecuting, sentencing, and incarcerating offenders. Perhaps the central function of these activities, however, is deterring individuals from participating in illegal activity in the first place.[1c]

Awareness of military and/or police presence discourages actions that threaten the social order by instilling fear of possible negative consequences. For example, fear of arrest and prison for stealing property can act to prevent the crime from occurring. For most Americans, deterrence is more important that the actual arrest. Military and police power influence behavior with the potential of use of coercion (deterrence), as well as actual coercion.[2]

In practice, military and police roles and responsibilities overlap. Military and police functions are reviewed separately below with a recognition that they, as other sources of power, are interrelated.

THE MILITARY

Article 1, Section 8 of the Constitution provides Congress authority "to raise and support Armies and to provide and maintain a Navy." Since the time of the writing of the Constitution the Marines and US Air Force have been added as part of the armed forces. The US Constitution continues to shape the conduct of the branches of the armed forces. Armed services members take the following oath:[3]

> I will support and defend the Constitution of the United States against all enemies, foreign and domestic.

As with the armed forces in other countries, the US armed forces "are institutions established by the state for the primary purpose of national defense against external threats and internal conflicts."[4] As the Geneva Center for Security Sector Governance notes:[5]

The armed forces are unlike any other state organization because they are allowed to do things that no other organization is permitted to do (such as use lethal force offensively), and their personnel are required to do things that no other employees are required to do (such as submit to military discipline or ultimately give up their lives in the line of duty).

In the US, as in many other of today's nations, the military is placed under civilian control. To be effective civilian governance must have a number of critical attributes. Among these are:[5]

- Clear chain of command
- Political neutrality
- Human rights protections
- Accountability

The military's role is not restricted to protecting our nation's physical borders. The armed services are deployed throughout the world to protect American interests. Currently, 200,000 active troops are deployed in more than 170 countries either to assist current allies or as part of international efforts (such as NATO).[7]

The American Armed Services today consists of approximately 2.1 million members.[8] Approximately 1.3 million are active service members with another 865,000 in reserves.[9] Using 2016 data, the Council on Foreign Relations provided the following breakdown of the military by branch: 471,171 Army, 320,101 Navy, 313,723 Air Force, and 183,501 marines.[10]

In addition to these servicemembers, some 434,000 Americans serve in the National Guard. While servicemen and women in the National Guard are under the control of the governors of their state or territory, they can be "federalized," that is, called to active duty, and deployed within the country or outside the country.[11] For example, during the Afghanistan and Iraq war, up to 48% of National Guard members were activated into national service.[12] Slightly more than 18.4 million Americans 18 years of age or older are veterans, or approximately 7.24% of the total US population of 251 million people 18 years of age or older.[13]

The military is also supported by a large number of civilian employees. The total number of military civilian employees in September 2019 was 755,386.[14] In addition, the military is supported by a number of "auxiliary" individuals and organizations, discussed below as part of the policing discussion.

The military protects the US from external threats from "foreign" countries. At the same time, it protects a variety of economic interests that could be harmed by actions in or by other countries. The America's military has taken on a variety of global roles to protect the economic and political interests of America. It is a major component of an apparatus that, along with the police, addresses the need for security.

The military, like other power centers in America, cannot be seen in isolation. It is the constitution and laws of the country that establish the military and police. America's economy relies on the enforcement of laws that protect economic interests both internationally and domestically. Exercise of military and police duties support and help achieve core elements of the American ideology.

POLICE

Police forces in America are extensive. They can be roughly divided into federal police, general purpose state and local police, and special jurisdiction police forces. These police forces are supported by a court system and by prisons and jails that enforce the consequences of violation of laws as well as by extensive private security.

FEDERAL

While the US does not have a federal police force as such, various organizations within the US federal government have personnel authorized to ensure compliance with laws and regulations, including the powers to arrest and apprehend.

Based on 2009 information, the Department of Justice estimated that 120,000 individuals had federal law enforcement powers in the United States.[15] This chart provides a breakdown.

AMERICA'S MILITARY/POLICE ORDER

Federal agencies employing 250 or more full-time personnel with arrest and firearm authority, September 2008

Agency	Number of full-time officers	Percent change 2004–2008
U.S. Customs and Border Protection	36,863	33.1
U.S. Customs and Federal Bureau of Prisons	16,835	10.7
Federal Bureau of Investigation	12,760	4.2
U.S. Immigration and Customs Enforcement	12,446	19.7
U.S. Secret Service	5,213	9.3
Administrative Office of the U.S. Courts*	4,696	13.8
Drug Enforcement Administration	4,308	-2.1
U.S. Marshals Service	3,313	2.5
Veterans Health Administration	3,128	29.1
Internal Revenue Service, Criminal Investigation	2,636	-5.1
Bureau of Alcohol, Tobacco, Firearms and Explosives	2,541	7.1
U.S. Postal Inspection Service	2,288	-23.1
U.S. Capitol Police	1,637	6.6
National Park Service - Rangers	1,404	-8.6
Bureau of Diplomatic Security	1,049	27.2
Pentagon Force Protection Agency	725	50.4
U.S. Forest Service	644	7.3
U.S. Fish and Wildlife Service	598	-15.5
National Park Service - U.S. Park Police	547	-10.6
National Nuclear Security Administration	363	24.3
U.S. Mint Police	316	-16.0
Amtrak Police	305	-3.8
Bureau of Indian Affairs	277	-13.4
Bureau of Land Management	255	2.4

Note: Excludes employees based in U.S. territories or foreign countries and offices of inspectors general (see table 3).

*Limited to federal probation officers employed in federal judicial districts that allow officers to carry firearms.

Source: Bureau of Justice Statistics, Census of Federal Law Enforcement Officers, 2004 and 2008.

There are 65 U.S. federal agencies and 27 offices of Inspector General that employ full time personnel authorized to make arrests and carry firearms. Every federal agency as well as the Congress and the court system have law enforcement officers.

According to the Bureau of Justice Statistics, in 2008 the largest employers of federally employed officers were Customs and Border Protection, Federal Bureau of Prisons, the Federal Bureau of Investigation (FBI), and Immigration and Customs Enforcement (ICE), each with more than 15,000 full-time law enforcement officers. Federal officers' duties include police response and patrol, criminal investigation and enforcement, inspections, security and protection, court operations, and corrections.[16] Some of these organizations are primarily concerned with enforcement of domestic laws and regulations; others act in support of the military in securing the nation's borders. Exact numbers of federal police enforcing federal laws and regulations is not currently available. However, data is available for the largest of these enforcement agencies.

The major organizations that have responsibility for enforcement of domestic laws and regulation are the (FBI), and the Drug Enforcement Administration (DEA) and border patrol agencies. The FBI as the law enforcement agency of the Department of Justice has general responsibility for enforcement of all US laws. "The FBI employs approximately 35,000 people, including special agents and support professionals such as intelligence analysts, language specialists, scientists, and information technology specialists."[17] The DEA, also part of the Department of Justice, is the primary enforcement agency for controlled substances. The DEA maintains 23 domestic field divisions with 222 field offices and 92 foreign offices in 70 countries. With a budget exceeding $3 billion, the DEA employs 10,169 people, including 4,924 Special Agents and 800 Intelligence Analysts.

The Bureau of Customs and Border Protection (CBP), the Bureau of Immigration and Customs Enforcement (ICE), United States Coast Guard, and the Transportation Security Administration (TSA) are major enforcement organizations protecting the US borders with approximately 169,000 employees. The CBP has approximately 60,000 employees.[18] ICE has approximately 20,000 employees. The Coast Guard has 40,992 men and women on active duty, along with 7,000 reservists, 31,000 auxiliarists, and 8,577 full-time civilian employees, for a total workforce of 87,569.[19] TSA has approximately 47,000 employees.[20]

While there is no federal police force as such, hundreds of thousands are deputized to enforce federal laws and regulations and are supported by thousands of others in their efforts.

STATE AND LOCAL POLICE

While the military focuses its attention on external threats and federal agents focus on enforcement of federal laws, state and local police ensure that local and state laws are followed. The 10th amendment of the Constitution gives states the right to establish and enforce laws to protect the health, welfare and safety of their residents and allows states to take action to enforce these laws. States, in turn, provide local communities with the ability of enact and enforce laws through their constitutions and laws. Police are called upon to ensure that individuals follow laws, both civil and criminal. If state or local police identify a legal infraction, they are empowered to take action to remedy the situation. In most cases their action requires far less than use of lethal force, but in specific situations, they are empowered to use lethal force. Police apprehend, take into custody, and bring people into court where they are tried and, if convicted, turned over to the correctional systems.

As in the case of federal government law enforcement officers, the police take an oath of office, in most states the same as other state elected officials, to protect the state's constitution and to uphold the laws of their state and/or locality. Almost all take the following oath of office.[21]

> An individual, except the President, elected or appointed to an office of honor or profit in the civil service or uniformed services, shall take the following oath: "I, AB, do solemnly swear (or affirm) that I will support and defend the Constitution of the United States against all enemies, foreign and domestic; that I will bear true faith and allegiance to the same; that I take this obligation freely, without any mental reservation or purpose of evasion; and that I will well and faithfully discharge the duties of the office on which I am about to enter. So help me God."

The determination of the numbers involved in law enforcement varies by whom is identified as "law enforcement." Based on 2012 data, there are more than 1.05 million individuals involved in state and local law enforcement, approximately 701,000 of whom are sworn police officers.[22]

In addition, there are another "specialized" law enforcement officers that are estimated to add another 200,000 other law enforcement personnel, such as university and transit police. These police are authorized to arrest in a narrow area of jurisdiction: universities, parks, or transit. Approximately 53% of sworn officers are local police, another 21% sheriffs, 7% state police, 7% specialized police and 12% federal law enforcement.[23]

COURTS

The federal, state and local courts, prisons, and jails are also part of the general policing function. At the present time, there are 94 federal district courts, 13 federal circuit courts, and one federal Supreme Court.[24] State courts totaled 346 in 2011.[25] There are municipal courts in most cities and villages in the United States which address violation of city ordinances and in certain cases minor crimes and civil issues.[25]. Each of these court systems has judges and support staff to assist in carrying out court functions. For example, state courts had 25,570 judges in 2011.

PRISONS AND JAILS

Prisons and jails are also part of the policing system.

> The American criminal justice system holds almost 2.3 million people in 1,719 state prisons, 109 federal prisons, 1,772 juvenile correctional facilities, 3,163 local jails, and 80 Indian Country jails as well as in military prisons, immigration detention facilities, civil commitment centers, state psychiatric hospitals, and prisons in the U.S. territories.[26]

It should be noted that this is a 2.3 million indicates those held at a specific time. Many more individuals go through the prison and jail system. The Prison Policy Initiative Reports notes that there is:[27]

> ...enormous churn in and out of our correctional facilities... Every year, over 600,000 people enter prison gates, but people go to jail 10.6 million times each year. Jail churn is particularly high

because most people in jails have not been convicted.

As in the case of courts, a large number of personnel are required to maintain the system. For example, the number of prison and jail guards is approximately 415,000[28] This number does not include the numerous support staff that work in the jails and prisons.

JOINT MILITARY AND POLICE POWER

While military and police powers most often operate separately, they can work together in specific situations. While the military is focused primarily on external threats, it can be deployed and join state and local police to address major internal rebellions, insurrections, or natural crises.[29] The military, and especially the Army, has been called upon to address a wide range of domestic issues from quelling rebellions, to assisting with disasters, to assuring civil rights protections. However, there are a number of constitutional and legal issues that limit the domestic uses of the military.[29a]

The Posse Comitatus Act, passed in 1878, prohibits the use of military force domestically with the exception of putting down an insurrection.[30] However, the President has the explicit authority to use federal forces or federalized militias to enforce the laws of the United States.[31] The ability of the president to involve local law enforcement is, however, limited.[32] While the National Guard units are under the control of state governors, the president has the authority to call them into national service in times of war, most recently the wars in Iraq and Afghanistan.[33]

PRIVATE SECURITY

Federal, state and local governments deploy an extensive policing force for law enforcement purposes. These keepers of law and order are supported by a number of organizations and individuals in private security. Private security is provided by employees of non-governmental organizations that offer their security services to individuals, businesses and governments, most often for pay.

Private policing is broadly construed and means the provision of security or policing services other than by public servants in the normal course of their public duties.[34]

Lack of trust and availability of public (police and military) law enforcement, protection of assets, and fear of crime are major motivators for use of private security.

A broad range of individuals from volunteers to off duty police officers provide security services.[35] Security services include a wide range of activities such as protection of individuals, employment screening, and cybersecurity to name a few occupations.[36]

Private security is most often provided by private security companies:

> A private security company is a business corporation, which provides armed and unarmed security services and expertise to private and public clients. Private security companies are defined by the U.S. Bureau of Labor Statistics as companies primarily engaged in providing guard and patrol services, such as bodyguard, guard dog, parking security and security guard services. Many of them (security companies) will even provide advanced special operations services if the client demands it. [37]

The relationships among and between public security and private security are "messy and complex."[38] In fact, it can be said that:

> Today, it is more accurate to suggest that policing is carried out by a network of public police and private security that is often overlapping, complimentary [sic] and mutually supportive. Within this context, it is increasingly difficult to distinguish between public and private responsibilities.[39]

Exact boundaries between police and private security are often difficult to define. While there are many benefits to increased private security capability, some express concerns regarding the growth of private security. Lack of accountability of private security officers, lessened protections of civil liberties, and unequal protections for those without resources to hire private security are often cited. At the same time, certain advantages have been pointed out such as increased protective services, ability to access specialized skills, and better protection of the poor since police can concentrate on those without resources to hire private security.[40]

AMERICA'S MILITARY/POLICE ORDER

While private security has been in place since ancient times, the private security industry has grown appreciably in the last 50 years. This growth in private security is global in nature. The number of individuals involved in private security is now large internationally as well as in the US[41] The Bureau of Labor Statistics (BLS) reports that, in 2018, 1,105,440 individuals were employed in the private sector security in America.[42]

The military and police, supported by court systems, prisons and jails, and extensive private security, work together and use their power and influence to maintain America's social order.

Notes

(1) What is the Difference Between the Police and the Military, Quora, https://www.quora.com/What-is-the-difference-between-the-police-and-the-military#targetText=They%20are%20different%20in%20what,is%20to%20kill%20their%20opponent.&targetText=Basically%20the%20police%20control%20the,control%20and%20enforce%20the%20borders.

(1a) See Deterrence, Lexico, Oxford, https://www.lexico.com/en/definition/deterrence and Deterrence, Miriam Webster, https://www.merriam-webster.com/dictionary/deterrence)

(1b) Specific Deterrence, Legal Dictionary, August 12, 2017 https://legaldictionary.net/specific-deterrence/

(1c) Aaron Chalfin and Justin McCrary, Criminal Deterrence: A Review of the Literature, Journal of Economic Literature, 2017 p. 1, https://www.aeaweb.org/articles?id=10.1257/jel.20141147

(2) See for example, Glen H. Snyder, Deterrence and Power, The Journal of Conflict Resolution, June 1960, https://journals.sagepub.com/doi/abs/10.1177/002200276000400201?journalCode=jcrb, and Kelli D Tomlinson, An Examination of Deterrence Theory: Where Do We Stand? Federal Probation, December 2016, https://www.uscourts.gov/federal-probation-journal/2016/12/examination-deterrence-theory-where-do-we-stand For more details on power, see Part 1, 2 Social Order and Power

(3) Ronald C. Johnson, Ph.D., The role of the US Constitution and the Armed Forces, Military, https://inmilitary.com/the-role-of-the-u-s-constitution-and-the-armed- forces/#targetText=Article%201%2C%20Section%208%20of,branches%20of%20the%20armed%20forces; (See Also, Major General H. Kujat, GEAF "The Role of the Military in a Democracy" Speech to the United Nations, NATO Information Center, July 2-3, 1998, https://www.nato.int/docu/speech/1998/s980702h.htm:

(4) The Armed Forces: Roles and responsibilities in good security sector governance, SSR Backgrounder, https://www.files.ethz.ch/isn/195684/DCAF_BG_10_The%20Armed%20Forces.11.15-1.pdf

(5) Ibid. p.4

(6) Ibid. p. 6

(7) Naill McCarthy, All the Countries Worldwide with a U.S. Presence, Forbes, May 28, 2017, https://www.forbes.com/sites/niallmccarthy/2017/03/28/all-the-countries-worldwide-with-a-u-s-military-presence-infographic/#554b2d8728cf

(8) United States Military Strength, Global Fire Power, https://www.globalfirepower.com/country-military-strength-detail.asp?country_id=united-states-of-america

(9) K.K.. Rebecca Lai, Troy Griggs, Max Fisher and Audrey Carlsen 'Is America's Military Large Enough?, New York Times, March 22, 2017, https://www.nytimes.com/interactive/2017/03/22/us/is-americas-military-big-enough.html#targetText=1%20Troops,fighting%20forces%20of%20any%20country.&targetText=The%20United%20States%20also%20has,in%20more%20than%20170%20countries.

(10) George M. Reynolds and Amanda Shendruk Demographics of the US Military, Council on Foreign Relations, April 24, 2018, https://www.cfr.org/article/demographics-us-military

(11) National Guard Fast Facts, CNN, Updated July 11, 2109 https://www.cnn.com/2013/08/09/us/national-guard-fast-facts/index.html

(12) United States National Guard, Wikipedia, https://en.wikipedia.org/wiki/United_States_National_Guard#Number_of_guardsmen_by_state,_territory_and_D.C.)

(13) Veteran Status 2019, US Bureau of the Census, https://factfinder.census.gov/faces/tableservices/jsf/pages/productview.xhtml?src=bkmk See also, Department of Veterans Affairs, CNN Library, Updated October 5, 2019, https://www.cnn.com/2014/05/30/us/department-of-veterans-affairs-fast-facts/index.html

(14) Number of Military and DOD appropriated DOD Appropriated Fund (APF) Civilian Personnel By Duty Location and Service/Location As of September 30, 2019, https://www.dmdc.osd.mil/appj/dwp/dwp_reports.jsp

(15) Brian A. Reaves, Federal Law Enforcement Officers, 2008, U.S Department of Justice, Bureau of Labor Statistics, June 2012, https://www.bjs.gov/content/pub/pdf/fleo08.pdf. Unfortunately this is the most recent overall study of the total number of federal law enforcement officers.

(16) Types of Law Enforcement Agencies, Discover Policing, https://www.discoverpolicing.org/explore-the-field/types-of-law-enforcement-agencies/#targetText=U.S.%20Federal%20Law%20Enforcement%20Agencies&targetText=Federal%20officers'%20duties%20include%20police,%2C%20court%20operations%2C%20and%20corrections.)

(17) How Many People Work for the FBI?, Federal Bureau of Investigation, https://www.fbi.gov/about/faqs/how-many-people-work-for-the-fbi#targetText=The%20FBI%20employs%20approximately%2035%2C000,join%20us%20at%20FBIJobs.gov.

(18) Bureau of Customs and Boarder Protection (CBP), https://www.cbp.gov/about#targetText=With%20more%20than%2060%2C000%20employees,lawful%20international%20travel%20and%20trade.

(18a) Cost of Immigration Enforcement and Border Security, American Immigration Council, October 14, 2019 https://www.americanimmigrationcouncil.org/research/the-cost-of-immigration-enforcement-and-border-security

(19) United States Coast Guard, Wikipedia https://en.wikipedia.org/wiki/United_States_Coast_Guard

(20))Transportation Security Administration, Wikipedia, https://en.wikipedia.org/wiki/Transportation_Security_Administration; See also Chad C. Haddal, Border Security: Key Agencies and Their Missions, Congressional Research Service, April 2009, https://fas.org/sgp/crs/homesec/RS21899.pdf

(21) Sheriff Larry American, What is the Legal Meaning of the Sheriffs Oath of Office, https://www.sheriffs.org/sites/default/files/uploads/Legal%20Meaning%20of%20Oath%20of%20Office.pdf; Section 3331. Oath of office 5 U.S. Code § 3331.Oath of office, https://www.law.cornell.edu/uscode/text/5/3331, See also, Pat Mason, The Oath of Office for Local Elected Officials, MSRC, November 26, 2019, http://mrsc.org/Home/Stay-Informed/MRSC-Insight/November-2013/The-Oath-of-Office-for-Local-Elected-Officials.aspx

(22) Shelley Hyland, Full-Time Employees in Law Enforcement Agencies, 1997-2016, Bureau of Justice Assistance, August 2018, https://www.bjs.gov/content/pub/pdf/ftelea9716.pdf See also, Duren Banks et alia, National Sources of Employment Data Revised October 4, 2016, https://www.bjs.gov/content/pub/pdf/nsleed.pdf)

(23) Daniel Bier, How Many Cops Are There In the United States? (2018 update), Skeptical Libertarian, August 24, 2018, https://blog.skepticallibertarian.com/2018/08/24/how-many-cops-are-there-in-the-united-states-2018-update/)

(24) Introduction To The Federal Court System, Office of the United States Attorney, https://www.justice.gov/usao/justice-101/federal-courts#targetText=There%20are%2094%20district%20courts,heard%20in%20the%20federal%20system.

(25) Rom Maglea et Alia, State Court Organization 2011, November 2013 https://www.bjs.gov/content/pub/pdf/sco11.pdf)

(26) City Court, Wikipedia, https://en.wikipedia.org/wiki/City_court
Wendy Sawyer and Peter Wagner, Mass Incarceration: the Whole Pie 2019, Prison Policy Initiative, March 19, 2019 https://www.prisonpolicy.org/reports/pie2019.html

(27) Ibid.

(28) Occupational Employment and Wages, May 2018, 33-3012 Correctional Officers and Jailers, Bureau of Labor Statistics, https://www.bls.gov/oes/current/oes333012.htm

(29) Lieutenant Colonel Craig E. Merutka, Use of the Armed Forces for Domestic Law Enforcement, US Army War College, March 2013, https://apps.dtic.mil/dtic/tr/fulltext/u2/a589451.pdf

(29a) See, for example, Paul J. Scheips, The Role of the Federal Military Forces in Domestic Disorders: 1945 to 1992, Center of Military History, 2005, https://history.army.mil/html/books/030/30-20/CMH_Pub_30-20.pdf

(30) Can the USA Military be used as a police force domestically? Law, https://law.stackexchange.com/questions/14813/can-the-usa-military-be-used-as-a-police-force-domestically

(31) Garri Benjamin Hendell, Domestic Use of the Armed Forces to Maintain Law and Order—posse comitatus Pitfalls at the Inauguration of the 44th President, Publius The Journal of Federalism, Spring 2011, https://academic.oup.com/publius/article-abstract/41/2/336/1905995?redirectedFrom=fulltext

(32) Jennifer K. Elsea, The President's Authority to Use the National Guard or the Armed Forces to Secure the Border, Congressional Research Service, April 19, 2018, https://fas.org/sgp/crs/natsec/LSB10121.pdf

(33) United States National Guard, Wikipedia, https://en.wikipedia.org/wiki/United_States_National_Guard

(34) Malcolm K Sparrow, Managing the Boundary Between Public and Private Security, New Perspectives on Policing, Harvard Kennedy School/National Institute for Justice, September 2014, p. 2, https://www.ncjrs.gov/pdffiles1/nij/247182.pdf)

(35) Kevin Strom et. alia., The Private Security Industry: A Review of the Definitions, Available Data Sources, and Paths Moving Forward, Department of Justice, December 2010, https://www.ncjrs.gov/pdffiles1/bjs/grants/232781.pdf

(36) Ibid. 4-1 to 4-26

(37) Private Security, Wikipedia, https://en.wikipedia.org/wiki/Security_company

(38) Managing the Boundary Between Public and Private Security op. cit., p. 1, see also, Charles P. Nemeth J.D., Ph.D., LL.M, Public and Private Law Enforcement in Private Security and the Law (Fourth Edition), 2012, https://www.sciencedirect.com/topics/computer-science/private-security-personnel)

(39) Ibid. p. 8

(40) Ibid. p. 9

(41) See for example, Niall McCarthy, Private Security Outnumbers The Police In Most Countries Worldwide (Infographic) Forbes, August 31, 2017, https://www.forbes.com/sites/niallmccarthy/2017/08/31/private-security-outnumbers-the-police-in-most-countries-worldwide-infographic/#7430aa18210f. See for example, Rudo Robinson, A Brief History of Private Security February 10, 2019, https://protectedbytrust.com/2019/02/10/a-brief-history-of-private-security/

(42) Security Guards and Gaming Surveillance Officer, Occupational Handbook Look, Bureau of Labor Statistics, Last Modified Date: Wednesday, September 4, 2019, https://www.bls.gov/ooh/protective-service/security-guards.htm#:~:targetText=Security%20Guards%20and%20Gaming%20Surveillance%20Officers,-Median%20annual%20wages&targetText=The%20lowest%2010%20percent%20earned,percent%20earned%20more%20than%20%2449%2C650.

VOLUNTARY ASSOCIATIONS AND RELIGION

The free association of individuals and freedom of religion are guaranteed by the United States Constitution. The First Amendment states:

> "Congress shall make no law respecting an establishment of religion, or prohibiting the free exercise thereof; or abridging the freedom of speech, or of the press; or the right of the people peaceably to assemble, and to petition the Government for a redress of grievances."

The First Amendment "protects the individual rights to freely exercise one's religion, speak freely, publish freely, peaceably assemble, and petition the government "[1] This right to assembly is guaranteed, is not absolute, and can be subject to conditions—but it remains a right[2] The Fourteenth Amendment to the Constitution clarified that states could not impinge on this right.

Voluntary association, and particularly the voluntary choice of one's religion, has a special place in American life and contributes significantly to the social order of the United States.

America has historically relied on voluntary association and action by voluntary groups. Alex de Tocqueville in his 1835 *Democracy in America*, noted:

Americans of all ages, all stations in life, and all types of disposition are forever forming associations. There are not only commercial and industrial associations in which all take part, but others of a thousand different types–religious, moral, serious, futile, very general and very limited, immensely large and very minute. . . . Nothing, in my view, deserves more attention than the intellectual and moral associations in America.[3]

Americans freely offer their time, money and skills and join with others to seek societal and personal goals.

What de Tocqueville reported regarding the significance of voluntary organizations in 1835 continued throughout American history and is found today.[4] There are voluntary or 'third sector' organizations in all countries and their number continues to grow. America's voluntary organizations are, however, the most extensive of all countries and have been major element of society for the longest time. While other countries, especially European countries, have seen a growth in nonprofit organizations, identified as nongovernmental organizations (NGOs), the presence and significance of nonprofit/nongovernmental organizations in other countries is not as extensive as in the US. [4a]

Through voluntary organizations, individuals act for a purpose without coercion and with no expectation of immediate personal gain.[5] At the most basic level, individuals volunteer to support their cause. They join others to improve a situation, solve a problem, or achieve a goal. There are multiple opportunities to join with others in voluntary organizations. Individuals can join with others on an ongoing basis to provide food, donate blood, contribute to a refugee organization, or address civic issues. Individuals can also join others on a one-time basis to carry out action to address a specific issue, e.g. build a levee. Once a need, a cause, or a belief is defined, people freely join together to achieve a goal. Involvement can extend from a one-time donation of a small amount of money or coming together for a few hours to significant contributions of time and money. Many show their commitment by contributing time as volunteers to the organizations they support. (See information on number and value of volunteers below.)

In the most general sense, a voluntary organization is any group of individuals who gather together for a specific purpose. Most voluntary groups establish a formal organization and register as a non-profit corporation in a state and seek tax-exempt status from the state and federal governments. Non-profit status allows the organization to collect money that is not taxed as income. In most cases, the money donated can be taken as a tax deduction by the donors.

Non-profit organizations/corporations are organized so that no income goes to members. The most common non-profit designation is identified in Internal Revenue Service (IRS) code as 501(c)3. This designation provides purposes for which tax-exempt status is provided:

> The exempt purposes set forth in section 501(c)(3) are charitable, religious, educational, scientific, literary, testing for public safety, fostering national or international amateur sports competition, and preventing cruelty to children or animals. The term *charitable* is used in its generally accepted legal sense and includes relief of the poor, the distressed, or the underprivileged; advancement of religion; advancement of education or science; erecting or maintaining public buildings, monuments, or works; lessening the burdens of government; lessening neighborhood tensions; eliminating prejudice and discrimination; defending human and civil rights secured by law; and combating community deterioration and juvenile delinquency.[6]

There are twenty-seven other purposes for which tax-exempt status is afforded through other IRS 501 designations. [7]

A large number of voluntary groups exist that are neither formally constituted nor have received nonprofit status. No real estimate of the number and size of these groups is available. However, it is possible to provide an overview of more formally-organized groups recognized by the federal and state governments.

The size and scope of the formal nonprofit or voluntary sector is summarized by Brice McKeever:[8]

- Approximately 1.54 million nonprofits were registered with the IRS in 2016, an increase of 4.5 percent from 2006.
- The nonprofit sector contributed an estimated $1.047.2 trillion to the US economy in 2016, composing 5.6 percent of the country's gross domestic product (GDP).

- Of the nonprofit organizations registered with the IRS, 501(c)(3) public charities accounted for just over three-quarters of revenue and expenses for the nonprofit sector as a whole ($2.04 trillion and $1.94 trillion, respectively) and just under two-thirds of the nonprofit sector's total assets ($3.79 trillion).
- In 2018, total private giving from individuals, foundations, and businesses totaled $427.71 billion (Giving USA Foundation 2019), a decrease of -1.7 percent from 2017 (after adjusting for inflation). According to Giving USA (2018) total charitable giving rose for consecutive years from 2014 to 2017, making 2017 the largest single year for private charitable giving, even after adjusting for inflation.
- An estimated 25.1 percent of US adults volunteered in 2017, contributing an estimated 8.8 billion hours. This is a 1.6 percent increase from 2016. The value of these hours is approximately $195.0 billion.

Giving USA calculated the amount given to non-profits in 2017 as $410.2 billion.[9]

Giving exceeded $400 billion in a single year for the first time, increasing 5.2 percent (3.0 percent adjusted for inflation) over the revised total of $389.64 contributed in 2016. The stock market and economic conditions helped drive solid growth in contributions across the board.

Initial 2018 data indicates that there was slightly less giving than in 2017 but still over $427 billion, due primarily to a slight reduction in individual giving, perhaps related to tax changes.[10] Non-profits receive their donations from a variety of sources.[11]

Source of Financial Contributions to nonprofit organizations

- 70% individual donations
- 9% Bequests
- 16% Foundations
- 5% Corporations

Individual giving is the largest source of funding for nonprofits. Based on tax returns, over 30 million households made charitable contributions.

Others may have made contributions but no data sources are available to document their contributions or the aggregate amount contributed.

In addition to charitable donations, non-profit organizations receive significant support from federal and state governments through grants, contracts, loans, and loan guarantees. A 2009 report from the Government Accounting Office (GAO) provides the following summary information: [12]

> Funding data sources identified the following as the approximate amounts of federal funds flowing to nonprofits in 2006 under different mechanisms, although most sources did not reliably classify nonprofit status of recipients:
>
> - $135 billion in fee-for-service payments under Medicare;
> - $10 billion in other types of fee-for-service payments;
> - $25 billion in grants paid directly to nonprofits;
> - $10 billion paid directly to nonprofits for contracts; and
> - $55 billion in federal funds paid to nonprofits by states from two grantprograms, including Medicaid. (GAO could not assess other programs.)
>
> In addition, approximately $2.5 billion in loan guarantees and $450 million in loans were issued to nonprofits, and approximately $50 billion in federal tax revenues were foregone due to tax expenditures related to nonprofits. More current summary information is not available but the amount provided by federal government to nonprofits has increased since the date of this report.
>
> Non-profit organizations also benefit from volunteering. An estimated 63 million Americans, 30% of adult Americans, volunteer to assist in causes they believe in. Using an average valuation of $25.43 per hour, American volunteers contributed over $203 million in labor to the organizations they support.[13]

Financial contributions are distributed to the following types of organizations:[14]

Type of Organizations of Receiving Charitable Gifts: 2017

	Amount Billions	%
Religion	$127.37	31%
Education	$ 58.90	15%
Human Services	$ 50.06	12%
Foundations	$ 45.89	11%
Health	$ 38.27	9%
Public-Society Benefits	$ 29.59	7%
International	$ 22.97	6%
Arts, Culture and Humanities	$ 19.51	5%
Environment	$ 11.83	3%

As noted above, the nonprofit sectors constituted 5.2% of the total GDP in 2016 and had expenditures of slightly over $1 trillion. In addition, nonprofits control more than $3.7 trillion dollars in assets.

The voluntary sector is also a major employer. Economists regularly consider any industry or economic sector that employs 5% of a country's workforce to be a "major" industry or sector. It is therefore notable that the 12.3 million paid workers were employed by US nonprofits as of 2016, accounting for a substantial 10.2% of the total US private workforce.[15] Using a different methodology and approach to identifying who are nonprofit employees, the Bureau of Labor Statistics identifies nonprofits as having "11,426,870 employees, 10.3 percent of total U.S. private sector employment," in their 2012 summary report. [16]

Religious groups represent the largest number of voluntary organizations. Estimates of the number of religious congregations in the United States range 350 to 410 thousand, with the average congregation size estimated at around 75 adults.[17] Based on recent PEW and Gallup surveys, 77% of Americans (some 188 million Americans) identified with a religious tradition, 71% Christian, 6% with other religious traditions.[18] Sixty-three percent adults belong to a church. While religious identification and church membership has decreased, especially among young people, religion still has the largest number of members of any type of voluntary association.

As indicated above, religious groups receive the largest percentage of charitable donations: more than $127 billion, 30% of total individual donations. Some have noted the strong linkage between religious belonging and charitable donations. For example, David King, director of the Institute on Faith & Giving, concludes from his research that:

> Someone with a religious affiliation was more than two times more generous than someone without a religious affiliation. And among those with a religious affiliation, religious intensity really matters. Those who attend services were much more likely to give, whether it's monthly or weekly. We really see the connection grow with continued involvement in a religious community."[19]

As noted above, freedom of religion is guaranteed by the First Amendment, and religion holds a special place in American society. While membership in religious congregations has decreased, 74% of Americans indicate membership in a religious denomination, and the vast majority of Americans indicate a belief of a god or higher power. Of the 26% of Americans who indicate no particular religious affiliation, the largest portion of this grouping have "no affiliation" (17%), i.e. not identifying with a specific denomination. The remaining 9% identify as being either atheist or agnostic. The pattern of belief in God mirrors religious identification, with approximately 80% indicating a traditional belief in God, another 10% indicating a belief in a higher power; and a final 10 % stating no belief in a higher power.[20] Regardless of belief, Americans support freedom of religion, even if their decision is to have no religion.

The voluntary sector is an important element of America's social order, involving a large percentage of Americans and a significant amount of financial resources. This sector provides employment to a large number of Americans who must abide by the rules of the voluntary organization. Voluntary associations set forth values, norms, and rules of behavior that must be adhered to and followed by their members.[21] Religion is the largest of voluntary organizations in America. Their power in terms of influence can extend to not only to immediate concerns and consequences but also to "in the next life."

Because of their extent and their multiple sources of power and influence, voluntary associations, and especially organized religion, are important forces in the American order.

Notes

(1) "Does the First Amendment Protect the Freedom of Association?" The Future of Freedom Foundation. October 29, 2012. Accessed June 05, 2021. https://www.fff.org/explore-freedom/article/does-the-first-amendment-protect-the-freedom-of-association/.

(2) "Right of Association." Legal Information Institute. Legal Information Institute. Accessed June 5, 2021. https://www.law.cornell.edu/constitution-conan/amendment-1/right-of-association.

(3) Tocqueville, Alexis de, Henry Reeve, and Francis Bowen. Democracy in America. Boston: J. Allyn, 1863.

(4) Gamm, Gerald, and Robert D. Putnam. "The Growth of Voluntary Associations in America, 1840-1940." The Journal of Interdisciplinary History 29, no. 4 (1999): 511-57. Accessed June 5, 2021. http://www.jstor.org/stable/206973.

(4a) Casey, J.. "Comparing Nonprofit Sectors Around the World: What Do We Know and How Do We Know It?" (2016). https://doi.org/10.18666/JNEL-2016-V6-I3-7583

(5) Voluntarism is obviously consistent with American's commitment to individual freedom and choice as well as promoting equal opportunity.

(6) "Exempt Purposes - Internal Revenue Code Section 501(c)(3)." Internal Revenue Service. Accessed June 5, 2021. https://www.irs.gov/charities-non-profits/charitable-organizations/exempt-purposes-internal-revenue-code-section-501c3.

(7) Fritz, Joanne. "How Does the IRS Classify Your Nonprofit Organization?" The Balance Small Business. Accessed June 5, 2021. https://www.thebalancesmb.com/how-the-irs-classifies-nonprofit-organizations-2501798.

(8) McKeever, Brice S. The Nonprofit Sector in Brief, Urban Institute: National Center for Charitable Statistic, December 3, 2019, https://nccs.urban.org/project/nonprofit-sector-brief, See also McKeever, Brice S., The Nonprofit Sector in Brief 2018: Public Charites, Giving, and Volunteering, Urban Institute, November 2018, https://nccs.urban.org/publication/nonprofit-sector-brief-2018#the-nonprofit-sector-in-brief-2018-public-charites-giving-and-volunteering and McKeever, Brice S., The Nonprofit Sector in Brief 2018, Urban Institute, December 13, 2018, https://nccs.urban.org/publication/nonprofit-sector-brief-2018#the-nonprofit-sector-in-brief-2018-public-charites-giving-and-volunteering

(9) Giving USA. "Giving USA 2018: Americans Gave $410.02 Billion to Charity in 2017, Crossing the $400 Billion Mark for the First Time: Giving USA." Giving USA | A public service initiative of the Giving Institute, August 1, 2018. https://giviångusa.org/giving-usa-2018-americans-gave-410-02-billion-to-charity-in-2017-crossing-the-400-billion-mark-for-the-first-time/.

(10) Eisenberg, Richard. "Charitable Giving Took A Hit Due To Tax Reform." Forbes. Forbes Magazine, June 18, 2019. https://www.forbes.com/sites/nextavenue/2019/06/18/charitable-giving-took-a-hit-due-to-tax-reform/#20ec0119f6ff).)

(11) Giving USA, op. cit.

(12) U.S. Government Accountability Office. (2009). Nonprofit sector: Significant federal funds reach the sector through various mechanisms, but more complete and reliable funding data are needed. GAO-09-193.

(13) "Volunteering Statistics and Trends For Nonprofits." Nonprofits Source. Accessed June 5, 2021. https://nonprofitssource.com/online-giving-statistics/volunteering-statistics/., "Value of Volunteer Time." Independent Sector. Accessed June 5, 2021. https://independentsector.org/value-of-volunteer-time-2021/.

(14) Giving USA, op. cit.

(15) Salamon, L. M., Newhouse, C. L. & Sokolowski, S.W. (2019). The 2019 nonprofit employment report. Johns Hopkins Center for Civil Society Studies, http://ccss.jhu.edu/wp-content/uploads/downloads/2019/01/2019-NP-Employment-Report_FINAL_1.8.2019.pdf.

(16) "Nonprofits Account for 11.4 Million Jobs, 10.3 Percent of All Private Sector Employment." U.S. Bureau of Labor Statistics. U.S. Bureau of Labor Statistics, October 21, 2014. https://www.bls.gov/opub/ted/2014/ted_20141021.htm.

(17) Brauer, S.G. (2017), How Many Congregations Are There? Updating a Survey-Based Estimate. Journal for the Scientific Study of Religion, 56: 438-448. https://doi.org/10.1111/jssr.12330. See also Fast Facts about American Religion. Accessed June 5, 2021. http://hirr.hartsem.edu/research/fastfacts/fast_facts.html#sizecong.

(18) "U.S. Public Becoming Less Religious." Pew Research Center's Religion & Public Life Project, May 30, 2020. https://www.pewforum.org/2015/11/03/u-s-public-becoming-less-religious/. Jones, Jeffrey M. "U.S. Church Membership Down Sharply in Past Two Decades." Gallup. com. Gallup, April 6, 2021. https://news.gallup.com/poll/248837/church-membership-down-sharply-past-two-decades.aspx. See also "How Often Respondents Attend Religious Service" GSS Data Explorer: NORC at the University of Chicago." GSS Data Explorer | NORC at the University of Chicago. https://gssdataexplorer.norc.org/trends/Religion%20&%20Spirituality?measure=attend.

(19) Giving USA. "Giving USA Special Report on Giving to Religion: Giving USA." Giving USA | A public service initiative of the Giving Institute, February 28, 2018. https://givingusa.org/just-released-giving-usa-special-report-on-giving-to-religion/.

(20) PEW, op. cit. See also, "How Religion Affects Everyday Life." Pew Research Center's Religion & Public Life Project, May 30, 2020. https://www.pewforum.org/2016/04/12/religion-in-everyday-life/. and "In U.S., Decline of Christianity Continues at Rapid Pace." Pew Research Center's Religion & Public Life Project, June 9, 2020. https://www.pewforum.org/2019/10/17/in-u-s-decline-of-christianity-continues-at-rapid-pace/.

(21) Giridharadas, Anand. *Winners Take All: the Elite Charade of Changing the World.* New York: Alfred A. Knopf, 2019. and Reich, Rob. *Just Giving: Why Philanthropy Is Failing Democracy and How It Can Do Better.* Princeton: Princeton University Press, 2020.

SUMMARY AND CONCLUSION: THE US SOCIAL ORDER

The United States, like other societies, has a social order, which is maintained by powers operating in the ideological, economic, political/governmental, military/police, and voluntary/religious realms.

US ideology exerts overarching powers, identifying desired goals and values. It employs a variety of critical influences that direct ideals to be pursued, and it defines acceptable and unacceptable behaviors.

The US economic system consists of powers that affect not only physical survival but also provide a wide array of criteria used in assessing one's societal position. The US economy is clearly enmeshed in the global economy. In the United States, private property is basic, and money is the common vehicle used to transfer property. Property exercises its influence through the US system of capitalism: a "mixed economy." In the US mixed economy, the general principles of capitalism are implemented, but government plays a strong role. While individuals and companies make fundamental operational decisions to seek profit, government has a hand in a significant number of roles.

Currently corporations conduct the vast majority of US economic activity, and they have grown in size and importance—particularly financial-sector corporations, which account for a disproportionate share of profits. Corporations have become the major controllers of private property, making decisions on how capital is deployed. Corporations, especially financial corporations, are the major economic actors and possess the greatest power in the US economic system.

While strongly influencing the direction of the economy, the political realm's influence extends beyond the economic realm. Based in the US Constitution, US laws draw their legitimacy and authority from the fact that those who enact laws are chosen by the citizens. Drawing their legitimacy and authority from the fact that they are chosen by the citizens, elected representatives then enact laws at the federal, state, and local-community levels. These laws, and the regulations stemming from them, influence US behavior in almost all aspects of an American's daily life. Of special importance are those laws that regulate the fiscal and monetary policies that direct the economy.

In addition to laws—and as part of their implementation—federal, state, and local governments account for approximately 20 percent of all US employment. Government is the largest US employer. Millions more are employed by companies that receive governmental contracting for goods and services. Along with employment and contracting, government determines and implements US monetary and fiscal policies that directly impact the economy.

The US Constitution and a wide range of federal laws, state laws and constitutions, and local-community laws have established and supported national military and local law enforcement. A force of 4.5 million individuals in the military and law enforcement are in place to influence and maintain social order. The federal government, states, and municipalities deploy police with extensive powers to enforce their laws and take actions against those who violate these laws. While circumscribed by laws, police and military have great discretion to exercise their power in concrete situations. To maintain social order, they can implement this power in a coercive and physical manner, up to and including death. A major component of military and police powers is deterrence (i.e., the awareness that action will be taken if laws are violated).

The voluntary sector employs a significant influence in the United States as well. The employees and volunteers in nonprofit organizations total over 80 million Americans. These Americans voluntarily join with others and provide their money and time to address chosen needs or to achieve goals. The voluntary sector is large in terms of size, finances, and employed individuals. Most voluntary organizations that continue to exist obtain federal and state tax-exempt status. These organizations must meet purposes that are designated in the tax code, purposes that the governments determine are important enough to allow individuals to make tax-deductible donations. Voluntary associations influence the minds and hearts of their members. Among voluntary associations, religion holds a special place.

The influence and power of ideological, economic, political/governmental, military/police, and voluntary/religious realms come from their power to meet human needs, each realm complementing and working together to satiate this range of human need in an organized fashion. While separable conceptually, these powers are not separable in their combined impact. Some elements, though, can be seen as having a greater impact on certain needs, as illustrated by the table below.

TABLE 1. Primary agents of social order in meeting human needs

Needs   Agents of Social Order

	Ideological	Economic	Political	Military/Police	Voluntary/ Religious
Physiological		X			
Security/Safety				X	
Social			X		
Esteem/ Recognition					X
Cognitive	X				
Self/Actual					

Self-actualization is somewhat unique in that it can occur in a variety of ways depending on the individual, and it does not seem possible to determine a single sphere that self-actualization dominates. Self-actualization, rather, can be found in all of the realms.

While giving primacy to individual realms, all are most often simultaneously involved. For example, in the United States, an individual who makes a lot of money and/or is wealthy may have a high social status, hire security guards, influence elections, give a large amount to charity, and serve as a deacon or elder of a church. This person has significant power.

A person who makes little income, has no wealth, depends on the public police force, just has time to vote, gives little to charity, volunteers with a group that feeds the hungry, and occasionally attends church, alas, has less power.

There are clear spheres of influence, nexuses of power, that maintain the US social order. As will be shown, this order and how it operates is responsible in large part for the patterns of inequality, mobility, and poverty that will now be discussed.

PART II: PATTERNS OF INEQUALITY, MOBILITY AND POVERTY (IMP) IN AMERICA

OVERVIEW

The economist Friedrich Hayek notes:

> There is no practical measure of the degree of inequality that
> is desirable here. We do not wish, of course, to see the position
> of individuals determined by arbitrary decision or a privilege
> conferred by human will on particular persons. It is difficult to see,
> however, in what sense it could ever be legitimate to say that any
> one person is too far ahead of the rest or that it would be harmful
> to society if the progress of some greatly outstripped that of others.
> There might be justification for saying this if there appeared great
> gaps in the scale of advance; but, as long as the graduation is more
> or less continuous and all the steps in the income pyramid are
> reasonably occupied, it can scarcely be denied that those lower
> down profit materially from the fact that others are ahead.[1]

Hayek presents the major issues of inequality today, and what he says
about inequality could also be true of mobility or poverty. If there is
no arbitrary decision or privilege involved, how can the outcome be
challenged? To what degree does inequality contribute to the good of all?
Are there gaps in the "pyramid" of income distribution, and, if so, what

are they? Can an ideal inequality be established?

Inequality is part of the ordering of all societies, including modern societies.[2] Those things that a society values are distributed in an orderly fashion to its members using the rules and processes established by the particular society. Different systems of social order in different societies produce different distributions of things, such as income, wealth, and status. In fact, inequalities are found in multiple areas. To encourage its members to carry out certain activities and maintain the society, societies offer rewards for different activities and punishments for others. Often the rewards get associated with a specific part of a group—for example, shamans, kings, warriors, merchants, etc. In certain societies such as the United States, the belief is that rewards are based, at least to a large degree, on merit and hard work.

Just what is social inequality? Various definitions are offered:

- Social inequality is the existence of unequal opportunities and rewards for different social positions or statuses within a group or society.[3]
- Social inequality refers to relational processes in a society that have the effect of limiting or harming a group's social status, social class, and social circle.[4]
- Social inequality occurs when resources in a given society are distributed unevenly, typically through norms of allocation, that engender specific patterns along lines of socially defined categories of persons. It is the differentiation preference of access to social goods in the society brought about by power, religion, kinship, prestige, race, ethnicity, gender, age, sexual orientation, and class.[5]

Within a society, the valued things, such as wealth and status, and the burdens, such as law enforcement and taxes, are not equally shared but unequally distributed throughout a society.[6] Each of these descriptions stresses a different element of inequality:

- Uneven opportunity
- Societal processes that limit or harm
- Uneven resource distribution due to power
- Uneven distribution of valued things and societal burdens

OVERVIEW

In the United States, as in most developed societies, inequalities can be found in a number of areas:

- Income
- Wealth
- Education and occupation
- Status

In truth there are numerous inequalities.[7]

Further review of inequalities requires the use of common distinctions. One distinction is absolute versus relative inequality. The relative/absolute distinction is most often used in economic areas but is also applicable in other areas. Absolute inequality is about differences; relative inequality is about ratios. If, for example, two incomes are $1,000 and $10,000 respectively, and they are increased to $2,000 and $20,000, the ratios would remain (i.e., 1 to 10). However, the absolute difference would double from $9,000 ($10,000 minus $1,000) to $18,000 ($20,000 minus $2,000).[8] Positional versus individual status inequality is another distinction. A boss has status (and power) because of his position in an organization. Status inequality, however, is distinct from position. For instance, a doctor is a doctor regardless of their position in an organization—although in a hospital, the doctor may also have positional power.[9] A person can be provided positive or negative status simply because of personal attributes over which they have no control, such as race or gender (i.e., ascribed status), or a person can achieve a certain status through merit (i.e., achieved status).[10] All of these various forms of inequality, while separately identifiable, often operate in conjunction.

To the extent possible, these various distinctions will be employed in discussing inequality and its various forms.

Notes

(1) Friedrich A. Hayek, "The Common Sense of Progress," in *The Constitution of Liberty* (Chicago: University of Chicago Press, 1960), 570.

(2) Most agree that inequalities are a part of all societies. See, for example, David B. Grusky, "The Past, Present, and Future of Social Inequality," in *Social Stratification: Class, Race, and Gender in Sociological Perspective*, 2nd ed. (Boulder: Westview Press, 2001), 3–51, http://homepage. ntu.edu.tw/~khsu/mobile/sup2.pdf; Richard B. Lee, "Primitive Communism and the *Origin of Social Inequality*," in *Evolution of Political Systems: Sociopolitics in Small-scale Sedentary Societies*

(Cambridge: Cambridge University Press, 1990), 225–46, http://hdl.handle.net/1807/18020; Irfan Habib, "Inequalities: A Social History," *Social Scientist* 43, no. 1/2 (January–February 2015): 3–8, http://www.jstor.org/stable/24372959.

(3) Kimberly Moffitt, "What Is Social Inequality in Sociology?—Definition, Effects and Causes," video, Study.com, February 6, 2015, https://study.com/academy/lesson/what-is-social-inequality-in-sociology-definition-effects-causes.html.

(4) "Social Inequality," *Science Daily*, https://www.sciencedaily.com/terms/social_inequality.htm. Previously published as "Social Inequality" on *Wikipedia*.

(5) *Wikipedia*, s.v. "Social inequality," https://en.wikipedia.org/wiki/Social_inequality.

(6) "Social Inequalities and Populations Dynamics," Department of Sociology and Human Geography, University of Oslo, https://www.sv.uio.no/iss/english/research/subjects/social-inequality/.

(7) Prudence L. Carter and Sean F. Reardon, "Inequality Matters," William T. Grant Foundation, Stanford University, September 2014, https://ed.stanford.edu/sites/default/files/inequalitymatters.pdf. In reviewing various dimensions of inequality, Carter and Reardon note, "We focus on four key interacting social domains: (1) socioeconomic (financial and human capital), (2) health (including physical and psychological), (3) political (access to power and political representation), and (4) sociocultural (identity, cultural freedoms, and human rights" (1).

PERCEPTIONS OF INCOME AND WEALTH INEQUALITY

A useful stating point in the discussion of inequality is a brief review of what Americans think about inequality. Perceptions are important. They reflect a general societal understanding and are guiding forces that strongly influence support or opposition to action-taking, decide which actions should be taken, and, if particular actions are taken, contemplate the organizations who should enact such actions, such as the government or private charities. However salient the data, perceptions play a large role in determining behavior.

> The general data on the perception of inequality in the United States have been focused on perceptions of income and wealth inequality. These perceptions are general in nature with a vague definition of income and wealth.

Perception of Income Inequality

Oliver P. Hauser and Michael I. Norton, in their essay, "(Mis)perceptions of Inequality," document that most Americans have a misperception of income distribution.[1] They state that "(mis)perceptions of inequality—but not actual levels of inequality—drive behavior and preferences for redistribution."[2] Americans share misperceptions of US income inequality with perceptions of citizen inequality in other developed countries. Americans also share with citizens in other countries a desire for a more equal distribution of income.[3]

Reports indicate that income inequality is actually greater than generally perceived. For example, economist Judith Niehues says that there is a general bias of citizens to see their society as more equitable, yet "many nationalities assume that the structure of their society is considerably less equitable than it really is."[4]

A Pew Research Center survey reveals that, while there appears to be a general concern about income inequality, Americans do not identify income inequality as a major concern. In fact, less than half of Americans view inequality as a significant problem.[5] Those who are "relatively poor" are not especially supportive of redistribution. Economist Christopher Hoy notes that a possible reason for this is that most Americans believe they are middle class, "a median bias," and it appears that telling people that they are poor makes them less willing to address income inequality.[6] Ilyana Kuziemko et al., in their working paper, "'Last-Place Aversion': Evidence and Redistributive Implications," suggest that low-income persons may not be supportive of redistribution because it might differentially help the group just below them.[7]

PERCEPTION OF WEALTH INEQUALITY

Norton and Ariely provide a graph (Graph 1) in their essay, "Building a Better America—One Wealth Quintile at a Time," summarizing their findings of Americans' estimate of wealth distribution and their ideal distribution, along with actual distribution perception.[8]

GRAPH 1. Actual, estimated, and desired wealth distribution in the United States

Source: Norton and Ariely (2011)

They end their discussion by noting that Americans prefer the income distribution of Sweden to that of the United States.

Bénabou and Ok in the *Quarterly Journal of Economics* ascribe the lack of desire for change in wealth distribution to Americans' "prospect of upward mobility" (POUM). Americans have a strong sense of optimism, an expectation for personal mobility, and a hope for a better future.[9] They say that a "super-majority will therefore oppose (perhaps through constitutional design) any redistributive policy that bears primarily on future incomes."[10]

Based on a review of the literature and their own research, Gimpelson and Treisman, in "Misperceiving Inequality," also state that misperception of wealth distribution is common across most developed countries.[11] They go further than simply offering descriptive data; they say that it is perception of income and wealth inequality, social mobility, and poverty that are primary in influencing personal behavior. At the end of their article, they suggest some possible causes of these perceptions: overgeneralizations from their immediate reference group, media influence (and travel), ideology, and psychological variables such as a desire to fit in or wanting to feel important.[12]

It is apparent that the current perception of income and wealth inequality are inaccurate. But exactly what is the current state of income and wealth inequality?

Notes

(1) Oliver P. Hauser and Michael I. Norton, "(Mis)perceptions of Inequality," special issue on inequality and social class, *Current Opinion in Psychology* 18 (December 2017): 21–25, https://www.hbs.edu/ris/Publication%20Files/Hauser%20%20Norton%20(2017)_5b0d07bb-f8d6-4edc-bddc-434ef6cd930e.pdf.

(2) Ibid., 21.

(3) Sorapop Kiatpongsan and Michael I. Norton, "How Much (More) Should CEOs Make? A Universal Desire for More Equal Pay," *Perspectives on Psychological Science* 9, no. 6 (2014): 587–93, https://www.hbs.edu/faculty/Publication%20Files/kiatpongsan%20norton%202014_f02b004a-c2de-4358-9811-ea273d372af7.pdf.

(4) Judith Niehues, "Subjective Perceptions of Inequality and Redistributive Preferences: An International Comparison," Cologne Institute for Economic Research, 2014, 1, https://pdfs.semanticscholar.org/1fa2/10b6340448329be06aca72950e7ad1105dcc.pdf.

(5) Bruce Stokes, "The U.S.'s High Income Gap Is Met with Relatively Low Public Concern," Fact Tank, Pew Research Center, December 6, 2013, http://www.pewresearch.org/fact-tank/2013/12/06/the-u-s-s-high-income-gap-is-met-with-relatively-low-public-concern/.

(6) Christopher Hoy, "Why Are Relatively Poor People Not More Supportive of Redistribution?" *Development Impact* (blog), World Bank Blogs, December 4, 2018, https://blogs.worldbank.org/impactevaluations/why-are-relatively-poor-people-not-more-supportive-redistribution-guest-post-christopher-hoy.

(7) Ilyana Kuziemko et al., "Last-Place Aversion: Evidence and Redistributive Implications" (working paper no. 17234, NBER, July 2011), https://www.nber.org/papers/w17234.pdf.

(8) Michael I. Norton and Dan Ariely, "Building a Better America—One Wealth Quintile at a Time," *Perspectives on Psychological Science* 6, no. 1 (January 2011): 9–12, http://www.people.hbs.edu/mnorton/norton%20ariely.pdf.

(9) Roland Bénabou and Efe A. Ok, "Social Mobility and the Demand for Redistribution: The POUM Hypothesis," *Quarterly Journal of Economics* (May 2001): 451, https://www.princeton.edu/~rbenabou/papers/d8zkmee3.pdf.

(10) Ibid., 449.

(11) Vladimir Gimpelson and Daniel Treisman, "Misperceiving Inequality," *Economics and Politics* 30, no. 2 (August 2017), https://www.researchgate.net/publication/319688441_Misperceiving_Inequality.

(12) Ibid., 25–26.

INCOME DISTRIBUTION

Income inequality refers, generally, to differences in the amount of income received by a person, family, or household.[1] Income is the money an individual receives from various sources to purchase goods and services or to invest.[2] In developed countries, the calculation of an individual's income is most often done on an annual basis. Currently, the dollar is the common measure of income, not only in the United States but throughout the world. Income sources are many.[3] Using the categories of the IRS, the Tax Foundation identifies the most prevalent sources of income in 2012 (see Table 1).[4]

TABLE 1: Top ten sources of total income on US individual income tax returns, 2012

Income type	Amount (in billions)
Salaries and wages	6,301
Capital gains less losses	623
Taxable pensions and annuities	612
Partnerships and S corporation net income	535
Business net income	304
Dividends	260
Taxable IRA distributions	231
Taxable Social Security benefits	224
Taxable interest	112
Unemployment compensation	71

Source: Data from IRS SOI Table 1.3 via Cole (2015).

Income from wages is by far the most common source of income reported to the IRS.

THE UNITED STATES IS A RICH COUNTRY

Regardless of source, it is apparent that Americans as a whole have a lot of income. Using gross domestic product (GDP)—the value of goods and services produced as a form of income measurement—the overall US income is the highest in the world. The US GDP was $19.3 trillion in 2017 and an estimated $20.66 trillion in 2018. The $19.3 trillion in 2017 was nearly 25 percent of the world's total income of $77.9 trillion. The United States has had, at least for the past twenty-five years, around 25 percent of the world's income.[5] While having 25 percent of the world's income, the United States, however, has slightly less than 4 percent of the world's population.

The Central Intelligence Agency (CIA) estimates that the average income per person in the United States in 2017 was $59,500.[6] This figure was obtained by dividing the total GDP by the total US population. According to the US Census Bureau report Income and Poverty in the United States: 2018, the median (midpoint) household income for the United States was $63,179 in 2018.[7] According to the IRS, the mean (average) household income was $89,143 in 2016.[8]

Median and average are measures of income-distribution middle points. They do not, however, say much about how income is broadly distributed among Americans. The issue of income distribution can become convoluted with overall increases in income within the population. In the United States, incomes for all have increased over the past forty-five years. The issue of distribution inequality is that, while the incomes of all have increased, incomes at all strata of the population have not increased at the same rate. For example, as will be shown, the incomes of the highest 20 percent of the population have increased at a greater rate than the incomes of the lower 80 percent of the population, and the largest increases are found primarily in incomes of the top 10 percent, 1 percent, and especially the top 0.1 percent.

UNEQUAL INCOME DISTRIBUTION IN THE UNITED STATES

A starting point in understanding income distribution in the United States is by comparing it with that of other countries. A common measure of societal income distribution is the Gini coefficient.[9] This coefficient is organized so that a zero (0) rating would indicate perfect equality, and a one (1) would indicate perfect inequality. Using this measure, the United States has a high Gini coefficient in relation to that of other developed countries. The US Gini coefficient is calculated to be 0.394 by the OECD and 0.45 by the CIA.[10] The US Census Bureau calculates a pretax US Gini coefficient of 0.485 and a posttax coefficient of 0.442.[11]

There are a variety of other commonly used methods employed to determine income distribution, such as the average-income ratio of the top 10 percent of households to the lowest 10 percent of households, as well as the average-income ratio of the top 20 percent of households to the lowest 20 percent of households. By all standard measures, the United States consistently ranks high in unequal income distribution among developed countries. On the other hand, it should be noted that the United States has much less income inequality than less developed countries that have a lower per capita income, smaller GDPs, and lower rankings on human development indices.

Table 2 below provides a general sampling of inequality using a number of the measures already noted.[12] The table shows that the United States ranks at or near the top in unequal distribution of wealth among the high-income and developed countries but has far less income inequality than many undeveloped countries.

TABLE 2. A sampling of income inequality using various measures*

Country	R/P 10%: Ratio: income top 20% to Poorest 10%	R/P 20%: Ratio: income top 20% to Poorest 10%	Gini index	United Nations Development Programme	CIA World Facebook
Finland	5.6	3.8	26.9	5.7	29.5
Sweden	6.2	4	25.0	6.2	23.0
India	8.6	5.6	36.8	8.6	36.8
France	9.1	5.6	32.7	8.3	32.7
Canada	9.4	5.5	32.6	9.5	32.1
Russia	12.7	7.6	39.9	12.8	42.3
UK	13.8	7.2	36.0	13.6	34.0
US	**15.9**	**8.4**	**40.8**	**15.0**	**45.0**
China	21.6	12.2	46.9	21.8	41.5
Mexico	24.6	12.8	46.1	24.6	48.2
Argentina	40.9	17.8	51.3	35.0	45.7
Brazil	51.3	21.8	57.0	49.8	56.7

Source: Wikipedia, s.v. "List of Countries by Income Inequality."

Also, using various analytic tools (e.g., GDP, Human Development Index [HDI], and CIA criteria), the United States is one of the few developed countries where inequality has increased since 1960.[13]

Within this broad international framework, a closer examination of income distribution within the United States can be carried out. *Income and Poverty in the United States: 2018*, published by the US Census Bureau, provides the following distribution of pretax income:[14]

TABLE 3. Percent of total income by households in income quintiles, 2018

Quintile					
Lowest (%)	Second (%)	Third (%)	Fourth (%)	Highest (%)	Top five percent (%)
3.1	8.3	14.1	22.6	52.0	23.1

Source: Semega et al. (2020).

The lowest 20 percent of US households (the lowest quintile) have 3.1 percent of the total income, while the highest 20 percent of households (the highest quintile) have 53 percent of the total income. To put it another way, the top 20 percent of households have 50 percent of the income, and 80 percent of the remaining households have the other 50 percent of the income.

Using the 2012 census, the Congressional Research Service report "The Distribution of Household Income and the Middle Class" by Craig K. Elwell displays similar results (see Table 4).[15] The Congressional Budget Office (CBO) reports on 2010 and 2014 income also provide basic information on income distribution on a pretax- and posttax-income basis, as well as a posttax analysis that includes the value of social programs (see Tables 5 and 6).[16]

TABLE 4. US Census Bureau estimate: distribution of household income by quintile, 2012

Quintile	Share of income (%)	Income range ($)	Number of households
Lowest	3.2	20,592 or less	24,492,000
Second	8.3	20,593–39,735	24,492,000
Third	14.4	39,736–64,553	24,492,000
Fourth	23.0	64,544–104,086	24,492,000
Highest	51.0	104,087 or more	24,492,000
Top 5 percent	22.3	191,150 or more	6,126,000

Source: US Census Bureau, 2012 Annual Social and Economic Supplement to the Current Population Survey via Elwell (2014).

TABLE 5. CBO estimate: distribution of pre- and posttax household income by quintile, 2010

Quintile	Lowest (%)	Second (%)	Third (%)	Fourth (%)	Highest (%)	Top five percent (%)
Share of pretax income	3.9	9.2	14.2	20.8	53.2	28.1
Share of pretax income	7.1	11.2	15.2	20.8	47.4	28.1

TABLE 6. CBO estimate: distribution of pre- and posttax household income by quintile, 2014

Quintile	Lowest (%)	Second (%)	Third (%)	Fourth (%)	Highest (%)	Top five percent (%)
Share of pretax income	3.6	8.6	13.4	20.3	55.3	30.2
Share of pretax income	6.9	10.9	14.6	20.8	48.7	25.1

Source: Perese et al. (2018).

Table 7, using information from the Tax Foundation, provides a more detailed analysis of income brackets, especially of those with the highest incomes. The report points out that those with extremely high incomes have a disproportionate share of income obtained by all those with high incomes.[17]

INCOME DISTRIBUTION

TABLE 7. US income breakdown, 2015

Percent of taxpayers*	Adjusted gross income ($ billions)	Percentage of adjusted gross income (%)
Lowest 50	1,144,545	11.28
Top 50	8,998,075	88.72
Top 25	6,997,737	68.99
Top 10	4,803,327	47.36
Top 5	3,658,556	36.07
Top 1	2,094,906	20.65
Total income tax paid	10,142,620	

Others have further broken down the income of the highest earners. Based on 2015 RS data and listing:[18]

TABLE 8. Breakdown of entry-level income levels for top 1 percent, .1 percent, .01 percent, and .001 percent, 2015

	Entry-level income ($)
Top 1 percent	1,483,596
Top .10 percent	7,318,955
Top .01 percent	35,070,892
Top .0001 percent	152,016,289

Source: Dungan (2018).

For example, the annual income required to be in the top 1 percent is $1,438,596. To be in the top .001 percent, one must earn $152,016,289 a year.

Of some importance is the income source for various income levels. Based on the 2014 annual average, 77.6 percent of the income for all households is from wages and salaries. For those ages twenty-five to thirty-four, salaries and wages account for 92.2 percent of their income. After the age of fifty-five, wages and salaries begin to decrease, falling to 14.9 percent for those seventy-five years and older when pensions and Social Security constitute 70.5 percent of income.[19]

Some, while not denying income inequality, question its degree.[20] For example, the Organization of Economic Cooperation and Development (OECD) notes that when taxes and transfer payments are counted, the US Gini index decreases—as does the Gini index of many other countries.[21] The American Enterprise Institute (AEI) developed a measure of inequality based on consumption. Using this method, while there are still inequalities, these inequalities are less than those identified when income alone is used. Using the AEI measures, the top 20 percent of income has about 40 percent of consumption expenditures, while the lowest 20 percent has roughly 10 percent of the consumption expenditures.[22] Using a different mode of consumption calculation, Jonathan D. Fisher et al., for the *American Economic Review*, conclude that consumption inequality grew about two-thirds the amount of pretax income inequality.[23] According to Fisher et al., "While not denying that income inequality rose, researchers dispute the extent of the increase, which depends on the resource measure used, the definition of the resource measure, the time period over which inequality is measured, and the population of interest."[24] Income inequality in the United States is evident, but there are some questions as to the degree of inequality and how this inequality should be measured.

INEQUALITY OF INCOME INCREASING?

Thomas Piketty and Emanuel Saez each use the share of income reported on individual income tax returns in their calculations of changes in income distribution.[25] They state that in 2012, the top 1 percent (1.3 million US taxpayers) accounted for 16.1 percent of income when Social Security and other transfer payments are excluded. Using income-tax data, Saez prepared a longitudinal analysis of income distribution since 1917. To summarize:

- From 1917 to 1941, 40–45 percent of total US earnings went to the top 10 percent of earners.
- From 1942 to 1982, 30–35 percent of total US earnings went to the top 10 percent of earners.
- Beginning in 1982, the percentage of earnings going to the top 10 percent has begun to increase.
- By 2000, the percentage of earnings going to the top 10 percent grew to 40 percent.

- By 2012, the percentage of earnings going to the top 10 percent grew to 51.6 percent.[26]

In Saez's analysis, when viewed in a historical perspective, high-income households in 2012 had a slightly higher percentage of the total US income than high-income earners did in 1929, the year with the highest percentage of income that went to the top 10 percent in the past hundred years.

On January 12, 2012, in his presentation to the Center for American Progress ("The Rise and Consequences of Inequality in the United States"), Alan B. Krueger, chairman of the Council of Economic Advisers, focused on rising inequality. He indicated that:

- From 1979 to 2010, the annual growth rate in real income for the top fifth of the population was twice that of those in the four-fifth and four times greater than the lowest fifth of the population.
- The (real) median income peaked in 1999 and has decreased since that time.
- While growth in real posttax incomes increased for all between 1979 and 2007, the top 1 percent had a 278 percent real increase, nearly four times the increase of those in the 81st to 99th percentiles and six times the increase in real income of the lowest quintile.
- The top 1 percent and the top 10 percent of earners currently have the greatest share of earned income since 1928.[27]

In their 2016 report, the CBO makes 1979 the baseline starting point for income levels of income quintiles and then plots the changes in total income pretaxes through 2013. While income quintiles are generally used, for this analysis, the top 1 percent was considered separately from the top decile. All groups had increases in income, but the percentage of increase varied. The lowest four quintiles showed a growth of approximately 35 percent; the 88–99 percentiles, all of the highest-income quintile (excluding the top 1 percent), had a growth of 65 percent; the top 1 percent had a 187 percent increase. When posttax income is plotted, the income increases for all groups are slightly higher.[28] In their 2016 blog, the Federal Reserve reaches a similar conclusion.[29] These data show that the largest income increase occurred for those with 1 percent of the income. As Forbes contributor Roberton Williams says, "CBO finds that over the past three decades, a growing fraction of income has gone to the top of the income distribution. The top fifth saw its share of pretax income rise from 43 percent (of total US income) in 1979 to more than 50 percent in 2010. Much of the gain went to the top 1 percent, whose share increased from 9 percent to 15 percent over that period (i.e., the period between 1979 and 2010.)"[30] In his study "Striking It Richer," Emmanuel Saez indicates that this upward trend has been observable since the mid-1970s.[31]

Using a comparable methodology and data set, the Center on Budget and Policy Priorities (CBPP) conducted an assessment that began with the same data set beginning in 1945. Its analysis is illustrated in the two charts below. They depict a generally equal percentage of increase for all income levels until the late 1970s and early 1980s. Starting in the 1980s, a major divergence in income increases for various income quintiles began and continues today, with noticeable increases going to those in the top 5 percent of income.[30]

Income Gains Widely Shared in Early Postwar Decades – But Not Since Then

Real family income between 1947 and 2016, as a percentage of 1973 level

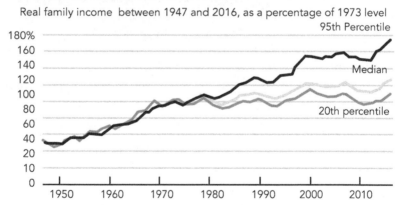

Note: In 2014 Census spit its semaple of survey respondents into two groups to test a set of redesigned income questions. In 2015 (reporting on 2014 income using the new questions), Census releases two estimates of 2013 incomes, one based on the old questions and one on the new. The chart uses the estimate based on the old questions, based on CBPP's jusdgement that, die in part to sample szie, it is likely more accurate for 2013
Source: CBPP calculations based on U.S. Census Bureau Data

CENTER ON BUDGET AND POLICY PRIORITIES I CBPP.ORG

Source: Stone et al. (2019).

Income Gains at the Top Dwarf Those of Low- and Middle-Income Households

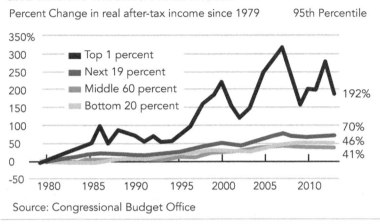

Percent Change in real after-tax income since 1979   95th Percentile

Source: Congressional Budget Office

CENTER ON BUDGET AND POLICY PRIORITIES | CBPP.ORG

The CBPP analysis focuses especially on the income increases in the top 1 percent of households. A number of other analyses point out the same pattern.[33]

Economist Robert J. Gordon, in his piece "Misperceptions About the Magnitude and Timing of Changes in American Income Inequality," writes that the median income has tracked pretty closely to productivity gains since 1980. He proposes that major increases in inequality ended by the late 1990s and early 2000s. A factor he considers important in exaggerations about rising inequality is the "use of common price indexes across income groups," arguing that prices paid for goods used by the rich have risen more rapidly than prices paid for goods by the poor. As a result, the consumption income of the more affluent is actually less, and therefore the differences simply based on income are not adequate. Gordon says that the increase in inequality should be ascribed principally to the top 1 percent and the top 0.1 percent.[34]

In his critique of Timothy Noah's 2012 book, *The Great Divergence*—a book that reflects the same income distribution patterns shown in the above CBO and CPPB analyses—Scott Winship of the Brooking Institute notes that the percentage increase in the 1 percent does not take inflation into consideration. Doing so, according to Winship, decreases the amount of income that goes to the top 1 percent from 80 percent to 53 percent during the 1980–2005 period. Winship also states that the purchasing power of the 1 percent is greatly reduced. [35]

Although they don't refute the presence of income inequality from 1917 to 2015, two analyses of increased inequality, one from 1917 to 1945 and another from 1962 to 2015, also depict an increase in equality that's not as great as that shown by Piketty and Saez. Both studies focus primarily on the top 1 percent. They make technical adjustments to the data based on a variety of factors, including the quality of data, the manner in which the IRS calculates income, and the changes in the demography of the US population. Using these factors, both studies find increases in inequality but, again, not at the rate of increase indicated by Piketty and Saez.[35a]

The most extensive and ongoing critiques about the extent of income-inequality growth comes from the Cato Institute and the Heritage Foundation. Both argue strongly that the growth in income inequality is overstated, particularly as it relates to the top 10 percent. Their biggest objections to what they see as an exaggeration to the growth of inequality can be summarized as:

- The top 1 percent shifts its income to obtain the best tax advantage and hence their amount of income after taxes is overstated. Shifting income from corporate tax returns to individual returns does not make the rich any richer but, rather, causes them to record their income as individual income versus corporate income This type of reporting began in the 1980s due to the impact of a number of changes in the tax code, such as the Tax Reform Act of 1986, the Revenue Reconciliation Acts of 1990 and 1993, and the Small Business Job Protection Act of 1996.
- The share of income of the top 5 percent has consistently fluctuated between 20 percent and 21 percent and has been flat since 1998.
- Salary has not been a big factor in the growth of income inequality.[36]

In his 2007 paper "Has US Income Inequality Really Increased?" Alan Reynolds keys in on the problems associated with using data from individual tax returns. He encapsulates his position in the following chart: [37]

TABLE 9. Factors affecting estimates of income from individual tax returns

Factor	Main effect of factors
Business income: There was a shift in business from corporate tax returns to individual tax returns after individual t ax rates fell.	A great expansion of income was recorded at the top.
Personal savings: There was a large expansion in the use of tax-favored savings, including 401(k)s and IRAs.	This reduced reported investment income among vehicles used by middle-income taxpayers, which raised the top's apparent income share.
Transfer payments: There was a large growth in transfer payments for low-income families—income that is excluded from most tax return-based studies.	This reduced the total-income denominator of income distribution in estimates of income shares at the top.
Capital gains: The boom-and-bust cycle of capital-gains realizations and stock-option exercises occurred as a result of the tax rate.	Comparisons of income-shares changes and stock-market trends between two atypical years need not represent sustained trends.
Stock options: There was a change in stock options for executives and workers from a type taxed as salary in response to changes in the tax rate.	In those studies that exclude capital gains, it increased top incomes when compared to capital gains and ordinary income in the 1970s.
Tax-rate changes: Marginal tax changes occurred in 1981, 1986, 1990, 1993, 2001, and 2003; income reported by high-income taxpayers is highly responsive to such rate changes due to changes in avoidance, evasion, and other behaviors.	Marginal tax-rate changes may have large effects on reported income at the top in situations where actual income may not have changed much.
AGI gap: The AGI gap of unreported income on tax returns has grown s ince 1988.	It may have exaggerated the apparent growth of top incomes due to a greater underreporting of other incomes.

Source: Reynolds (2007).

Reynolds summarizes his position in an extensive 2012 working paper, "The Misuse of Top 1 Percent Income Shares as a Measure of Inequality," as follows: "I estimate that more than half of the increase in the top 1 percent's share of pretax, pretransfer income since 1983, and all of the increase since 2000, is attributable to behavioral reactions to lower marginal tax rates on salaries, unincorporated businesses, dividends and capital gains. After reviewing numerous data sources, I find no compelling evidence of any large and sustained increase in the inequality of disposable income over the past two decades."[38] Analyzing a wide range of official and academic statistics, Reynolds finds no clear trend toward an increase in income inequality after 1988 in:

- Distribution of disposable income
- Consumption
- Wages
- Wealth

Robert Rector and Christine Kim, in their 2008 report, "How the Wealth Is Spread: The Distribution of Government Benefits, Services and Taxes by Income Quintile in the United States," argue that income inequality, in practice, should not be viewed simply by looking at income-distribution figures.[39] In particular, they propose that income inequality should be viewed after the distribution of tax benefits. Per Rector and Kim, "The present analysis suggests that one trillion dollars in resources is transferred from the two highest income household quintiles to the rest of the population. Roughly speaking, this sum would represent about 15 percent of income of the higher income households. Further, public good expenditures (such as national defense and scientific research) and interest payments on the debt are financed solely by the two highest income quintiles. Lower income households benefit from these expenditures but do not pay sufficient taxes to support them."[40] They say that looking only at income before considering taxes and the redistribution of state- and federal-government transfers paints an inaccurate picture of inequality.

Ryan Messmore, a Heritage Fellow, summarizes a similar position in his 2012 article for *National Affairs*:

Once employee health benefits and government transfers are added, the effects of taxation are accounted for, and quintiles are adjusted to contain equal shares of population, the picture looks much different: According to Census Bureau data from the past decade, the ratio of the incomes of the top quintile to the bottom quintile drops from about $15 to one dollar down to just over $4 to one dollar. Hederman and Rector have also calculated that if the adults in each quintile worked the same number of hours at current income levels, the ratio of incomes between the quintiles would fall further, to $2.91 to one dollar.

> Moreover, as a group led by Richard Burkhauser of Cornell University recently showed, the rise in income inequality in America since early 1990s has been smaller and has grown more slowly than in the two decades before. After adjusting the US Census Bureau's Current Population Survey data for a practice called top-coding (by which all incomes above a certain level in the survey are scored as equal to that level, to protect the identities of the wealthiest Americans), Burkhauser and his colleagues found that "the increase in American income inequality since 1993 has been significantly slower than in the previous two decades.[41]

There is a clear pattern of income inequality in the United States. The United States has a high Gini coefficient absolutely and when compared to the Gini coefficients of other developed countries. The lowest 50 percent of Americans have approximately 12 percent of the US income, while the upper 50 percent have 88 percent of the income. The top 5 percent has 36 percent of the income, and top 1 percent has 21 percent of the income. Using other-than-straightforward statistical measures, they also point to an increase in inequality since 1980 but to a lesser degree.

While there are differences in identifying the degree of inequality and its increase, there is recognition that inequality is present and growing to some degree in the United States.[42] As Gordon states in his critique questioning the magnitude and timing of income inequality: "The evidence is incontrovertible that American income inequality has increased in the United States since the 1970s."[43]

Depending on the measures and methodology used, different

conclusions are reached regarding the extent to which inequality is growing and the periods of most significant growth. Underlying this debate is the question of how income is calculated, if and how other factors should be considered (e.g., taxes and cost of consumption), and to what degree social programs should be counted as income. Of particular interest here is the pattern of growth since 1970. This topic will be returned to later.

Notes

(1) Individual, family, and household incomes are discussed here. In addition to these personal incomes, entities can also earn income (e.g., corporations).

(2) Julia Kagan, "Income," Investopedia, last modified August 20, 2019, https://www.investopedia.com/terms/i/income.asp#:~:targetText=Income%20is%20money%20(or%20some,sources%20of%20income%20for%20retirees.).

(3) "LB&I Concept Unit: Knowledge Base—International," PowerPoint, IRS, last modified April 12, 2017, https://www.irs.gov/pub/int_practice_units/ftc_c_10_02_05.pdf.

(4) Alan Cole, "The Top Ten Sources of Personal Income," Tax Foundation, February 2, 2015, https://taxfoundation.org/top-ten-sources-personal-income/.

(5) "List of Countries by Projected GDP," map and table, *Statistics Times*, last modified March 2019, http://statisticstimes.com/economy/countries-by-projected-gdp.php.

(6) "Country Comparison: GDP Per Capita PPP," *World Factbook, CIA*, https://www.cia.gov/library/publications/the-world-factbook/rankorder/2004rank.html.

(7) Jessica Semega et al., *Income and Poverty in the United States*: 2018 (Washington, DC: US Census Bureau, September 2019), https://www.census.gov/content/dam/Census/library/publications/2019/demo/p60-266.pdf.

(8) "HINC-02. Age of Householder-Households, by Total Money Income, Type of Household, Race and Hispanic Origin of Householder," US Census Bureau, https://www.census.gov/data/tables/time-series/demo/income-poverty/cps-hinc/hinc-02.2016.html#par_textimage_10.

(9) Jim Chappelow, "Gini Index," Investopedia, last modified September 18, 2019, https://www.investopedia.com/terms/g/gini-index.asp.

(10) "OECD Income Distribution Database (IDD): Gini, Poverty, Income, Methods and Concepts," OECD, http://www.oecd.org/social/income-distribution-database.htm; see *World Factbook*, CIA, https://www.cia.gov/library/publications/the-world-factbook/rankorder/2172rank.html.

(11) Semega et al., *Income and Poverty*.

(12) *Wikipedia*, s.v. "List of Countries by Income Inequality," http://en.wikipedia.org/wiki/List_of_countries_by_income_equality.

(13) Lowell R. Ricketts and Christopher J. Waller, "U.S. Income Inequality May Be High, but It Is Lower Than World Income Inequality," Federal Reserve Bank of St. Louis, July 2014, https://www.stlouisfed.org/~/media/Files/PDFs/publications/pub_assets/pdf/re/2014/c/income_inequality.pdf. While US income inequality is high compared to other developed countries, it should be noted that when viewed from the average of all countries—including developed, developing, and underdeveloped countries—US inequality is lower than the average. Also, as already indicated, the lowest incomes in the US are higher than the

lowest incomes in other countries. For example, "the poorest 10 percent of the U.S. income distribution hold a median income that is more than seven times that of the poorest 19 developing nations."

(14) Semega et al., *Income and Poverty*, 7.

(15) Craig K. Elwell, "The Distribution of Household Income and the Middle Class," Congressional Research Service, March 10, 2014, https://fas.org/sgp/crs/misc/RS20811.pdf.

(16) Kevin Perese et al., *The Distribution of Household Income*, 2014 (Washington, DC: CBO, March 2018), https://www.cbo.gov/system/files/115th-congress-2017-2018/reports/53597-distribution-household-income-2014.pdf; see also "Household Income Quintiles," table, Tax Policy Center, March 24, 2020, http://www.taxpolicycenter.org/statistics/household-income-quintiles; Table 2.1, "Personal Income and Its Disposition," BEA, https://www.bea.gov/iTable/iTable.

(17) Tax Foundation Fiscal Fact no. 540, February 2017; https://taxfoundation.org/summary-federal-income-tax-data-2017/

(18) Adrian Dungan, "Individual Income Tax Shares, 2015," *IRS Statistics of Income Bulletin*, IRS, 2018, https://www.irs.gov/pub/irs-soi/soi-a-ints-id1801.pdf; Aimee Picchi, "How Much Do the 1, .01 and .001 Really Earn?" *CBS MoneyWatch*, CBS News, February 27, 2018, https://www.cbsnews.com/news/how-much-do-the-1-01-and-001-percent-really-earn/.

(19) "Wages and Salaries Were 92 Percent of Income before Taxes for Consumer Ages 25 to 34 in 2014," bar graph and table, *TED: The Economics Daily*, US Bureau of Labor Statistics, June 28, 2016, https://www.bls.gov/opub/ted/2016/wages-and-salaries-were-92-percent-of-income-before-taxes-for-consumers-ages-25-to-34-in-2014.htm.

(20) Drew DeSilver, "The Many Ways to Measure Income Inequality," *Fact Tank*, Pew Research Center, September 22, 2015, http://www.pewresearch.org/fact-tank/2015/09/22/the-many-ways-to-measure-economic-inequality/.

(21) "OECD Income Distribution Database (IDD)."

(22) Kevin A. Hassett and Aparna Mathur, *A New Measure of Consumption Inequality* (Washington, DC: American Enterprise Institute, June 2012), http://www.aei.org/wp-content/uploads/2012/06/-a-new-measure-of-consumption-inequality_142931647663.pdf.

(23) Jonathan D. Fisher, David S. Johnson, and Timothy M. Smeeding, "Measuring the Trends in Inequality of Individuals and Families: Income and Consumption," American Economic Review 103, no. 3 (May 2013): 184–88, https://www.aeaweb.org/articles?id=10.1257/aer.103.3.184.

(24) Ibid., 188.

(25) Thomas Piketty, Capital in the Twenty-First Century, trans. Arthur Goldhammer (Cambridge: Belknap Press of Harvard University Press, 2014); Emmanuel Saez, "Striking It Richer: The Evolution of Top Incomes in the United States," UC Berkeley, last modified March 2, 2019, https://eml.berkeley.edu/~saez/saez-UStopincomes-2017.pdf. A major source of data for the discussion on income inequality arises from the works of Thomas Piketty and Emanuel Saez, as well as Gabriel Zucman (see below). Their work serves as a vital resource and starting point for the topic of changing income inequality. Piketty's book *Capital in the Twenty-First Century* is an oft-cited reference when it comes to studies on income and wealth inequality. Piketty and Saez continue to update their information as additional income data become available.

(26) Emmanuel Saez and Gabriel Zucman, "*Wealth Inequality in the United States Since 1913*," PowerPoint, UC Berkeley, October 2014, https://eml.berkeley.edu/~saez/SaezZucman14slides.pdf; see also Wojciech Kopczuk, Emmanuel Saez, and Jae Song, "Earnings Inequality and Mobility in the United States: Evidence from Social Security Data Since 1937," *Quarterly Journal of Economics* 125, no. 1 (February 2010): 91–128, https://eml.berkeley.edu/~saez/kopczuk-saez-songQJE10mobility.pdf.

(27) Alan B. Krueger, "The Rise and Consequences of Inequality in the United States," (speech to the Center for American Progress, Washington, DC, January 12, 2012), https://obamawhitehouse. archives.gov/sites/default/files/krueger_cap_speech_final_remarks.pdf, https://obamawhitehouse. archives.gov/sites/default/files/speech_2012_01_12.pdf.

(28) Kevin Perese et al., *The Distribution of Household Income and Federal Taxes*, 2013 (Washington, DC: CBO, June 2016), https://www.cbo.gov/publication/51361.
(29) Michael T. Owyang and Hannah G. Shell, "Measuring Trends in Income Inequality," Federal Reserve Bank of St. Louis, March 30, 2016, https://www.stlouisfed.org/publications/regional-economist/april-2016/measuring-trends-in-income-inequality.

(30) Roberton Williams, "CBO Details Growing US Income Inequality," Forbes, December 9, 2013, http://www.forbes.com/sites/beltway/2013/12/09/cbo-details-growing-u-s-income-inequality/#322910d03242.

(31) Saez, "Striking It Richer."

(32) Chad Stone et al., "A Guide to Statistics on Historical Trends in Income Inequality," Center on Budget and Policy Priorities, last modified August 21, 2019, http://www.cbpp.org/research/poverty-and-inequality/a-guide-to-statistics-on-historical-trends-in-income-inequality.

(33) See, for example, Ricketts and Waller, "U.S. Income Inequality May Be High"; "Dividing the Pie," *Economist*, February 2, 2006, https://www.economist.com/finance-and-economics/2006/02/02/dividing-the-pie; "The Rich, the Poor and the Growing Gap between Them," *Economist*, June 15, 2006, https://www.economist.com/special-report/2006/06/15/the-rich-the-poor-and-the-growing-gap-between-them.

(34) Robert J. Gordon, "Misperceptions About the Magnitude and Timing of Changes in American Income Inequality" (working paper series no. 15351, NBER, September 2009), https://www.nber.org/papers/w15351.pdf.

(35) Scott Winship, "Making Sense of Inequality," Brookings, August 3, 2012, https://www.brookings.edu/opinions/making-sense-of-inequality/. Winship also notes that the median family income tracks well with productivity, but this argument does not seem to address the issue of income going to the top 1 percent.

(35a) Gerald Auten and David Splinter, "Income Inequality in the United States: Using Tax Data to Measure Long-term Trends" (working paper, on David Splinter's personal website, December 20, 2019), http://davidsplinter.com/AutenSplinter-Tax_Data_and_Inequality.pdf; Vincent Geloso et al., "How Pronounced Is the U-Curve? Revisiting Income Inequality in the United States, 1917–1945," SSRN, February 4, 2018, http://dx.doi.org/10.2139/ssrn.2985234.

(36) Michael D. Tanner, "Five Myths About Income Inequality in America," Cato Institute, September 7, 2016, https://www.cato.org/publications/policy-analysis/five-myths-about-economic-inequality-america; Kate Walsh O'Beirne and Robert Rector, "Dispelling the Myth of Income Inequality," Heritage Foundation, June 6, 1989, https://www.heritage.org/civil-society/report/dispelling-the-myth-income-inequality; Robert Rector, "Understanding Poverty and Economic Inequality in the United States," Heritage Foundation, September 15, 2004, https://www.heritage.org/welfare/report/understanding-poverty-and-economic-inequality-the-united-states.

(37) Alan Reynolds, "Has US Income Inequality *Really* Increased?," Cato Institute, January 8, 2007, https://www.cato.org/publications/policy-analysis/has-us-income-inequality-really-increased.

(38) Alan Reynolds, "The Misuse of Top 1 Percent Income Shares as a Measure of Inequality" (working paper no. 9, Cato Institute, October 4, 2012), 2, https://object.cato.org/sites/cato.org/files/pubs/pdf/WorkingPaper-9.pdf.

(39) Robert Rector and Christine Kim, "How the Wealth Is Spread: The Distribution of Government Benefits, Services and Taxes by Income Quintile in the United States," Heritage Foundation, September 7, 2008, http://www.heritage.org/taxes/report/how-the-wealth-spread-the-distribution-government-benefits-services-and-taxes-income.

(40) Ibid., 24.

(41) Ryan Messmore, "Justice, Inequality, and the Poor," *National Affairs*, Winter 2012, https://nationalaffairs.com/publications/detail/justice-inequality-and-the-poor; see also http://www.nationalaffairs.com/doclib/20111220_Messmore_Indiv.pdf.

(42) It is unfortunate that the discussion of income inequality, and in particular the discussion around trends in inequality, have taken a decidedly political taint. Those who represent a more conservative view argue that there is little increase; those from a more liberal perspective tend to show higher amounts of inequality and growth. When the causes of income inequality are explored, this intrusion of political bias will be in evidence, especially concerning whether action should be taken and, if so, what actions should be considered.

(43) Gordon, "Misperceptions," 1.
in evidence, especially concerning whether action should be taken and, if so, what actions should be considered.

(43) Gordon, "Misperceptions," 1.

WEALTH

Wealth in the United States grew from $1.17 trillion in 1950 to $106 trillion in 2018. Even after taking inflation into consideration, this is remarkable growth.[1] As is the case with income, the United States currently has the greatest share of the world's wealth—over $98 trillion, with 31 percent of the world's $317 trillion of wealth.[2] The population of the United States is 326 million; the world population is approximately 7.6 billion. That's roughly 4.3 percent of the world's 7.6 billion population holding close to a third of the total global wealth. Of the world's 42.2 million millionaires, 17.4 million (41.2 percent) are Americans.[3] According to Money Watch, the median net worth of the average US household is $97,300.[4] The mean net worth is nearly $404,000, making the United States one of the highest mean net-worth countries in the world.[5]

While there is disagreement about both the size of income inequality and its growth, almost no disagreement exists regarding the degree of wealth concentration and the growth of wealth inequality in the United States. The US wealth inequality is one of the highest in the world. The percent of wealth held by the top 10 percent of Americans is among the highest in the entire developed world. Only the United States, Switzerland, and Denmark have 70 percent or more of the wealth owned by 10 percent of the population.[6] Carlotta Balestra and Richard Tonkin, in a report for the

OECD, note that "wealth inequality is twice the level of income inequality on average."[7]

While wealth inequality has always been present in the United States, it is clear that this inequality has increased since the 1970s.[8] The following chart illustrates this increase:

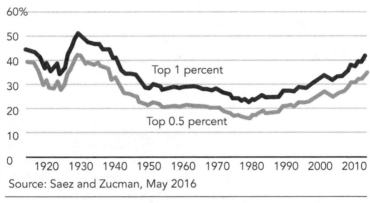

Wealth Concentration Has been Rising Toward Early 20th Century Levels

Share of total wealth held by the wealthies families, 1913-2012

Source: Saez and Zucman, May 2016

CENTER ON BUDGET AND POLICY PRIORITIES I CBPP.ORG

Source: Stone et al. (2019).

As economist Edward N. Wolff states in a report for the National Bureau of Economic Research, wealth has concentrated at the top.[9] A number of other analyses have supported this position.[10] At the present time, there is a consensus that the top 10 percent of the US population has approximately 75 percent of the total US wealth.[10a] The top 1 percent has approximately 40 percent of the US wealth.[11] A few examples illustrate wealth differences: As of 2020, households at the midpoint of wealth have, on average, approximately $141,000. Those at the 90 percent level have $1.219 million in wealth. Those at the 99 percent level have $11.099 million. And those at the 99.9 percent level have $43.207 million. However, those in the lowest 10 percent of wealth distribution actually have, on average, a negative net worth of -$467, and those at the 20 percent of distribution have $6,318 in wealth.[12]

WEALTH

A report by labor-economics specialist Linda Levine for the Congressional Research Service, "An Analysis of the Distribution of Wealth Across Households, 1989–2010," shows both increasing median and mean household net worth. Recognizing the anomalies of the Great Recession, the report depicts a growing "median-to-mean" ratio, an indicator that more wealth is concentrated at the upper end of wealth distribution. This report also provides a summary of the wealth-distribution percentage held by various population segments. The amount of wealth held by the top 10 percent escalated from 67.2 percent in 1989 to 74.5 percent in 2010; the wealth held by the top 1 percent escalated from 30.1 percent to 34.5 percent. Of all US households in 2010, 50 percent held 1 percent of wealth. The next 40 percent held 24.3 percent of wealth. The highest 10 percent of households held 40 percent of wealth. And, finally, the top 1 percent held 34.5 percent of wealth.[13] When discussing the causes of the increase in wealth concentration, the major reason given in the report is additional savings. While four out of five (80 percent) of the top 10 percent saved income, only one in three (33 percent) in the lowest 20 percent saved.[14]

The liberal Economic Policy Institute identifies even greater wealth concentration. According to their analysis, the top 1 percent possesses greater collective wealth than the entire bottom 90 percent. While the overall wealth pie shrank during the Great Recession, wealth distribution was simultaneously becoming more unequal. In 2009, the wealthiest 20 percent of households controlled 87.2 percent of all wealth, up from 85 percent in 2007. The top 1 percent controlled 35.6 percent of all wealth, up from 34.6 percent in 2007.[15]

Noteworthy is the fact that the wealth of ethnic and racial minorities has decreased. While the overall distribution of wealth to the top .1 percent, 1 percent, and 10 percent is increasing, the median wealth of the white population, as compared to minorities, has increased eightfold in the past twenty years.[16]

There seems to be little disagreement that US wealth concentration and inequality are sizeable and have increased since the 1970s. The amount of wealth held by the top 10 percent of the population has progressed, while the percentage of wealth held by the lowest 50 percent has actually decreased. Today, the 50 percent of households with the lowest amount of wealth hold less than 2 percent of the total wealth, while the top 10 percent hold 71 percent of the wealth. The percentage of wealth held by middle-income individuals and families has been cut in half to 17% of the aggregate wealth.

Notes

(1) "Households and Nonprofit Organizations; Net Worth, Level," line chart, FRED Economic Data, Federal Reserve Bank of St. Louis, https://fred.stlouisfed.org/series/TNWBSHNO.

(2) Anthony Shorrocks, Jim Davies, and Rodrigo Lluberas, *Research Institute: Global Wealth Report 2018* (Zurich, Switzerland: Credit Suisse AG, October 2018), https://www.credit-suisse.com/corporate/en/research/research-institute/global-wealth-report.html; see also Kathrin Brandmeir et al., *Allianz Global Wealth Report 2018* (Munich: Allianz, September 26, 2018), https://www.allianz.com/en/economic_research/publications/specials_fmo/agwr18e.html; Edward Yardeni, Debbie Johnson, and Mali Quintana, "US Financial Accounts: US Household Wealth," Yardeni Research, Inc., April 1, 2021, https://www.yardeni.com/pub/fofhhwealth.pdf.

(3) Shorrocks, Davies, and Lluberas, *Global Wealth Report*, 11.

(4) Dayana Yochim, "What's Your Net Worth, and How Do You Compare to Others?," NerdWallet, MarketWatch, January 23, 2020, https://www.marketwatch.com/story/whats-your-net-worth-and-how-do-you-compare-to-others-2018-09-24.

(5) Shorrocks, Davies, and Lluberas, *Global Wealth Report*, 40; see also *Wikipedia*, s.v. "List of Countries by Wealth per Adult," https://en.wikipedia.org/wiki/List_of_countries_by_wealth_per_adult.

(6) James B. Davies et al., "Estimating the Level and Distribution of Global Household Wealth" (research paper no. 2007/77, United Nations University, November 2007), https://www.wider.unu.edu/sites/default/files/rp2007-77.pdf.

(7) Carlotta Balestra and Richard Tonkin, "Inequalities in Household Wealth across OECD Countries: Evidence from the OECD Wealth Distribution Database" (working paper no. 88, OECD, June 20, 2018), 7, https://www.oecd.org/officialdocuments/publicdisplaydocumentpdf/?cote=SDD/DOC(2018)1&docLanguage=En; see also Markus Jäntti and Eva Sierminska, "Survey Estimates of Wealth Holdings in OECD Countries: Evidence on the Level and Distribution across Selected Countries (WIDER research paper no. 2007/17, United Nations World Institute for Development Economics Research, April 2007), https://www.econstor.eu/bitstream/10419/63571/1/537399062.pdf.

(8) Chad Stone et al., "A Guide to Statistics on Historical Trends in Income Inequality," Center on Budget and Policy Priorities, last modified August 21, 2019, https://www.cbpp.org/research/poverty-and-inequality/a-guide-to-statistics-on-historical-trends-in-income-inequality.

(9) Edward N. Wolff, "Household Wealth Trends in the United States, 1962 to 2016: Has Middle Class Wealth Recovered?" (working paper no. 24085, NBER, November 2017), http://www.nber.org/papers/w24085. For a summary of Wolff's report, visit https://www.nber.org/digest/jan18/w24085.shtml.

(10) See Gabriel Zucman, "Wealth Inequality," Stanford Center on Poverty and Inequality, 2016, https://inequality.stanford.edu/sites/default/files/Pathways-SOTU-2016-Wealth-Inequality-3.pdf; Emmanuel Saez and Gabriel Zucman, "Wealth Inequality in the United States Since 1913: Evidence from Capitalized Income Tax Data" (working paper series no. 20625, NBER, October 2014), https://www.nber.org/papers/w20625.pdf.

(10a) See, for example, Jesse Bricker et al., "Changes in U.S. Family Finances from 2013 to 2016: Evidence from the Survey of Consumer Finances," *Federal Reserve Bulletin* 103, no. 3 (September 2017), https://www.federalreserve.gov/publications/files/scf17.pdf; PK, "Average, Median, Top 1%, and All United States Net Worth Percentiles," DQYDJ, https://dqydj.com/net-worth-brackets-wealth-brackets-one-percent/; Jake Johnson, "'What a Rigged Economy Looks Like': Top 10% Now Own 77% of American Wealth," BillMoyers.com, September 29, 2017, https://billmoyers.com/story/top-10of-percent-wealth/.

(11) Christopher Ingraham, "The Richest 1 Percent Now Owns More of the Country's Wealth Than at Any Time in the Past 50 Years," *Washington Post*, December 6, 2017, https://www.washingtonpost.com/news/wonk/wp/2017/12/06/the-richest-1-percent-now-owns-more-of-the-countrys-wealth-than-at-any-time-in-the-past-50-years/?utm_term=.0096d8e087ca.

(12) PK, "Average, Median, Top 1%."

(13) Federal Reserve - Wealth and Income Concentration in the SCF: 1989–2019 https://www.federalreserve.gov/econres/notes/feds-notes/wealth-and-income-concentration-in-the-scf-20200928.htm

(14) https://www.pewresearch.org/social-trends/2020/01/09/trends-in-income-and-wealth-inequality/.

(15) "The Great Recession Exacerbated Existing Wealth Disparities in U.S.," press release, Economic Policy Institute, March 29, 2011, https://www.epi.org/press/news_from_epi_th_great_recession_exacerbated_existing_wealth_disparities_in/.

(16) Rakesh Kochhar and Anthony Cilluffo, "How Wealth Inequality Has Changed in the U.S. Since the Great Recession, by Race, Ethnicity and Income," Fact Tank, Pew Research Center, November 1, 2107, http://www.pewresearch.org/fact-tank/2017/11/01/how-wealth-inequality-has-changed-in-the-u-s-since-the-great-recession-by-race-ethnicity-and-income/.

EDUCATION AND EMPLOYMENT

Inequality is often spoken of in terms of education and occupation. While both are related to income and wealth, it is possible to separate education and occupation for purposes of analysis. Education is most commonly examined in terms of number of years of education and degree type. Occupations are classified in a number of ways, typically by salary and/ or type of license or certification required for the job at hand. Extensive literature exists on both. This discussion will summarize education and occupation only in relationship to inequality and will be limited to a review of adult education.

Education level is often used to identify inequality. It is thought that more education is more valuable than less education. The division by education is usually done through the amount of formal education, in terms of years, one possesses. The following table, using US Census Bureau data, provides an overview of adult (twenty-five years and older) education levels.[1]

TABLE 1. Formal educational attainment of Americans twenty-five years and older, 2015

Educational attainment	Number	Percentage (%)
Less than high school	24,600,000	11.6
High school or GED	187,500,000	88.4
Some college or more	124,900,000	58.9
Associate degree or more	89,700,000	42.3
Bachelor's degree or more	68,900,000	32.5
Master's degree, doctorate, or professional degree	25,500,000	12.0

Source: US Census Bureau, 2015 Current Population Survey via Ryan and Bauman (2016).

A number of points here are noteworthy:

- Over 40 percent of Americans exclusively have a high-school diploma or less (high-school graduates plus those who did not complete high school), with no college schooling.
- Nearly 60 percent of Americans have some college education (58.9 percent, specifically).
- Roughly two-thirds of those who graduate from high school have taken some college courses.
- Of those who enter college, 16.6 percent do not receive any degree.
- Of those who have a college degree, 32.5 percent have a bachelor's degree.
- In total, 12.0 percent of American adults have a master's degree, doctorate, or professional degree.

Additional data are available regarding the 11 percent of the adult population who have less than a high-school education (25.584 million individuals).[2]

TABLE 2. Less than a high-school education for persons over twenty-five years of age, 2015

Years of school	Number (in millions)	Percent (%)
0 to 4	2,601	10.5
5 to 8	7,295	29.7
9 to 11	14,688	59.7

Source: US Census Bureau (2017).

Approximately 40 percent of those without a high-school education have only completed grade school, while 60 percent have completed grade school but have not completed high school.

The number and percentage of Americans who have completed both high school and college has increased significantly over the years. In 1950, for example, the total US population was 152 million. The population over the age of twenty-five represented 58.4 percent of the total population, or 88.8 million Americans. Of this twenty-five-years-and-older population, 34 percent, or 32.2 million Americans, had a high-school diploma. Those with a college degree accounted for 6.2 percent, or 5.5 million Americans.[3]

By 2015, the US population had grown to 321 million.[4] Almost 67 percent of this population, 212 million Americans, was twenty-five years and older. Of this population, 88.4 percent, or 187 million Americans, were high-school graduates, and 32.5 percent, some 68.9 million Americans, were college graduates. As the United States has grown in population so, too, has the overall education level of its citizens.[5]

The relationship of education to occupation to income is evident. A wide body of literature correlates low educational achievement to income. For example, in their report on the working poor for 2013, the US Bureau of Labor Statistics states that the higher the education level, the smaller the percentage of those living in poverty.[6] Other data show that for persons sixteen years and older, unemployment was less than 10 percent for those with a post-high-school education, while it was between 30 percent and 40 percent for those without a high-school education.[7]

Education level is highly determinative of the occupational opportunities an individual can access. Occupational requirements for higher-wage jobs are, alas, based primarily on education.[8] Meeting the basic educational requirements is necessary for a number of high-paid occupations.[9] Some authors even point out the value of education both immediately and over a lifetime in terms of its effects on earnings.[10]

While education by itself can be used for determining inequality, it is often grouped with occupation and income to divide the population into various levels. The so-called educational divide relates to many other inequalities, but it is especially akin to occupational differences.

Americans also identify occupational inequalities, with certain occupations being valued more highly than others. To a large extent, more valued occupations are those that require higher education levels. The graph below illustrates the relation of wages to education: the higher the education level, the higher the salary.[11] The vast majority of occupations in the United States are linked to education level.[12]

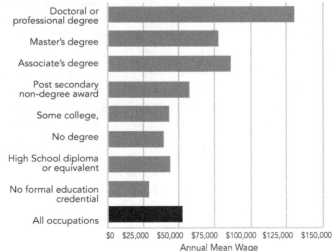

Annual mean wages by typical entry-level educational requirement May 2017

Source: U.S. Bureau of Labor Statistics, Occupational Employment Statistics program.

Source: US Bureau of Labor Statistics (2018).

In 2016, the most available jobs, in terms of numbers, were those that required the least education. A US Bureau of Labor Statistics report provides an overview of the requirements for entry-level jobs.[13]

TABLE 3: Employment by typical entry-level educational requirement, as a percentage of total employment, May 2016

Typical entry-level education requirement	Percent of total employment (%)
Doctoral or professional degree	2.5
Master's degree	1.7
Bachelor's degree	21.3
Associate degree	2.4
Postsecondary nondegree award	6.0
Some college, no degree	2.6
High-school diploma or equivalent	35.8
No formal educational credential	27.7

Source: US Bureau of Labor Statistics (2017).

In 2016, 27.7 percent of available jobs were available for those without a high-school education, 35.8 percent for those with at least a high-school education, and 36.5 percent required post-high-school training.[14]

However, it is apparent that the greatest growth in high-income jobs will be for positions that require a college education. A 2017 report from the Department of Labor depicts the growth in jobs by education level.[15] Clearly the good-paying jobs of today and of the near future will require additional skill training.

TABLE 4: Shifts in education-level requirements for entry-level jobs, since 2007

Typical entry-level education requirement	Employment change (in millions)		
	May 2007-May 2010	May 2010-May 2016	May 2017 May 2016
Doctoral or professional degree	0.1	0.3	0.5
Bachelor's or master's degree	0.3	3.7	4.0
Associate degree	0.0	0.4	0.5
Postsecondary nondegree award	-0.1	0.8	0.7
Some college, no degree	-0.2	0.0	-0.2
High-school diploma or equivalent	-4.8	3.5	-1.3
No formal educational credential	-2.5	4.5	2.0
All occupations	-7.3	13.3	6.0

Source: US Bureau of Labor Statistics, Occupational Employment Statistics program via Watson (2017).

Americans are differentiated by education levels, occupation, and the income received from any given occupation. Americans thus rank others by their education level and occupation.

Notes

(1) Camille L. Ryan and Kurt Bauman, "Educational Attainment in the United States: 2015," US Census Bureau, May 2016, https://www.census.gov/content/dam/Census/library/publications/2016/demo/p20-578.pdf.

(2) "Educational Attainment in the United States: 2016," US Census Bureau, last modified March 31, 2017, https://www.census.gov/data/tables/2016/demo/education-attainment/cps-detailed-tables.html.

(3) Frank Hobbs and Nicole Stoops, Demographic Trends in the 20th Century: Census 2000 Special Reports (Washington, DC: US Census Bureau, 2002), https://www.census.gov/prod/2002pubs/censr-4.pdf; "A Look at the 1940s Census," PowerPoint, United States Census Bureau, https://www.census.gov/newsroom/cspan/1940census/CSPAN_1940slides.pdf; "Chapter 4. Population Change in the U.S. and the World from 1950 to 2050," Pew Research Center, January 30, 2014, https://www.pewresearch.org/global/2014/01/30/chapter-4-population-change-in-the-u-s-and-the-world-from-1950-to-2050/; "Chapter 10: Education," US Census Bureau, https://www.census.gov/population/www/cen2000/censusatlas/pdf/10_Education.pdf.

(4) "U.S. and World Population Clock," live clock, US Census Bureau, https://www.census.gov/popclock/.

(5) Ryan and Bauman, "Educational Attainment"; "Population Distribution by Age," interactive graphic, KFF, https://www.kff.org/other/state-indicator/distribution-by-age/?currentTimeframe=0&sortModel=%7B%22colI d%22:%22Location%22,%22sort%22:%22asc%22%7D.

(6) "A Profile Of The Working Poor, 2013," BLS Reports, US Bureau of Labor Statistics, July 2015, https://www.bls.gov/opub/reports/working-poor/archive/a-profile-of-the-working-poor-2013.pdf#targetText=the%20 labor%20force%20for%20half,11.1%20percent%20a%20year%20earlier.

(7) Stephanie Hugie Barello, "Consumer Spending and U.S. Employment from the 2007–2009 Recession through 2022," *Monthly Labor Review*, US Bureau of Labor Statistics, October 2014, https://doi.org/10.21916/mlr.2014.34.

(8) "Occupational Requirements in the United States—2017" (news release, US Bureau of Labor Statistics, November 29, 2017), https://www.bls.gov/news.release/archives/ors_11292017.pdf.

(9) "Annual Mean Wages by Typical Entry-Level Educational Requirement, May 2017," table, US Bureau of Labor Statistics, last modified March 30, 2018, https://www.bls.gov/oes/2017/may/education3.htm. However, 40 percent of entry-level jobs still require a high-school diploma or an equivalent.

(10) Christopher R. Tamborini, ChangHwan Kim, and Arthur Sakamoto, "Education and Lifetime Earnings in the United States," *Demography* 52, no. 4 (2015): 1383–1407, doi: 10.1007/s13524-015-0407-0; Anthony P. Carnevale, Stephen J. Rose, and Ban Cheah, *The College Payoff: Education, Occupations, Lifetime Earnings* (Washington, DC: Georgetown University Center on Education and the Workforce, 2014), https://cew.georgetown.edu/wp-content/uploads/2014/11/collegepayoff-complete.pdf.

(11) "Annual Mean Wages."

(12) Standard Occupational Classification Structure, US Bureau of Labor Statistics, https://www.bls.gov/soc/2018/soc_structure_2018.pdf.

(13) "37 Percent of May 2016 Employment in Occupations Typically Requiring Postsecondary Education," *TED*, US Bureau of Labor Statistics, June 28, 2017, https://www.bls.gov/opub/ted/2017/37-percent-of-may-2016-employment-in-occupations-typically-requiring-postsecondary-education.htm.

(14) See also "Education and Training Assignments by Detailed Occupation," table, Employment Projections, US Bureau of Labor Statistics, 2018, https://www.bls.gov/emp/tables/education-and-training-by-occupation.htm. In discussing employment, it is recognized that there are a great diversity of industries that hire, and there are occupations within and across that great diversity of industries.

(15) Audrey L. Watson, "Employment Trends by Typical Entry-level Education Requirement," *Monthly Labor Review*, US Bureau of Labor Statistics, September 2017, https://doi.org/10.21916/mlr.2017.22.

STATUS STRATIFICATION

Income, wealth, educational, and occupational inequalities are most often used in discussions of inequality because their quantitative nature facilitates comparison.[1] For example, if a person earns twenty dollars per hour and another ten dollars per hour, we can say that the first person earns twice the hourly wage of the other. The person who has a wealth of $1 million has ten times the wealth of a person who has $100,000. Education can be ordered in by levels that are, while not exact, ordered numerically and progressively, such as first grade, second grade, and so on. Occupations, especially when linked to education (as is often the case), can also be placed in a hierarchal order, such as line workers, supervisors, or chief executive officers.

However, other important societal inequalities exist that are not so quantifiable. While many of these other inequalities sometimes relate to inequalities in income, wealth, education, and occupation, they are separately recognizable.

One of the first to point out this separation of status from quantitative measures was the German sociologist Max Weber. "In contrast to classes, *status groups* are normally communities," Weber states. "They are, however, often of an amorphous kind. In contrast to the purely economically determined 'class situation' we wish to designate as 'status situation' every typical component of the life fate of men … is determined by a specific, positive or negative, social estimation of *honor*."[2] This honor can be connected with any quality that a social group deems as important. Weber says that, independent of one's economic position, individuals within groups receive prestige and honor on noneconomic bases, such as sex, race, ethnicity, religion, and birthplace. He mentions, but does not develop, the obverse: individuals can have positions that are not honored but are instead held in low esteem, or even disrespected.

Simply put, social status, per the *Encyclopaedia Britannica*, is "the relative rank that an individual holds."[3] Social status is not a biological phenomenon but is found in a social order of a particular society. Status refers to the relative rank that an individual holds in a social hierarchy. Rights, duties, and lifestyle are part of this hierarchy.[4] Status reflects the norms and behaviors that are established to maintain the status order. For example, the ways one relates to a teacher or a boss reflects the status of the student/teacher or the worker/boss.

In talking about status, a distinction is usually made between achieved status and ascribed status. Achieved status is one that an individual achieves through effort or competition. A doctor, for instance, achieves status by completing medical school, or an elected official achieves status by winning an election. Achieved status is often based on education, occupation, or other accomplishments. All achievements need not be economic. A priest, minister, or rabbi is offered recognition not only within a specific religion but also by society in general. The person carrying out charitable activities is esteemed for the "good work" that they do. While their status is achieved, it is not related to economics. The noble poor, the people who do without much income, the hard-working parents who take care of their children and teach them good behavior, the helpers of the needy, the men of God, the women of principle— all are seen as worthy of honor and respect. And all of these are admired and honored independently of their level of income or wealth.

Status can also be ascribed (i.e., assigned without any relation to abilities or achievements). Ascribed status is typically based on sex, age, race, family relationships, or birthplace.[5] Ascribed status is, according to *Wikipedia*, "the social status a person is assigned at birth or assumed involuntarily later in life. It is a position that is neither earned nor chosen but assigned."[6] Sex, race, nationality, and immigration status are often used in ascribing achieved statuses. Although there is a general agreement on equal opportunity in the United States, women, minorities, and immigrants can sometimes be identified as "less than" men, non-Hispanic whites, and/or natives. Men, white people, and native-born citizens can be seen as "better," as higher in the social order.[7]

Sociologist Cecilia L. Ridgeway of Stanford University argues that status as just described is a force independent of economic or political power. Status, she says, arises from the systematic interaction of processes at multiple levels, which she identifies as "cultural" processes.[8] She depicts social status as "inequality based on differences in honor, esteem, and respect" accorded to a person.[9] Two factors make status difficult to analyze: cultural beliefs, rather than material arrangements, cause certain statuses, and these statuses "work their effects on inequality primarily at the social relational level by shaping people's expectations for themselves and others."[10] Through these relationships, a "durable inequality" of categorical differences is put in place. These durable inequalities then become a status difference, and this status difference becomes a separate factor that generates material inequalities between people above and beyond their personal control of resources.[11]

Status becomes an autonomous dynamic. It "operates primarily at the social relational level of self-other expectations, judgments, and behavior," Ridgeway continues.[12] Status positions are written into material organizations. Widely shared beliefs "become a powerful, independent force for the perpetuation of patterns of inequality based on social difference," says Ridgeway.[13]

Beyond mere quantitative measures, other inequalities are found in status. The bases of this esteem are both earned (i.e., achieved) and attributed to individuals due to certain characteristics (i.e., ascribed). The presence of status leads to differentiations that impact the pattern of social relationships in the United States. Society recognizes the difference between men and women, ethnic minorities and birthplace. These are not simply biological distinctions but ones developed and embodied through relationships and evidencing power and influence—or the lack thereof.

Notes

(1) Income and wealth provide data that are interval in nature (i.e., there are exact differences between various levels).

(2) Max Weber, From *Max Weber: Essays in Sociology* (New York: Oxford University Press, 1958), 186–87. Max Weber addresses status as a source of power, independent of economic power. Power is acknowledged in this book further when we talk about social order and the necessity of

power to maintain this social order. See also Tony Waters and Dagmar Waters, "Are the Terms 'Socio-economic Status' and 'Class Status' a Warped Form of Reasoning for Max Weber?," *Palgrave Communications* 2, article no. 16002 (2016), https://www.nature.com/articles/palcomms20162; *Wikipedia,* s.v. "Social Status," https://en.wikipedia.org/wiki/Social_status. Wikipedia provides the following definition of social status: "Social status is a measurement of a social value. Some writers have also referred to a socially valued role or category a person occupies as a 'status' (e.g., gender, race, having a criminal conviction, etc.). Status is based in *beliefs* about who members of a society believe holds comparatively more or less social value. By definition, these beliefs are broadly shared among members of a society."

(3) *Encyclopaedia Britannica Online,* s.v. "Social Status," https://www.britannica.com/topic/social-status.

(4) Ibid.

(5) Ibid.

(6) *Wikipedia,* s.v. "Ascribed Status," https://en.wikipedia.org/wiki/Ascribed_status.

(7) See Anthony P. Carnevale, Stephen J. Rose, and Ban Cheah, *The College Payoff: Education, Occupations, Lifetime Earnings* (Washington, DC: Georgetown University Center on Education and the Workforce, 2011), https://www2.ed.gov/policy/highered/reg/hearulemaking/2011/collegepayoff.pdf. The level of ascribed status is often related to economic status. For example, on average, women who work full time for a full year earn 25 percent less than men, even at similar education levels. At all levels of educational attainment, Black people and Hispanics earn less than white people. Black people and Hispanics with master's degrees have lifetime earnings lower than white people with bachelor's degrees.

(8) Cecilia L. Ridgeway, "Why Status Matters for Inequality," *American Sociological Review* 79, no. 1 (2014): 1–16, https://www.asanet.org/sites/default/files/savvy/journals/ASR/Feb14ASRFeature.pdf.

(9) Ibid., 2.

(10) Ibid., 3.

(11) Ibid.

(12) Ibid., 4.

(13) Ibid., 5.

INCOME INEQUALITIES

Inequalities in the United States are manifold.

Income and wealth inequalities, for one, are often the topics most discussed in public-opinion polls. In general, the degree of income and wealth inequality is not accurately perceived. Americans identify less inequality in their country than actually exists. While most Americans desire to reduce income and wealth inequality, decreasing inequality is not, for the majority, a priority.

The data show, and most agree, that there is a clear pattern of income inequality in the United States. The United States has a high Gini coefficient both absolutely and when compared to the Gini coefficients of other developed countries. The lowest 50 percent of Americans have approximately 12 percent of the US income, while the upper 50 percent of Americans have 88 percent of the income. The top 5 percent has 36 percent of income, and the top 1 percent has 21 percent of income. Using straightforward statistical measures, the majority of studies point to a growth in income inequality Some, while agreeing that income inequality exists and has grown, question the degree of inequality and its growth.

There seems, however, to be little disagreement that wealth concentration the United States is large and has increased since the 1970s. The amount of wealth held by the top 10 percent of the population has grown, while the wealth of the lowest 50 percent has actually decreased so that now the lowest 50 percent of households hold 1 percent of the wealth, while the top 10 percent hold 74.5 percent of the wealth.

In addition to income and wealth, Americans occupy positions in the educational and occupational order. In general, a higher education level is seen as valuable. Education level is strongly related to occupations and the salary provided to individuals in that occupation. Americans, thus, rank other Americans by their education level and occupation.

Wealth, education and occupation, and other inequalities, along with quantitative measures of income, are found in status (i.e., the esteem in which individuals are held). The bases of this esteem are both earned (i.e., achieved) and ascribed (i.e., placed on individuals with certain characteristics). The presence of these forms of status lead to differentiations that impact the overall pattern of social relationships in the United States. Society recognizes differences based on gender, ethnicity, and birthplace, as types of ascribed status. These differences are not biological distinctions but are developed and embodied through relationships.

Patterns of inequality are found throughout the US social order. These inequalities are best seen in combination, and they are a cause, and a result, of the overall US social order.

AMERICANS' PERCEPTION OF MOBILITY

Perceptions of mobility focus primarily on economic mobility. The majority of the studies revolving around mobility perception conclude that Americans overestimate economic mobility and see mobility in the United States as greater than in other developed countries.[1] Alas, Americans believe they live in a country that is significantly more equal and upwardly mobile than it actually is. While there is no absolute consensus, most analysts confirm that Americans overestimate economic mobility, although there is some disagreement on the degree of their misperception.[2]

The differences in degree of mobility misperception rest, to a large degree, on the method used to determine mobility—and to some degree the population sampled.[3] While there is disagreement about over- or underestimating mobility, there appears to be agreement that upper-income individuals tend to overestimate upward mobility, while those with lower incomes tend to underestimate upward mobility.[4] It also appears that Americans' perceptions of direction and degree of mobility may be related to their political beliefs.[5] In the 2018 article "Intergenerational Mobility and Preferences for Redistribution," the authors summarize that, through a cross-country survey and experimental data, "our randomized treatment shows pessimistic information about mobility and increases support for redistribution, mostly for 'equality opportunity' policies. We find strong political polarization. Left-wing respondents are more pessimistic about mobility: their preferences for redistribution are correlated with their mobility perceptions; and they support more redistribution after seeing pessimistic information. None of this is true for right-wing respondents, possibly because they see the government as a 'problem' and not as the 'solution.'"[6]

There is not a complete consensus on mobility perception in the United States. As Swan et al. state in their article, "How Should We Measure Americans' Perceptions of Socio-economic Mobility?": "Both effects—that Americans either over- or underestimate social mobility in the U.S., ostensibly depending on (a) the accuracy comparator [basis of comparison] and on (b) how one asks the question—appear to be genuine, albeit somewhat smaller in magnitude than both original reports suggested."[7]

A 2018 Gallup poll points out that nearly two-thirds of Americans are satisfied with their ability to get ahead. Yet approximately two-thirds are also dissatisfied with income distribution.[8] Acceptance of inequality seems tied to Americans' ideals of meritocracy and upward mobility.[9] Shariff et al., in their research for *Perspectives on Psychological Science* journal, also notice that if people believe there is mobility, they are more accepting of inequality. "We find support for both the prospect of upward mobility," the authors say, "and the view that peoples' economic station is the product of their own efforts, as mediating mechanisms."[10]

In general, Americans perceive that there is a large degree of mobility. However, differences in perception are found. One's income and political affiliation affect one's perception of mobility. Americans' belief in meritocracy and upward mobility appears to influence their overestimation of mobility.

Notes

(1) Shai Davidai and Thomas Gilovich, "How Should We Think About Americans' Beliefs About Economic Mobility?," *Judgment and Decision Making* 13, no. 3 (May 2018): 302, http://journal.sjdm. org/17/17911b/jdm17911b.pdf. The authors identify a high degree of overestimation and note the "old rule of psychology": people's actions are guided not by how the world is but by how it seems.

(2) See, for example, Sondre S. Nero et al., "Still No Compelling Evidence That Americans Overestimate Upward Socio-economic Mobility Rates," *Judgement and Decision Making* 13, no. 3 (May 2018): 305–8, http://journal.sjdm.org/17/17911br/jdm17911br.pdf.

(3) Davidai and Gilovich, "Americans' Beliefs About Economic Mobility," 297.

(4) Ibid.; Nero et al., "Still No Compelling Evidence."

(5) John R. Chambers, Lawton K. Swan, and Martin Heesacker, "Perceptions of U.S. Social Mobility Are Divided (and Distorted) along Ideological Lines," *Psychological Science* 26, no. 4 (April 2015): 413–23, https://doi.org/10.1177/0956797614566657.

(6) Alberto Alesina, Stefanie Stantcheva, and Edoardo Teso, "Intergenerational Mobility and Preferences for Redistribution," *American Economic Review* 108, no. 2 (2018):521, https://doi.org/10.1257/aer.20162015.

(7) Lawton K. Swan et al., "How Should We Measure Americans' Perceptions of Socio-economic Mobility?," *Judgment and Decision Making* 12, no. 5 (September 2017): 510, http://journal.sjdm.org/16/16506b/jdm16506b.pdf.

(8) Frank Newport, "Majority in U.S. Satisfied with Opportunity to Get Ahead," Gallup, March 7, 2018, https://news.gallup.com/poll/228914/majority-satisfied-opportunity-ahead.aspx; see also Frank Newport, "Americans' Satisfaction with Ability to Get Ahead Edges Up," Gallup, January 21, 2016, https://news.gallup.com/poll/188780/americans-satisfaction-ability-ahead-edges.aspx.

(9) Davidai and Gilovich, Davidai and Gilovich, "Americans' Beliefs About Economic Mobility," 297.

(10) Azim F. Shariff, Dylan Wiwad, and Lara B. Aknin, "Income Mobility Breeds Tolerance for Income Inequality: Cross-national and Experimental Evidence," *Perspectives on Psychological Science* 11, no. 3 (May 2016): 373, https://www.researchgate.net/publication/286243068_Income_Mobility_Breeds_Tolerance_for_Income_Inequality_Cross-National_and_Experimental_Evidence.

ACTUAL MOBILITY PATTERNS IN THE UNITED STATES

To guide the discussion of social mobility in the United States, some general comments on the nature of social mobility are helpful. Social mobility, as defined by *Wikipedia*, is "the movement of individuals, families, households, or other categories of people within or between social strata in a society. It is a change in social status relative to one's current social location within a given society."[1] In the section on inequality, a variety of ways in which ordering occurs were reviewed, such as wealth, education, and social esteem. Social mobility is a change in one's position on one or more of these factors. In Forbes, economist Aparna Mathur writes, "The concept of economic mobility is relatively simple to grasp. Over the course of a lifetime, can people move up the rungs of the income ladder? Are children doing better than their parents when it comes to standards of living? How do we help people access opportunities that we know can make the climb easier?"[2]

Social mobility can be horizontal or vertical. Horizontal mobility is about moving within a social class—a factory worker becomes a construction worker or a waitress becomes a store clerk. Vertical mobility is about moving up or down the class structure of a society—a line worker becomes a plant manager, a waitress become the manager of a chain of restaurants, or a supervisor becomes a custodian. The concepts of horizontal and vertical social mobility depend on a society's existing stratification. The focus in this section will be vertical mobility.

In discussing vertical mobility, two important sets of definitions are essential: 1) absolute and relative mobility and 2) intragenerational and intergenerational mobility. Wikipedia provides a good description of absolute and relative mobility:

- Absolute mobility measures whether (and by how much) living standards in a society have increased—often measured by what percentage of people have higher incomes than their parents.
- Relative mobility refers to how likely children are to move from their parents' place in income distribution.[3]

Absolute mobility can simply mean making more income. If, for example, a person's income increases from $32,000 at the beginning of their career to $38,000 a decade later, that person has $6,000 more income and has experienced absolute upward mobility, assuming that the dollars are adjusted for inflation.

Relative mobility refers to the fluidity of a society. If you are extremely poor, did you move up the income ladder to become part of the middle class? If you were one of those in the lowest 20 percent of income distribution, did you become part of the 60 percent that makes up the middle class? Relative mobility is what is often called a zero-sum game: if one person moves up in relative terms, another, by definition, must move down.

Absolute and relative mobility have little to do with each other. High absolute-mobility rates can coexist with highly unequal relative-mobility chances. An economy can have a lot of absolute mobility. For instance, all make more money but with little relative mobility, or the lowest 20 percent don't move to the middle 60 percent. At the same time, you can have an economy with a lot of relative mobility. For instance, people moving from the 20 percent to the 60 percent group with little absolute mobility, or the economy did not grow.

Mobility can occur within a generation or between generations.

- Intragenerational mobility refers to mobility within the same generation. One starts with an income of $30,000 and ends with an income of $100,000.
- Intergenerational mobility refers to mobility between generations.

ACTUAL MOBILITY PATTERNS IN THE UNITED STATES

The parents had an annual income of $25,000 per year. A child of these parents has an annual income of $100,000, and this moves the child from the second-quintile income level occupied by the parent to the fourth-quintile income level.

We will use the above descriptions as a guide in the following discussion.

Economic mobility is a fact of life in the United States. There are three related, but separate, areas in which economic mobility occurs:

1. **Family income**: all taxable income including wages and cash transfers
2. **Family wealth:** all assets minus liabilities, sometimes called net worth
3. **Family earnings**: all income from wages

Mobility goes both ways, up and down.

A number of studies have reviewed the issue of intergenerational social mobility both internationally and in the United States. A review of these studies can serve as a starting point. There have been criticisms of each of the studies, all of which are similar in core elements. After going over some of these recent studies, critiques of such efforts will be considered.

In a 2006 research paper, Markus Jäntti et al. conduct a comparison of income mobility across the United States, the United Kingdom, Finland, Norway, and Sweden. Their major conclusions are that 1) substantial increases in earnings can be found across generations in each country, and 2) mobility in the United States is lower than the United Kingdom, and both the United States and the United Kingdom have less mobility than Finland, Sweden, and Norway. In addition, the study states that in the United States, a disproportionate percentage of sons of the poorest who remain in the lowest-income quintile and sons of the highest earners are very "unlikely" to show significant downward mobility.[4]

Jo Blanden, Paul Gregg, and Stephen Machin, in their essay, "Intergenerational Mobility in Europe and North America," indicate that intergenerational mobility in the United States and the United Kingdom is much less than in Canada and the Nordic countries. They posit that the decline in mobility is due to an increasing relationship between family income and educational attainment, especially in one's access to higher education. They also say that family income in one's childhood years makes a "genuine difference to educational outcomes." Their prescription is to support the pursuit of early education, assist less-economically advantaged parents, and promote postsecondary education.[5]

Canadian economist Miles Corak concludes that social mobility in terms of earnings in both Canada and Australia is nearly twice that of the United States and the United Kingdom. He suggests that mobility is higher where there is lower income inequality but adds that a number of interactive forces are at play, such as how families, markets, and government policy work together to determine life chances of children. He also recommends that, along with addressing inequality, it is important to address family function, the educational development of disadvantaged children in terms of human capital, and interactions within the labor market.[6]

Alan Krueger, chairman of the Council of Economic Advisers, points out that there is a growing body of knowledge that, over longer periods, higher correlations between parental and children's incomes are found.[7] In his remarks, he makes note of the intergenerational income elasticity (IGE) index, which correlates parental income to their children's chances to obtain additional income.[8] As income inequality among parents increases, the concentration of income at higher levels and less mobility at the highest levels seem inevitable.

In the report Pursuing the American Dream: Economic Mobility across Generations, the Pew Charitable Trusts use the comparative data found in the Panel Study of Income Dynamics, a data set that has followed families since 1968, to track changes in intergenerational mobility. Among the report's major findings are:

INCOME

- It is pretty clear that absolute intergenerational mobility is a fact (i.e., children's incomes exceeded their parents).
- Having more income does not always result in a change of rank in society in relative mobility. This lack of mobility is especially true for the lowest and highest quintiles. Those in the lower quintile stay in the lower quintile, whereas those in the higher quintile remain in the higher. Some 66 percent in the lowest and highest quintiles remain in their quintile. Only 4 percent of the lowest rises to the top quintile; only 8 percent in the highest quintile falls to the lowest quintile.

ACTUAL MOBILITY PATTERNS IN THE UNITED STATES

EARNINGS

- Personal earnings of all increase across generations for persons at the same age. While the average is a 59 percent increase, 85 percent of those in the bottom quintile show an increase in earnings.
- Those at the top and those at the bottom tend to stay with the highest earnings and lowest earnings.

WEALTH

- Family wealth increases for half of the population, with 72 percent of those at the bottom having more absolute wealth than their parents.
- At the same time, 66 percent of those in the bottom and 66 percent of those at the top remain in the same quintile of wealth. [9]

"The Decline in Intergenerational Mobility after 1980" by Jonathan Davis and Bhash Mazumder, published by the Federal Reserve Bank of Chicago, reviews available data on mobility and concludes, "We demonstrate that intergenerational mobility declined sharply for cohorts born in the early 1960s compared to those born around 1950. The former entered the labor market largely after the large rise in inequality that occurred around 1980."[10]

SUMMARY AND CONCLUSION

In general, Americans perceive that there is more intergenerational mobility in the United States than actually exists. In fact, mobility in the United States is much less than that in other countries. Mathur states it simply: "The U.S. is one of the four high income economies amongst 50 economies with the lowest rates of relative upward mobility."[11] Looking at things on a national level, it appears that in the United States, intergenerational vertical mobility (i.e., the poor becoming rich) is very low, especially when compared to other industrialized countries. In the United States, parents with high incomes pass their place in the social order to their children, while in other countries such as Canada and Denmark, the advantage high-income parents provide to their children is much lower. Most agree that after 1970 or 1980, there was a decrease in intergenerational mobility. Moving up to achieve the American Dream is not as prevalent as most believe.

Notes

(1) *Wikipedia*, s.v. "Social Mobility," https://en.wikipedia.org/wiki/Social_mobility.

(2) Aparna Mathur, "The U.S. Does Poorly on Yet Another Metric of Economic Mobility," Forbes, July 16, 2018, https://www.forbes.com/sites/aparnamathur/2018/07/16/the-u-s-does-poorly-on-yet-another-metric-of-economic-mobility/#738cca036a7b.

(3) *Wikipedia*, s.v. "Economic Mobility," https://en.wikipedia.org/wiki/Economic_mobility#Relative_vs._absolute.

(4) Markus Jäntti et al., "American Exceptionalism in a New Light: A Comparison of Intergenerational Earnings Mobility in the Nordic Countries, the United Kingdom and the United States," (discussion paper no. 1938, IZA, January 2006), http://ftp.iza.org/dp1938.pdf.

(5) Jo Blanden, Paul Gregg, and Stephen Machin, "Intergenerational Mobility in Europe and North America," Centre for Economic Performance, April 2005, 2–3, https://www.suttontrust.com/research-paper/intergenerational-mobility-europe-north-america/.

(6) Miles Corak, "Social Mobility and Social Institutions in Comparison: Australia, Canada, the United Kingdom, the United States" (PowerPoint, Sutton Trust/Carnegie Foundation seminar on social mobility, London, UK, May 21/22, 2012), on Miles Corak's personal website, https://milescorak.files.wordpress.com/2012/05/social_mobility_summit_v3.pdf
.

(7) Alan B. Krueger, "The Rise and Consequences of Inequality in the United States," (speech/presentation, Center for American Progress, Washington, DC, January 12, 2012), https://pages.wustl.edu/files/pages/imce/fazz/ad_10_1_krueger.pdf. For an alternative analysis, see Chul-In Lee and Gary Solon, "Trends in Intergenerational Income Mobility," *Review of Economics and Statistics* 91, no. 4 (November 2009): 766–72, https://msu.edu/~solon/trends208.pdf.

(8) For more details on the IGE, see Juan C. Palomino, Gustavo A. Marrero, and Juan Gabriel Rodríguez, "Intergenerational Mobility in the US: One Size Doesn't Fit All," *Vox EU*, January 3, 2019, https://voxeu.org/article/intergenerational-mobility-us.

(9) Susan K. Urahn et al., *Pursuing the American Dream: Economic Mobility across Generations* (Washington, DC: Pew Charitable Trusts, July 2012), https://www.pewtrusts.org/~/media/legacy/uploadedfiles/wwwpewtrustsorg/reports/economic_mobility/pursuingamericandreampdf.pdf

(10) Jonathan Davis and Bhash Mazumder, "The Decline in Intergenerational Mobility after 1980" (working paper no. 2017-05, Federal Reserve Bank of Chicago, last modified January 19, 2019), https://www.chicagofed.org/publications/working-papers/2017/wp2017-05.

(11) Mathur, "U.S. Does Poorly."

AMERICANS' PERCEPTION OF POVERTY

> In America, if you work hard, you will succeed. So those who
> do not succeed have not worked hard. —Matthew Desmond,
> *New York Times Magazine*[1]

In general, Americans are responsive to those whom they identify as the "deserving poor" or the "truly needy." In 2018, charitable contributions totaled over $410 billion with over $50 billion going to addressing human needs.[2]

While "deserving poor" is not specifically defined, it commonly means the elderly, those with severe disabilities, and young children without sufficient income. As Robert L. Fischer, the codirector of the Center on Urban Poverty and Community Development in Cleveland, notes in his review of poverty: The Trump administration's approach "identifies certain categories of poor as more deserving of assistance because they are victims of circumstance. These include children, widows, the disabled and workers who have lost a job. Other individuals who are perceived to have made bad choices—such as school dropouts, people with criminal backgrounds or drug users—may be less likely to receive sympathetic treatment in these discussions."[3]

Other experts key in on similar issues within the topic of poverty. Martin Levine, a principal at a consulting group focused on organizational change, puts forth that the deserving/undeserving poor has become a consistent framework for the discussion of poverty in the United States.[4] Noah D. Zatz, a law professor at UCLA, says that this distinction reflects, and has often taken on, a moralistic tone.[5] Economist Robert A. Moffitt of Johns Hopkins University argues that this distinction is found in the governmental funding of programs. As he states, "(A)lthough aggregate spending is higher than ever, there have been redistributions away from non-elderly and nondisabled families to families with older adults and to families with recipients of disability programs; from non-elderly, nondisabled single-parent families to married-parent families; and from the poorest families to those with higher incomes. These redistributions likely reflect long-standing, and perhaps increasing, conceptualizations by U.S. society of which poor are deserving and which are not."[6] He adds: "These developments constitute a new type of 'diverging destinies,' although in this case not between those from low-income and middle-income families, but between different types of families within the low-income population."[7]

General surveys on the perception of those in poverty do not formally address the issue of who exactly are "those in poverty" when Americans are asked to share their perceptions. As a result, it is difficult to determine exactly what group of Americans they have in mind when those surveyed respond about who the poor are, whether to assist them, and what might be done if assistance is provided. With the realization that there is a lack of a clear definition, recent surveys about perception of poverty can be reviewed accordingly.

Americans' perception of people who are poor fall into two general categories:

1. People are poor because they fail to act responsibly and morally.
2. People are poor because of the operation of the economy, societal systems, and social policies that hinder the poor.

In early 2001, two thousand Americans eighteen years of age and older were asked (in a national poll conducted by NPR, the Kaiser Family Foundation, and Harvard's Kennedy School), "Which is the bigger cause of poverty today: that people are not doing enough to help themselves out of poverty, or that circumstances beyond their control cause them to be poor?" About 50 percent of the more-affluent people polled believed that the poor are not doing enough to help themselves; 39 percent of the poor did also. Poor people were more likely to blame "circumstances" than themselves for their financial hardship. Overall, respondents were roughly equally divided between "people not doing enough" (48 percent) and "circumstances" (45 percent).[8]

A 2012 Salvation Army survey provides similar findings:

- If poor people really want a job, they can always find a job (43 percent).
- Poverty is a trap some Americans just can't escape no matter how hard they try (59 percent).
- If we gave poor people more assistance, they would take advantage of it (47 percent).
- Giving people more assistance can help them escape poverty (60 percent).
- A good work ethic is all you need to escape poverty (49 percent).[9]

A 2014 *Wall Street Journal*/NBC News poll shows Americans' attitudes toward poverty have shifted dramatically over the last two decades. In 1995, Americans were twice as likely (60 percent to 30 percent) to believe poverty results from people not doing enough to help themselves rather than attributing poverty to external forces. "Fast forward 19 years, and those views have undergone a significant transformation," an article about this poll reports. "The latest [*Wall Street*] Journal poll of 1,000 adults, conducted June 11–15, found Americans are now as likely to blame poverty on circumstances beyond people's control than they are to believe the poor aren't doing enough to dig themselves out of it, 46% to 44%."[10]

However, there are some obvious differences among those who espouse differing positions. For example, the WSJ/NBC News poll proves that there is a near split on identifying whether personal or societal causes of poverty are primary. Some 60 percent of those who identified themselves as Democrats said forces outside of an individual's control cause poverty, while only 27 percent of those who described themselves as Republicans did so.

A 2017 Pew Research Foundation poll reflects the same division. When asked if the government should help the poor even if it meant that the country would go into debt, 50 percent responded yes, 48 percent said no. Breaking down responses into "Republican/Leaning Republican" and "Democrat/Leaning Democrat" shows 28 percent of the "Republican/Leaning Republican" agreed on providing help even if it meant "going into debt," and 71 percent of the "Democrat/Leaning Democrat" agreed on providing help even if it meant going into debt.[11] A more recent Pew study, conducted in 2020, finds that perhaps even more Americans believe that people are poor due to "circumstances." According to the study, 65 percent identified circumstances as being the main reason for poverty rather than a lack of hard work.[11a] Based on the data, it would seem that Americans are still virtually divided on whether the role of the individual's actions or the role of factors outside the individual is primary, possibly with a growing majority that sees social circumstances rather than individual effort as primary.

The same differences are found in a variety of other reports and studies that signify conservatives, Republicans, and those who are more affluent focus on individual responsibility; liberals, Democrats, and those who are less affluent identify social-policy solutions—the exception being affluent Democrats.[12]

It is noteworthy that surveys of perceptions of the poor differ from surveys of perceptions of inequality and mobility. Surveys of poverty do not normally seek respondents to identify the extent of poverty but, instead, seek to determine perceptions of poverty's nature and causes. A primary focus is on what respondents consider to be the main cause of poverty: individual behavior or social barriers?

Survey data on what individuals consider to be the causes of poverty fall roughly into two groups: those who place the burden of poverty on individual behaviors and those who suggest social factors. The difference in perception appears to be strongly related to economic status and political affiliation. Those who identify personal responsibility tend to be those with higher incomes and/or leaning Republican; those with a lower income and/or leaning Democrat tend to identify social causes. Two vastly different perceptions emerge. To some degree, this difference might be attributable to who the respondents view as the poverty population.

Notes

(1) Matthew Desmond, "Americans Want to Believe Jobs Are the Solution to Poverty. They're not," *New York Times Magazine*, September 11, 2018, https://www.nytimes.com/2018/09/11/magazine/americans-jobs-poverty-homeless.html.

(2) Ruth McCambridge, "The Very Good and Very Bad News in Giving USA's Report on Philanthropy in 2017," *Nonprofit Quarterly*, June 12, 2018, https://nonprofitquarterly.org/the-very-good-and-very-bad-news-in-giving-usas-report-on-philanthropy-in-2017/.

(3) Robert L. Fischer, "Why the War on Poverty in the US Isn't Over, in 4 Charts," charts, *Conversation,* July 20, 2018, https://theconversation.com/why-the-war-on-poverty-in-the-us-isnt-over-in-4-charts-99927.

(4) Martin Levine, "The Deserving and Undeserving Poor: A Persistent Frame with Consequences," *Nonprofit Quarterly*, June 23, 2018, https://nonprofitquarterly.org/the-deserving-and-undeserving-poor-a-persistent-frame-with-consequences/.

(5) Noah D. Zatz, "Poverty Unmodified?: Critical Reflections on the Deserving/Undeserving Distinction," UCLA Law Review 59 (2012): 550–97, https://www.uclalawreview.org/poverty-unmodified-critical-reflections-on-the-deservingundeserving-distinction-2/.

(6) Robert A. Moffitt, "The Deserving Poor, the Family, and the U.S. Welfare System," Demography 52, no. 3 (2015): 729, https://doi.org/10.1007/s13524-015-0395-0.

(7) Ibid., 743; see also Patricia Cohen, "Aid to Needy Often Excludes the Poorest in America," New York Times, February 16, 2015, https://www.nytimes.com/2015/02/17/business/economy/aid-to-needy-often-excludes-the-poorest-in-america.html; Kimberly J. McLarin, "The Nation; For the Poor, Defining Who Deserves What," New York Times, September 17, 2015, section 4, 4, https://www.nytimes.com/1995/09/17/weekinreview/the-nation-for-the-poor-defining-who-deserves-what.html?module=inline.

(8) Daniel T. Lichter and Martha L. Crowley, "American Attitudes About Poverty and the Poor," PRB, May 30, 2002, http://www.prb.org/Publications/Articles/2002/AmericanAttitudesAboutPovertyandthePoor.aspx; "Poverty in America," NPR/Kaiser/Kennedy School poll, NPR, https://news.npr.org/programs/specials/poll/poverty/staticresults.html.

(9) "National Salvation Army Week—Perceptions of Poverty Report: Key Findings and Messages," Salvation Army, May 16, 2012, https://centralusa.salvationarmy.org/usc/news/national_salvation_army_week_2012/.

(10) Patrick O'Connor, "Attitudes Toward Poverty Show Dramatic Change—WSJ/NBC Poll," *Wall Street Journal,* June 20, 2014, https://www.wsj.com/articles/BL-WB-46744.

(11) "The Partisan Divide on Political Values Grows Even Wider," Pew Research Center, October 5, 2017, https://www.pewresearch.org/politics/2017/10/05/the-partisan-divide-on-political-values-grows-even-wider/.

(11a) "Most Americans Point to Circumstances, Not Work Ethic, for Why People Are Rich or Poor," Pew Research Center, March 2, 2020, https://www.pewresearch.org/politics/2020/03/02/most-americans-point-to-circumstances-not-work-ethic-as-reasons-people-are-rich-or-poor/.

(12) See, for example, Francis O. Adeola, "Racial and Class Divergence in Public Attitudes and Perceptions About Poverty in USA: An Empirical Study," *Race, Gender and Class* 12, no. 2 (2005): 53–80, https://www.jstor.org/stable/41675161?seq=1#page_scan_tab_contents; "Perceptions of People Living in Poverty and Racial Attitudes: Section 4," Opportunity Agenda, 2016 https://www.opportunityagenda.org/explore/resources-publications/window-opportunity-ii/poverty-racial-attitudes; Christopher Howard, 'What Americans Think About Poverty and How to Reduce It," Scholars Strategy Network, March 21, 2018, https://scholars.org/contribution/what-americans-think-about-poverty-and-how-reduce-it.

PATTERNS OF POVERTY IN THE UNITED STATES

The perceptions of the "poor" and "poverty" by the general population and policymakers most often lack a basic starting point—that of a clear definition of poverty. Here, the US federal guidelines' definition of poverty, those with an income of $21,330 annually for a household of three, will be used, and the poverty population will be reviewed using this criterion.[1] The US Census Bureau's definition annually adjusts the poverty income level for households.[2]

After a precipitous drop from approximately 22 percent of the total US population in 1960, the percentage of the total population in poverty in the United States has ranged between 12 percent and 15 percent for the past fifty years, slipping slightly below 12 percent around 1973 and 2000 (see Graph 1 below for figures through 2017).[3] Most authors agree that the decrease in poverty in the 1960s was due in some part to the Great Society programs.[4]

It has been noted that inequality has increased, and mobility has decreased. On the other hand, poverty has remained relatively constant. Changes found in the poverty rate are associated with the economy's status. Poverty increases during recessionary periods and decreases when the economy is strong. While there have been changes related to the state of the economy, 12 percent to 15 percent of the population has consistently remained below the poverty level.

Poverty guidelines provide a starting point, this starting point being that all persons in poverty share a fundamental characteristic: not enough income to continually obtain the basics, such as housing, utilities, food, transportation, and health care. But when we go behind this starting point, major differences exist.

GRAPH 1. Sustaining progress against poverty

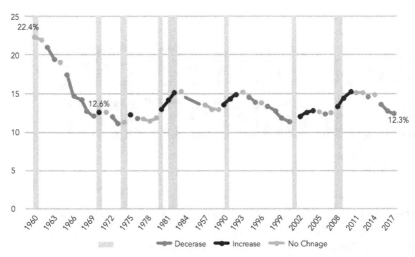

Source: U.S. Census Bureau, Current Population Survey, 1960 to 2018 Annual Social and Economic Supplements

Source: Edwards (2018)

Poverty is obviously not monolithic. Those identified as "impoverished" are not all the same. They differ in:

- Age
- Sex
- Race
- Health
- Geographical location
- Household living arrangements
- Education level of household members
- Work status

In fact, we have multiple poverty populations in the United States. There are many different groups of people with very different individual characteristics, living in different social situations at different stages of their lives. For example, the poor can be young, middle aged, or old. They can be healthy persons or persons with disabilities and/or acute or chronic illnesses. They can live in different regions of the country, in different states, in rural, urban, or suburban communities. They can live alone, in families, or in other household arrangements. They can be non-Hispanics, Black people, Hispanics, Asians, Native Americans, or members of other minority groups.[5]

There are also sizeable differences in income levels of persons in poverty, their time in poverty, and their near environs. Many live far below the official poverty-income line, having incomes below 50 percent of the poverty line, such as, for example, a family of three living off of an annual income of $11,650. There are differences in the time spent in poverty. Some are at the poverty level for a year or less. Others spend a large portion or all their lives with incomes below the poverty level. Some reside in areas where many others are in poverty. Others live in areas where most residents are not low income. All of these factors result in different life experiences.[6]

To say that someone is "in" poverty provides an extremely incomplete picture of this person's living situation. Multiple patterns and groupings of poverty emerge when we take the above factors into consideration. In reality, the United States has many poverties.

One way to view those in poverty is by race. While there are persons in poverty of all races, it is evident from the statistical data that Black people, Hispanics, and Native Americans have significantly larger percentages of their population in poverty.[7] Poverty rates for Black people ranged anywhere from approximately 21 percent to 27 percent during the period between 2002 and 2018, while the poverty rate for non-Hispanic whites hovered around 8 percent to 10 percent. During the same period, Hispanic poverty ranged roughly around 18 percent and 26.5 percent.[8] Native Americans have a poverty rate comparable to those of Black people and Hispanics (i.e., approximately 26 percent).[9] There is a stable pattern of Black people, Hispanics, and Native Americans having a higher poverty rate than the non-Hispanic white population.

Another perspective is to identify those who are in "deep poverty," those whose annual incomes are less than 50 percent of the poverty level. Data are available for those who are identified as being in "deep" poverty. A 2018 US

Census Bureau report puts the number of those in deep poverty as 17.3 million people, approximately 5.3 percent of the total US population and approximately 45 percent of the total poverty population.[10] Reviewing the period between 1968 and 2012, Liana Fox et al. discover that deep poverty ranged from 5.3 percent to 6.6 percent, stating, "We find that deep poverty rates have been fairly constant over the past fifty years, both overall and for families with children."[11]

They add, however, that "this overall stability obscures changes in the demographics of individuals and families in deep poverty, as well as the role of government policy."[12] They also say that most of the change in the deep-poverty population composition occurred prior to 1977.[13] "We find that single parents with children have experienced large declines in the likelihood of deep poverty; their deep poverty rates decreased from 19.0 percent in 1968 to 12.0 percent in 2011," the authors write. "However, much of this decline occurred prior to 1977; deep poverty rates for this group have been relatively flat since then."

As is the case with overall poverty, deep poverty is especially high in Black and Hispanic households. [14] While the generally available census data does not include a breakdown of information for Native Americans, an Annie E. Casey Foundation analysis gives the following breakdown for children (age zero to eighteen years) in deep poverty in 2017: Native American, 17 percent; Black people, 16 percent; Hispanics, 10 percent; and non-Hispanic whites, 5 percent.[15] Similar patterns can be found in Supplemental Poverty Measure data [16]

Data on poverty present a relatively stable poverty-population pattern over the past fifty years. Diversity within the poverty population is often not recognized and can be a barrier to understanding the many types of poverties. Within the poverty population, the higher rates of poverty for minorities, as well as the persistence of a large segment that has an income of less than 50 percent of the poverty level, are clear and striking patterns. As one looks at poverty, subgroups are of special significance.

Notes

(1) "U.S. Federal Poverty Guidelines Used to Determine Financial Eligibility for Certain Federal Programs," ASPE, last modified January 11, 2019, https://aspe.hhs.gov/poverty-guidelines.

(2) While we have used the US Census Bureau's poverty guidelines, it should be acknowledged that many alternatives to this federal guideline have been used. The most common alternatives are the Supplemental Poverty Measure (SPM) and the consumption-poverty measure. The SPM is prepared by the US Census Bureau, while the other is privately developed and utilized by many conservative analysts and policy institutes. For more information on consumption poverty, see, for example, Bruce D. Meyer and James X. Sullivan, "Annual Report on US Consumption Poverty: 2016," AEI,

September 13, 2017, https://www.aei.org/research-products/report/annual-report-on-us-consumption-poverty-2016/; Bruce D. Meyer and James X. Sullivan, "Annual Report on U.S. Consumption Poverty: 2017," University of Notre Dame, October 31, 2018, https://www3.nd.edu/~jsulliv4/2017%20Consumption%20Poverty%20Report%20Meyer%20Sullivan%20final.pdf.

(3) Ashley Edwards, "Poverty Rate Drops for Third Consecutive Year in 2017," September 12, 2018, US Census Bureau, https://www.census.gov/library/stories/2018/09/poverty-rate-drops-third-consecutive-year-2017.html

(4) See, for example, Ajay Chaudry et al., *Poverty in the United States: 50-Year Trends and Safety Net Impacts* (Washington, DC: ASPE, March 2016), https://aspe.hhs.gov/system/files/pdf/154286/50YearTrends.pdf; History.com editors, "Great Society," History, last modified Aug. 28, 2018, https://www.history.com/topics/1960s/great-society.

(5) For more details, see George Gerharz, *Show Me the Cash: Engaging Families to Help Very Poor Children Succeed* (Caritas Communications, 2018).

(6) Ibid.

(7) "Historical Poverty Tables: People and Families—1959 to 2019," tables, US Census Bureau, https://www.census.gov/data/tables/time-series/demo/income-poverty/historical-poverty-people.html. It should be noted that the largest number of persons in poverty are non-Hispanic whites.

(8) "Table 2. Poverty Status of People by Family Relationship, Race, and Hispanic Origin: 1959 to 2019," US Census Bureau, https://www.census.gov/data/tables/time-series/demo/income-poverty/historical-poverty-people.html.

(9) See "American Indian and Alaska Native Heritage Month: November 2017," US Census Bureau, October 6, 2017, https://www.census.gov/content/dam/Census/newsroom/facts-for-features/2017/cb17-ff20.pdf; Jens Manuel Krogstad, "One-in-four Native Americans and Alaskan Natives Are Living in Poverty," *Fact Tank*, Pew Research center, June 13, 2014, https://www.pewresearch.org/fact-tank/2014/06/13/1-in-4-native-americans-and-alaska-natives-are-living-in-poverty/.

(10) Jessica Semega et al., *Income and Poverty in the United States: 2018* (Washington, DC: US Census Bureau, September 2019), 18, https://www.census.gov/content/dam/Census/library/publications/2019/demo/p60-266.pdf.

(11) Liana Fox et al., "Trends in Deep Poverty from 1968 to 2011: The Influence of Family Structure, Employment Patterns, and the Safety Net," *Russell Sage Foundation Journal of the Social Sciences* 1, no. 1 (November 2015): 26, 14, https://muse.jhu.edu/article/603797/pdf.

(12) Ibid., 14.
(13) Ibid., 22.

(14) Semega et al., *Income and Poverty,* Table B-3, 52.

(15) "Children in Extreme Poverty (50 Percent Poverty) by Race and Ethnicity in the United States," table, Kids Count Data Center, Annie E. Casey Foundation, https://datacenter.kidscount.org/data/tables/8783-children-in-extreme-poverty-50-percent-poverty-by-race-and-ethnicity#detailed/1/any/fa

SUMMARY AND CONCLUSION: INEQUALITY, MOBILITY, AND POVERTY

INEQUALITY

Inequalities in the United States are manifold.

Income and wealth inequalities, for one, are the topics most often surveyed and discussed. In general, Americans do not accurately perceive the degree of income and wealth inequality, nor do they notice the changes in wealth and inequality distribution that have occurred. While most have some desire to reduce income and wealth inequality, doing so is not a high priority for most Americans.

A pattern of income inequality exists in the United States. The United States has a high Gini coefficient both absolutely and when compared to the Gini coefficients of other developed countries. To put it another way, the top 20 percent of US households have 50 percent of the total income, and 80 percent of the remaining households have the other 50 percent of income. The top 5 percent of the population has 36 percent of income, and the top 1 percent has 21 percent of income. Depending on the measures and methodology used, different conclusions are reached regarding the exact extent of income inequality, the rate at which income inequality is growing, and the periods that have the most significant inequality growth. The fact that income inequality exists and is flourishing seems to be accepted by all.

The current disagreements focus on how much income inequality is actually increasing.

There is a general consensus that US wealth inequality is large and has increased since the 1970s. The amount of wealth held by the top 10 percent of the population has grown, while the wealth of the lowest 50 percent has actually decreased. Of the households with the lowest amount of wealth, 50 percent of them hold approximately 1 percent of the total wealth, while the top 10 percent hold 74.5 percent of the wealth. The percentage of wealth held by middle-income individuals and families has decreased from 29.3 percent of the total wealth in 1989 to 24.3 percent in 2012.

In addition to income and wealth, Americans are commonly categorized by education and occupation. Americans often ask others, "What do you do for a living?" This question speaks to the issue of occupational inequality and, in most cases, educational inequality, or the education required for a given occupation. Americans, indeed, rank others by education level and occupation.

Over and above more quantitative measures, other inequalities are found in status (i.e., the esteem in which individuals are held in a particular society). The bases of this esteem are both earned (i.e., achieved) and ascribed (i.e., attributed to individuals or groups based on characteristics they cannot change). Status leads to differentiations that impact the overall pattern of social relationships in the United States. Differences between men and women, between the majority and ethnic minorities, and between citizens by birth and immigrants are present in US society. These distinctions are not just biological but developed and embodied in relationships and evidenced in power differentials.

The number of inequalities present in the US social order should be seen in their totality, for they are interrelated.

MOBILITY

In general, Americans perceive a greater vertical, especially upward, social mobility than actually exists. Differences among Americans' perceptions are, however, identifiable. One's income, wealth, and political affiliation affect one's perception of mobility. Americans' belief in meritocracy and upward mobility appears to influence the US perception of mobility.

Looking at things on a national level, intergenerational vertical mobility in the United States (i.e., the poor becoming rich) is considerably low when compared to the mobility of other industrialized countries. In the United States, parents with high incomes and wealth pass their place in the social order to their children, while in other countries such as Canada and Denmark, the advantage of high-income parents when it comes to providing for their children is much lower than that afforded in the United States. Achieving the American Dream is not as prevalent as most believe. *Forbes* contributor Aparna Mathur states it simply: "The U.S. is one of only four high income economies amongst 50 economies with the lowest rates of relative upward mobility."[1]

POVERTY

It is noteworthy that surveys about the perception of the poor differ in outcome from surveyed perceptions of inequality and mobility. These surveys about poverty normally want respondents not to identify the extent of poverty, but, rather, they want to determine the respondents' perceptions of poverty's nature. A central focus of these surveys is: What do respondents consider to be the primary cause of poverty? Individual behavior or social barriers?

Survey data fall roughly into two groups: those who think individual behaviors cause poverty and those who identify social barriers as being at fault. The differences in perception appear to be strongly related to the economic status and political affiliation of the respondents. Those who believe personal responsibility is to blame tend to be those with higher incomes and/ or are Republican-leaning; those with lower incomes and/or are Democratic-leaning tend to identify social causation. To some degree, this difference may be attributable to who is viewed as the poverty population.

The overall data indicate a relatively stable pattern of poverty over the past fifty years. A great diversity in the poverty population is often overlooked. Within this diversity, certain sizeable subgroups can be identified. The percentage of those in poverty that are minorities, as well as the existence of a large group whose incomes are 50 percent of the poverty level, are of special significance.

Three conclusions have been reached. In the United States, there are clear and documentable elements present:

- Great inequality
- Low mobility
- Stable poverty

These are elements of the major patterns of the overall US social order. If one is able to determine how these larger patterns can be changed, then it is possible to propose solutions to decrease inequality and poverty and increase mobility. The next section will pinpoint causes, and the following section will propose solutions that address these causes.

Notes

(1) Aparna Mathur, "The U.S. Does Poorly on Yet Another Metric of Economic Mobility," *Forbes*, July 16, 2018, https://www.forbes.com/sites/aparnamathur/2018/07/16/the-u-s-does-poorly-on-yet-another-metric-of-economic-mobili

PART III: CAUSES OF INEQUALITY AND SOME SOLUTIONS

CAUSES OF INEQUALITY, MOBILITY, AND POVERTY

A. OVERVIEW

Previous sections outlined the US social order and its inequality, mobility, and poverty (IMP) patterns. Here, the causes of IMP will be identified and explored in the context of the US social order.

A few introductory comments will help frame the discussion that follows. First of all, ideological, economic, political/governmental, military/police, and voluntary/religious patterns are interrelated; they complement and support each other. While all are interrelated and supportive, it is possible to notice which of the patterns have a stronger impact in one or more areas of life. Secondly, while all societies have patterns of order, the US social order and its IMP are uniquely American. Elements in other social orders can be similar to those in the United States, but these elements are not the same—individually or as a group. Causes of IMP specific to the United States need to be identified. Thirdly, an initial working assumption is that the same causes impact inequality, social mobility, and poverty. Some have argued that the IMP patterns in US society have, in fact, different causes. The approach that will be covered contends that the same causes work to create and sustain IMP pattens.

Finally, multiple lists of IMP causes have been proposed.[1] Many, if not most, are included in the discourse that follows. What differs here is their placement in the context of US sources of power and social order. The review of causes begins with a discussion of one of the most prominent causes of inequality, lack of mobility, and poverty in the United States: wealth concentration.

B. CONCENTRATION OF WEALTH: A PRIMARY CAUSE

"Money to create power; power to protect money."—Medici[1]

Concentrated wealth is one of the major causes, if not the only cause, of IMP patterns. Those with wealth maintain old patterns and create new patterns to protect and increase wealth for themselves, their families, their children, their friends, and their associates.

Those with wealth establish more wealth for themselves to the detriment of the incomes and wealth of other Americans who possess little or no wealth. The wealthy then retain and pass on wealth to their children so that their children can have special benefits to the detriment of the mobility of others. As a consequence of wealth concentration, less income and a decreased ability to create wealth are available for those of a lower class, resulting in continuing inequality, low mobility, and a permanent poverty population with significantly less wealth.

A plethora of policies and practices constitute the patterns that support wealth accumulation by those with wealth:

- Money accumulation in a variety of ways (e.g., more income from capital rather than labor)
- Financialization of the economy
- Fewer, but larger, corporations
- Executive pay
- Lobbying efforts
- "Crony" capitalism
- Tax policies
- Voluntary sector
- Ideology
- Governmental fiscal and monetary policy

While intimately interrelated, they are distinguishable and will be reviewed separately.

CAUSES OF INEQUALITY, MOBILITY, AND POVERTY

MONEY MAKES MONEY

As pointed out in the section on inequality, wealth in the United States is concentrated, and a pattern of increasing wealth concentration is evident. If an individual or group has wealth, this wealth can be deployed to increase wealth in a number of ways, including, for example, interest gains, dividends, or capital gains. This pattern of wealth producing wealth is illustrated by recent Tax Foundation data on how individuals obtain income. For those with incomes of $200,000 or less, wages account for approximately 75 percent of their incomes. For those with incomes over $10 million, wages account for only 16 percent of their incomes while 62 percent of their incomes comes from dividends and capital gains. These data are evidence of another point: the more income a person has, the greater their ability to retain and invest to create more wealth.[2] If one has exceedingly high wages, one will have the money to invest or save rather than consume.

Thomas Piketty, in his book *Capital in the Twenty-First Century* (2014), reveals a trend of increasing amounts of income deriving from returns on capital. He describes how capital returns in the United States are greater than overall productivity and how more and more of the benefits of productivity accrue to capital rather than to wages.[4] In their article for VoxEU, economists Branko Milanovic and Roy van der Weide note, "Inequality is bad for income growth of the poor (but not for that of the rich.)" The concentration of wealth, they suggest, retards overall economic growth.[4]

FINANCIALIZATION

A growing and more profitable financial sector supports and is supported by high returns on capital investment (i.e., the deployment of wealth). The size of traditional, federally insured financial institutions, such as banks of various kinds, has grown dramatically in the past fifty years. During this time period, a new set of private organizations, the so-called shadow-banking sector, has evidenced exponential growth. Now, according to most, shadow banking exceeds the size of the traditional banking system. Both the traditional and shadow-banking systems offer a wide range of services to those with wealth, developing and deploying a spectrum of instruments to increase the wealth of the wealthy (e.g., hedge funds and venture capital).

Financial organizations, services, and instruments develop, legitimize, and implement ways for money to make money from money. Their wealthy customers come to them to increase wealth by investing their wealth. Success comes from creating new wealth for those who have wealth. The entire financial sector has grown appreciably and now accounts for 30 percent of all US profits.[5]

While there is a debate regarding the impact of globalization on IMP in general, there is one element of globalization that has a direct impact on wealth concentration: financialization. Financialization—the ability to move capital throughout the world, from country to country, and use it where it can be most profitable—is a critical element of globalization. Global financialization is supported by technology and international regulations that set the rules for the use of money and wealth.

MEGACORPORATIONS

In this book's earlier review of the US economy, it was pointed out that more and more of the economy is now driven by large corporations. Through growth and, more significantly, mergers and acquisitions, large corporations, most of which are international, now dominate the US economy. These corporations generate a large percentage of US profits. In 2000, corporate profits were $786.517 billion. In 2018, the total profits were $2.074 trillion.[6] While corporations make up 5 percent of businesses, they earn 62 percent of revenues.[7]

More and more of corporate income is earned by "pass-through" corporations.[8] Various forms of pass-through corporations exist, such as limited liability companies and S corporations. (8a) These corporations now account for over 50 percent of US profits. The largest of these pass-through businesses are owned primarily by higher-income persons who use pass-through corporations to lower or avoid taxes.[9]

CHIEF EXECUTIVE OFFICER (CEO) PAY

CEOs of large corporations have received significant compensation, much of which is stock or stock options to purchase stock in their own corporation.[10] CEO pay is based on the promise or actual return on investment (ROI) to shareholders—in other words, the creation of wealth for those that have wealth. Those with wealth, the shareholders, acting through the board of directors, employ managers to create additional wealth for them. In almost all cases, the CEO is already a holder of wealth, most frequently in the company that they manage. Wealth creation is a clear benefit to the manager's own wealth creation since additional stock value is added to their wealth.[11]

POLITICAL CONTRIBUTIONS AND LOBBYING EFFORTS

Those with wealth-support policies may back political candidates that will support their wealth and its creation. While wealth has always been a major factor in politics, the 2008 Supreme Court decision (Citizens United v. Federal Election Commission [FEC]) has allowed corporations to become directly involved in US elections. The wealthy and corporations are now able to direct governmental policies through political action committees, often referred to as PACs or super PACs.[11a] Between January 2017 and March 2018, PACs collected $1.9 billion and dispersed $1.6 billion to influence numerous elections.[11b] Large donors do not have to be identified, and there is no limit on how much they can donate. The biggest limitation is that PACs cannot make donations to individual candidates or parties, and they cannot formally coordinate their actions with a candidate or party.

In addition, after elections, massive sums are spent on lobbying, primarily by large corporations and business trade associations. In 2017, for one, $3.4 billion was spent on lobbying activities. The vast majority of these expenditures were for specific interests of businesses and their profits.[12] Lobbying has always been a factor, but since the 1970s, it has grown appreciably, especially corporate lobbying.[13]

CRONY CAPITALISM

"Crony capitalism is capital generated not by innovation and risk taking," says Barry Ritholtz, the cofounder, chairman, and chief investment officer of Ritholtz Wealth Management LLC, "but rather through the unholy alliance between the business and political class."[14] A consequence and a goal of lobbying is the carving up of the "public sphere for private Interest." The bulk of lobbying efforts have benefited those at "the very top of the income distribution," writes Steven Teles for *National Affairs* journal.[15] Teles summarizes it this way: "We have seen an explosion in regulations that shower benefits on the very top of the income distribution. Economists call these 'rents,' which we can define for simplicity's sake as legal barriers to entry or other market distortions created by the state that create excess profits for market incumbents."[16]

Those with power and influence obtain a variety of benefits not through merit but through government intervention, such as special grants for research or assistance with the development of a manufacturing plant, among other forms of special assistance. Perhaps the consequences of crony capitalism are most evident in the changes to tax policy.

TAX POLICY: RETAINING WEALTH THROUGH GOVERNMENTAL POWER

Since the 1980s, US tax policy has decreased taxation on both wealth and those with higher incomes. Those with wealth have, through a variety of lobbying activities, achieved large tax reductions.

Numerous examples help illustrate this point:

- Individual-income tax rates on upper incomes have, with few exceptions, decreased since the 1960s.
- Employment taxes on wages (FICA) are currently capped at a level of $132,000 so that those with higher incomes pay FICA taxes only on wage income up to $132,000.
- Taxes on dividends for high-income individuals are taxed at a lower rate than wage income.
- Capital gains are taxed at a lower rate than wage income.
- Taxes on "carried interest," income earned from hedge-fund management, are taxed at the capital-gains rate, not the tax rate of wage income.
- The amount exempted from inheritance tax has grown since the 1950s so that more wealth is passed down to heirs.
- Corporate tax rates have been significantly reduced since the 1950s. Recently the corporate tax rate was reduced to 20 percent. Corporations on average pay 18 percent due in large part to a number of tax deductions.[17]
- Tax law allows the transfer of money up to certain limits via gifts to family members without the gift recipient paying any taxes.
- Dynasty trusts allow the placement of all or major portions of a

family's wealth into a trust that lasts "in perpetuity." "The biggest advantage of a dynasty trust is that it can save your descendants a significant amount of money in estate taxes," says Mary Randolph, JD. "The assets you put in the trust (plus any increase in their value over the years) are subject to the federal gift/estate tax just once, when you transfer them to the trust. They are not taxed again, even though multiple generations benefit from them."[17a]

- Charitable contributions allow for the deductions of charitable contributions, a deduction that disproportionately benefits large donors.

Each of these tax approaches individually has a positive impact on increasing wealth retention by those with wealth. Together, these tax policies work synergistically to have a cumulative impact.[18]

VOLUNTARY SECTOR

The larger nonprofit organizations depend upon major gifts from wealthy individuals, foundations, and corporations.[19] These gifts are fostered by the tax deductions provided to donors. Wealth accumulation, thus, is a major benefit to the nonprofit sector that seeks donations from the wealthy. While recipient organizations do not necessarily support wealth concentration, they don't usually favor a change in wealth accumulation since they rely upon it. In practice, the voluntary sector is a silent promoter of wealth accumulation.

MEDIA AND IDEOLOGY

The media extols success, especially the success of those who have developed great wealth. In addition, major media outlets, liberal and conservative, are reliant upon business interests to purchase advertising, providing them the revenue needed for their operation.[20] Most media organizations are not in a position to fundamentally criticize those who purchase advertisements from them. At the same time, though, most media organizations are themselves corporations seeking to gain profits (i.e., additional wealth) for their shareholders. Accumulated wealth is of great benefit to mainstream media—both to generate revenue and to provide their investors with profits.

GOVERNMENTAL FISCAL AND MONETARY POLICIES

Along with specific policies, federal monetary and fiscal policies in the United States generally support wealth creation.[21] In the US mixed economy, the political element is an essential ingredient in establishing wealth creation.

CONCLUSION

A vast array of mutually supportive patterns operates together to encourage the development and concentration of wealth.

C. OTHER PATTERNS CAUSING IMP

The patterns by which wealth is currently deployed, accumulated, and protected are tremendous causes of the current IMP pattern. However, many other patterns in US society create and support IMP. While clearly related to economic patterns, they are not themselves solely or even predominantly economic. Status ascription and segregation, skill gaps, lack of personal responsibility, and luck are additional factors impacting IMP.

STATUS, SOCIAL, AND SPATIAL SEGREGATION

Throughout this book's review of IMP, it has been noted that Black people, Latinxs, and Native Americans are disproportionately found to have lower incomes, less mobility, and greater poverty. This is due in large part to the negative status ascribed to these populations.

Ascribed status—the categorization of people based on characteristics assigned at birth—is prevalent in the United States. There are a number of personal characteristics that cannot be changed, such as gender, race, and immigration status. In multiple contexts, these status designations result in individuals being negatively perceived and subsequently hindered in their ability to achieve through merit. In many cases, laws to remove these obstacles have been established. Legal changes alone, however, are not sufficient enough to eliminate these barriers. Conscious and unconscious attitudes continually support behaviors that are not consistent with the law and, in turn, have negative effects.

Women, minorities, and immigrants are often negatively perceived and seen as unequal, less capable of upward mobility, and appropriately belonging in poverty, thus blocking or retarding their access to opportunities. Ascribed negative personal characteristics hinder or even prevent the chance to achieve in the United States.

Ascribed statuses, notably race and immigrant statuses, are significant contributors to spatial segregation. Individuals of similar race or immigrant status, especially those with lower incomes, live in spatially segregated communities, inner cities, minority-dominated suburbs, and tribal reservations. These communities not only have fewer resources but are also cut off from social relationships with those living in other communities that possess more resources. As a result, those who are cut off do not have the broader understandings and relationships that would facilitate larger incomes, increased mobility, and, ultimately, an escape from poverty.[22]

In the case of gender, women are typically not offered equal or commensurate treatment. While many legal changes have been put in place regarding gender discrimination—such as Title VII of the Civil Rights Act of 1964, the Equal Employment Opportunity Act of 1972, and Title IX of the Education Amendments Act of 1972 Act—disparities between men and women are still evident. [22a] Inequalities are found most strikingly in wages. Numerous studies point out the wage difference between men and women, with women making less than men..[22b] These differences appear even when other explanatory variables are considered. [22c] Occupations with a predominance of female workers are occupations that have lower wages.[22d]

While women are slightly over 50 percent of the population, they account for approximately 25 percent of all federal and state legislators.[22e] Other less-quantifiable differentiations of the status of women and men are also obvious (e.g., family roles, health status, etc.).[22f] A majority of the population still believes that one should "look up to men who are manly or masculine," as reported in a 2017 survey from the Pew Research Center. [22g] As is the case with other issues, there is a sizeable partisan gap on the current level of discrimination. For example, while half of Americans believe more should be done to achieve gender equality overall, nearly 70 percent of Democrats believe more should be done, while only 26 percent of Republicans share the same sentiment. [22h]

SKILLS GAPS AND LOW QUALITY OF EDUCATION

While occupational skills have always been important, employment rewards are increasingly divided by skill levels. There is growing evidence that the need and demand for "middle-skilled" workers are decreasing.[23] The driving factor, most economists agree, has been technological change and the consequent lowering of the demand for middle-skilled workers.

In the United States today, employment has shifted from manufacturing to services, from stable, long-term employment to multiple employers, from groups of employees to individuals operating on their own (i.e., the so-called gig economy). The number of low-skill jobs have increased, but they continue to provide low pay.

In the current economic environment, higher skill levels are required to procure employment that can provide good family incomes. An increasing number of individuals must have a postsecondary education merely to get the types of jobs that will allow them to meet their needs, be able to save, and to invest in the their children's social capital. If an individual's access to education and the development of needed skills are limited, individuals will not be able to succeed.

But prior to postsecondary education and skill development, individuals must have a solid, basic educational foundation provided through the K-12 system. There is little question that those with lower incomes have, in general, less access to high-quality preschools, elementary schools, and high schools. Lack of this access makes it difficult to succeed in postsecondary education and gain the range of intellectual and social skills necessary for success.

Even with the needed skills, the price of a postsecondary education is a barrier for those with limited individual or family resources. Postsecondary education costs continue to rise, and pursuing a postsecondary education requires individuals to temporarily give up the income required to support themselves or their families. School expenses and foregoing or reducing employment while in school are extremely difficult for those who are older and/or have existing familial responsibilities.

A lack of skills is not simply an individual issue of individual success. Rather, it has noticeable impacts on the US economy. The shortage of qualified, skilled individuals to fill critical employment positions retards the overall efficiency and growth of the economy.

INDIVIDUAL AND PARENTAL RESPONSIBILITY

Not all causes of IMP are brought about by social patterns. Placing all the causes of IMP on social patterns provides a distorted and incomplete picture.

Individuals must be responsible for their own lives. Parents must take responsibility not only for themselves but for the cultivation, protection, and development of their children.

Adequate data exist to establish the clear correlation—not necessarily the cause, or at least not the total cause—of certain individual characteristics to poverty, characteristics that also relate strongly to inequality and mobility. One of the better-documented correlations are those identified by Ron Haskins and Isabel Sawhill in their respective testimonies before the US Ways and Means Committee. They link poverty to three factors: failure to complete high school, lack of employment, and out-of-wedlock births.[24] Their analysis concludes with "three elementary rules" for success:

1. Complete high school, at minimum
2. Work full time
3 Be married but wait until the age of twenty-one, at least, before getting married and having children [25]

These "rules" have gained broad public acceptance due in some degree to their simplicity and for seemingly being "common sense."

As Sawhill notes, however, her and Haskins's work really only shows correlation, not causality, and it is probably just part of the explanation of poverty status.[26] Some have pinpointed additional individual factors. For example, August Turak, a contributor to *Forbes*, includes a fourth factor: alcohol or drug abuse. He also signifies that there has been a tendency to attach normative, prescriptive weight to the listed factors, identifying them as what people should do.[27]

Author Michael Tanner, whose research focuses on poverty and social-welfare policy, among other domestic policies, questions the "overreliance on this explanation [of these individual factors]." He points to the importance of the circumstances in which the poor make their choices. As he notes, "Focusing on the choices and not the underlying conditions [such as the context in which these choices occur] is akin to a doctor treating only the visible symptoms without dealing with the underlying disease." Tanner says that it is common in economic literature to recognize "constrained choice."[28] Constrained choice happens when an economic agent must determine the optimal combination of choice variables (given some relationship between combinations of those variables and payoffs) in the face of constraints of

(22e) Rachel B. Vogelstein and Alexandra Bro, "Women's Power Index," interactive index, Council on Foreign Relations, last modified January 30, 2020, https://www.cfr.org/article/womens-power-in dex?gclid=EAIaIQobChMIp8XJn6nW5wIVg8DACh1fdQ2tEAAYASAAEgLQfPD_BwE; "Women in State Legislatures for 2019," graph and chart, National Conference of State Legislatures, July 25, 2019, https://www.ncsl.org/legislators-staff/legislators/womens-legislative-network/women-in-state-legislatures-for-2019.aspx.

(22f) Dorothy E. McBride and Janine A. Parry, *Women's Rights in the USA*: Policy Debates and Gender Roles, 5th ed. (New York: Routledge, 2016).

(22g) Kim Parker, Juliana Menasce Horowitz, and Renee Stepler, "On Gender Differences, No Consensus on Nature vs. Nurture," Pew Research Center, December 5, 2017, https://www.pewsocialtrends.org/2017/12/05/on-gender-differences-no-consensus-on-nature-vs-nurture/.

(22h) Kim Parker, Juliana Menasce Horowitz and Renee Stepler, "Wide Partisan Gaps in U.S. Over How Far the Country Has Come on Gender Equality," Pew Research Center, October 18, 2017, https://www.pewsocialtrends.org/2017/10/18/wide-partisan-gaps-in-u-s-over-how-far-the-country-has-come-on-gender-equality/.

(23) "Upper Bound," *Economist*, April 17, 2010, https://www.economist.com/united-states/2010/04/15/upper-bound.

(24) See Ron Haskins, *Testimony of Ron Haskins, Brookings Institution and Annie E. Casey Foundation, Before the Subcommittee on Human Resources, Committee on Ways and Means, US House of Representatives, Hearing on Challenges Facing Low-Income Individuals and Families* (Washington, DC, February 11, 2015), https://www.brookings.edu/wp-content/uploads/2016/06/2-11-15-lowincome-families-haskins-testimony.pdf; Isabel Sawhill, *Isabel Sawhill, Senior Fellow and Cabot Family Chair, Economic Studies, The Brookings Institution, Before the Ways and Means Committee, Income Security and Family Support Subcommittee, United States House of Representatives, "Solutions to Poverty"* (Washington, DC, April 26, 2007), https://www.brookings.edu/wp-content/uploads/2016/06/20070426-1.pdf.

(25) Turak, "Is the American Dream Dead?" Many others have voiced agreement with the "three elementary rules." August Turak, for example, agrees but makes his own contribution to the rules, stating, "There are two additional points I would add. First a fourth rule: Don't abuse alcohol and drugs. Second, the most critical of Haskins' rules is 'get married, stay married, and give your children the incredible leg up that only a home that includes a father can provide.'" As to causes of poverty: "The fundamental causes of income inequality are illegitimacy, divorce, single parent households, promiscuity, and a cultural miasma that treats fathers as ancillary and largely superfluous sperm donors."

(26) In fact, the correlations provided account for only a third of the total explanation.

(27) Turak, "Is the American Dream Dead?"

(28) Michael D. Tanner, "The Success Sequence—and What It Leaves Out," *Cato Unbound*, May 9, 2018, https://www.cato-unbound.org/print-issue/2355.

(29) Thomas Gale, Encyclopedia.com, s.v. "Constrained Choice," last modified 2008, https://www.encyclopedia.com/social-./applied-and-social-sciences-magazines/constrained-choice.

(30) David M. Kreps and Evan L. Porteus, "Temporal Resolution of Uncertainty and Dynamic Choice Theory," *Econometrica* 46, no. 1 (January 1978): 185–200, https://www.jstor.org/stable/1913656?seq=1

WHY CHANGE? AND CHANGE TO WHAT?

Before suggesting specific changes to reduce inequality and poverty and increase mobility and personal responsibility, two preliminary questions need to be addressed:

- Why change?
- And if change, change to what?

Why try to change things? Change is difficult.[1] Change contains an element of risk and often elicits fears.[2] Change causes unease and a loss of comfort as it alters how things are done. With change, there is an element of uncertainty about what will actually happen. Change can cause tension, evoke anger, and, in many causes, arouse opposition.

Social change, as with all change, is difficult, but it includes the dimension of altering social patterns. In the broadest sense, social change is a change within social relationships.[3] It transforms the existing social order.[4] Individuals and organizations that possess power will oppose changes to the social order, seeing them as challenges to their vested interests and, at least potentially, resulting in a loss of their power and prestige.[5] Those with resources/power in the current system of social patterns will act to maintain the system as it currently operates, especially if the changes will result in the redistribution of resources and power.[6]

In their essay, "Social Change and Social Problems," sociologists Jackson T. C. B. Jack and Theophilus C. Akujobi provide more detail on social change, quoting others who have also examined social change:

> Social change … is ubiquitous and inevitable as change is the only permanent phenomenon. According to Defleur et al. (1977 cf Anele 1999) 'social change is the alterations in the pattern of social organization of specific groups within a society or even of the society itself'. Deducing from the definition above Ekpenyong (1993: 190) posits that alterations in the social organization of a group and or society refer to the development of new norms, the modification of role expectations, a shift to new types of sanctions, the development of different criteria for ranking and the introduction and use of new production techniques. Anele (1999) further asserts that a change in any part of the society or social organization affects other parts and the society generally at large.[7]

Social change reworks patterns of interaction, rules of behavior, organization of activities, and, often, existing values. A frequent distinction of types of changes is between those changes that maintain a system and those which modify a system. For example, to maintain social order, more police may be hired or more sophisticated security systems put in place to enhance the current safety of a community. On the other hand, the laws may be changed so that what was previously considered a crime, a deviation from social order, is changed, such as the legalization of marijuana in many states. The changes that will be reviewed next are those that would modify the social order.

In terms of social change within IMP, few Americans, if any, would advocate for more inequality and poverty, less mobility, or decreased individual responsibility, but many are comfortable with the status quo. For them, the current pattern of IMP is just part of how the ideological, economic, and political orders work in the United States. Alas, most Americans are comfortable with how things are. According to a 2019 Gallup poll, 56 percent of Americans reported as being very satisfied with their personal lives, another 30 percent said they are somewhat satisfied, and only 14 percent claimed that they are dissatisfied. However, there exists notable differences between subgroups of Americans. Of those who identify as Republicans, 70 percent indicated that they are very satisfied, whereas 50 percent of

Democrats said the same of their own situations. A mere 40 percent of those between the ages of eighteen and twenty-nine indicated that they are very satisfied, while 68 percent of those over the age of sixty-five said that they are very satisfied. Among white Americans, 61 percent deemed themselves very satisfied, while 47 percent of POC Americans said the same.[8]

When asked specifically about income distribution and available opportunities to get ahead, somewhat different patterns emerge. According to a 2018 Gallup survey, more than two-thirds (68 percent) of Americans believe there is too much income inequality, but nearly the same amount (63 percent) believe there is ample opportunity to get ahead. Differences, again, exist among subgroups. While 86 percent of those who identify as Republican believe there is ample opportunity to get ahead, only 50 percent of Democrats agree. Historical data for this discrepancy have been available since 2001. "As was the case for views of the opportunity to get ahead," writes Frank Newport for Gallup, "the gap between Republicans' and Democrats' satisfaction [with income and wealth distribution] has reached its highest point this year [2018], as Republicans have become more positive and Democrats less so. The spread is now 40 points—57% of Republicans are satisfied, compared with 17% of Democrats. From 2014 through 2017, the spread was in the range of 20 points." [9]

Available data point out that Americans are not satisfied with the federal government's efforts to address poverty. In 2015, only 16 percent of Americans were satisfied with federal effort. Little difference existed between Republican/Republic leaning individuals and Democrat/Democrat leaning individuals.[10] And yet poverty and the income gap are not seen by most as major problems.[11] Some willingness of Americans to change in these areas are present, but there is no overwhelming desire to alter the way things are.

Many changes can be made without destroying long-standing foundations, thus providing continuity of the basic US social order. Some who generally oppose change may see a particular change as "overthrowing" the entire social order. Others may see the change as creating a brand-new order. Both tend to exaggerate.[12] Short of revolution, most changes can be incorporated into the US social order and, in some cases, result in improvement of this order. Changes can be made in ways that support and strengthen the overarching patterns of the US social order. It is these changes that are offered here.

Three rationales are often put forth when considering reasons for social change: economic, political, and moral/ideological.

> **The Economic Reason:** Change will promote greater
> prosperity for all.
> **The Political Reason:** Change will improve the security, safety,
> and tranquility of all.
> **The Moral/Ideological Reason**: It's the right thing to do.

An economic rationale identifies ways in which the change could economically benefit individuals and/or the society as a whole. The political rationale identifies ways in which social order could be improved or social disruptions avoided or decreased. The moral/ideological rationale identifies an enhancement of the general values supported by a society.

In the case of IMP, economic changes can be offered to improve the economic situation of individuals and to promote the improvement and growth of the economy. Political changes can be offered to better improve current relationships between people and to diminish or avoid social disruptions in the future. Moral/ideological changes can be offered to better implement the American Dream, especially in the areas of equal opportunity and fairness.

With this perspective, the goals of change offered here can be examined and then some specific changes offered.

CHANGE TO WHAT?

The goals of the specific changes proposed here are **greater fairness, opportunity, merit, and responsibility for all Americans.** The way to achieve these goals is to alter social patterns so that they can contribute to these goals while simultaneously fostering individual responsibility.

It is impossible to set specific numerical goals for changes to IMP. Specifying an "ideal state" would be highly speculative—and probably wrong—as change is continually occurring. Specifying, for example, that individuals should be distributed in a certain way by income levels, or that a certain percentage of the population should be upwardly mobile, is neither feasible nor desirable. The US social order is, and always will be, changing. No final static points can or should be defined.

The goals, it must be recognized, are not to achieve total equality, absolute mobility, elimination of poverty, or assumption of full responsibility by all.

WHY CHANGE? AND CHANGE TO WHAT?

No inequality, unrestricted mobility, obsolete poverty, and a perfect populace are unrealistic expectations. Such a state would be social chaos, the loss of social order, and the failure to meet human needs. Societies need to have a functioning social order, a set of patterns for its members follow. Social order requires that various types of inequality exist and that mobility occurs in some ordered fashion. There will always be those who have less resources for a number of reasons, be it because of limited capability, poor health, old age, or simply bad luck. And in any order, all may not be fully responsible.

In determining specific proposed changes, a selection of criteria was employed. In addition to achieving the goals stated, the proposed changes should:

- Maintain and enhance the US social order
- Be consistent with US ideology
- Change current patterns of income, mobility, and poverty and promote merit, opportunity, fairness, and responsibility
- Occur with an awareness that the changes will take time
- Be informed of the interconnected nature of social patterns
- Support and enhance individual responsibility

The changes that will be proposed are clearly reformist in nature. They are not designed to encourage or support a revolution. If implemented, they should be able to enhance the US economy and further stabilize its political order. Significant changes can occur while still maintaining the basic US social order.

Any changes also need to be consistent with the US ideology. As noted earlier, the core American values are:

- The belief that the United States is a great country
- Individual freedoms: speech, press, religion, and the right to bear arms
- Privacy
- Choice
- Private property
- Individualism
- Self-reliance
- Achievement
- Competition

- Hard work
- Merit
- Pragmatism
- Better future
- Material wealth
- Equality of opportunity
- Rule of law
- Fairness
- Voluntarism
- "Religiosity"

The basics of the US ideology remain. Various elements of this ideology have received differing emphasis over time. In addressing IMP, special attention to fairness, merit, and equalizing opportunity are required, but this emphasis cannot occur without recognizing the other core ideological elements in the United States.

The changes selected must be able to have a noticeable impact and also be feasible within the current social order. In reviewing possible changes, it is important not only to assess potential benefits but to also be wary of potential negative consequences. A number of objective criteria can be used to evaluate the changes, such as economic, political, and moral criteria. But a subjective criterion is also important: the support of the majority of Americans. If changes are to be accepted, they must be seen as consistent with American values—the things Americans believe in and the goals to which they aspire.

Because of their nature, the recommended changes will take time to implement. The recommendations seek change in social patterns, but social patterns are embedded elements of American life. Change in these patterns do not normally happen quickly. However, with consistent effort the proposed changes can be effective.

Attention must also be given to the interconnectedness of changes. Changes to the economy and government, for example, have sizeable impacts on each other. If, say, marijuana is legalized, policing systems will shift, what was once a previous crime will not be prosecuted, and an "illegal" market that operated "in secret" will now be operating in the open. Those who sell marijuana will have legal employment and pay employment taxes, and the businesses selling marijuana will be subject to appropriate business taxes.

Finally, any changes will require and should enhance individual responsibility. All individuals must take responsibility for their own actions. For parents, responsibility extends to being responsible for their children. Individual responsibility does not take place in a vacuum, though. Individuals differ in multiple ways: intellectually, emotionally, physically, and socially. Social contexts vary. Given an individual's abilities and situation, each person needs to take responsibility accordingly. Any social change should promote this individual responsibility. No matter what social changes are made, no progress on IMP can occur without individuals taking responsibility for their actions.

With these criteria in place, the specific recommended changes will now be outlined.

Notes

(1) Katherine Schreiber, "Why Is Change So Hard?," *Psychology Today*, August 8, 2016, https://www.psychologytoday.com/us/blog/the-truth-about-exercise-addiction/201608/why-is-change-so-hard.

(2) Max Weigand, "Why Change Is So Hard: The Chemistry of Habits," personal blog, Medium, November 4, 2017, https://medium.com/@MaxWeigand/why-change-is-so-hard-the-chemistry-of-habits-f0c226f00bff.

(3) William Form et al., *Encyclopaedia Britannica Online*, s.v. "Social Change," https://www.britannica.com/topic/social-change.

(4) "28 Important and Dangerous Causes of Resistance to Change," Entrepreneurship in a Box, https://www.entrepreneurshipinabox.com/223/factors-that-causes-resistance-to-organizational-change/.

(5) "Resisting Social Change," *CliffsNotes*, https://www.cliffsnotes.com/study-guides/sociology/social-change-and-movements/resisting-social-change.

(6) Stuart R. Levine, "Why Is Implementing Change So Hard?," in Stuart Levine and Associates LLC official website, August 22, 2017, https://stuartlevine.com/articlesbystuart/why-is-implementing-change-so-hard/. Originally published in Credit Union Times, August 11, 2017, https://www.cutimes.com/2017/08/11/why-is-implementing-change-so-hard/.

(7) Jackson T. C. B. Jack and Theophilus C. Akujobi, "Social Change and Social Problems," In Major Themes in Sociology: An Introductory Text, ed. E. M. Abasiekong, F. A. Sibiri, and N. S. Ekpenyong (Benin City: Mase Perfect Prints, 2017), 492.

(8) Justin McCarthy, "Six in Seven Americans Satisfied with Their Personal Lives," line charts, Gallup, February 5, 2019, https://news.gallup.com/poll/246326/six-seven-americans-satisfied-personal-lives.aspx.

(9) Frank Newport, "Majority in U.S. Satisfied with Opportunity to Get Ahead," March 7, 2018 Gallup Poll, https://news.gallup.com/poll/228914/majority-satisfied-opportunity-ahead.aspx.

(10) Jeffrey M. Jones, "U.S. Satisfaction with Federal Poverty Efforts at New Low," Gallup, May 7, 2015, https://news.gallup.com/poll/183023/satisfaction-federal-poverty-efforts-new-low.aspx.

(11) "Most Important Problem," line chart and tables, Gallup, https://news.gallup.com/poll/1675/Most-

Important-Problem.aspx.

(12) See, for example, *Stanford Encyclopedia of Philosophy*, s.v. "Equality," https://plato.stanford.edu/entries/equality/; Michael D. Tanner, "Five Myths about Economic Inequality in America," Cato Institute, September 7, 2016, https://www.cato.org/policy-analysis/five-myths-about-economic-inequality-america; Brian Gallagher, "Is There an Ideal Amount of Income Inequality?," *Nautilus*, September 28, 2017, http://nautil.us/issue/52/the-hive/is-there-an-ideal-amount-of-income-inequality.

SUMMARY AND CONCLUSION: SPECIFIC CHANGES

The US social order—how it meets social needs and how power maintains this order—was reviewed. The major ideological, economic, political/governmental, military/police, and voluntary/religious organizations, and the patterns that maintain this order, were discussed. Inequalities, mobility patterns, and poverty patterns, as part of this order, were then examined.

Changes in these patterns can occur without destroying or causing sizeable disruptions. While specifics of "ideal" end states cannot be identified, it is possible to move toward more fairness, increased opportunity, a stronger reliance on merit, and enhanced personal responsibility. These elements are already present in the current US social order and can be strengthened.

In general, the types of changes required are changes in power relationships and how such power operates in a society. Power pervasively works throughout the entire social order, keeping things as they are and retarding or blocking social changes. This power is supported by socialization processes and, consequently, the American identities formed by socialization. Change will, out of necessity, require activation of new or reenergized sources of power.[1]

In deciding what specific changes should be proposed, a number of criteria were employed. In summary, society must:

- Maintain the overriding social order
- Support and enhance the mixed economy and political system of the United States (i.e., capitalism)
- Be sensitive to possible negative consequences
- Be aware of the interconnected nature of social patterns

The proposed changes here are clearly reformist in nature. They are not designed to encourage or support a revolution. Rather, they are designed to enhance the US economy and further stabilize its political order. While challenging the current set of social patterns and power relationships, awareness of the potential negative consequences from such changes was a consideration. The changes are offered with the knowledge that they are interconnected. Governmental and economic changes can have large impacts on each other. For example, with the passage of the Volstead Act in 1919, it was illegal to sell alcoholic beverages. Law enforcement took actions to arrest and prosecute those who did so. A "secret" market nevertheless grew to provide alcohol to customers. With the abolishing of this act in 1933, those who now sell alcohol have become legitimate businesses and pay employment, sales, and income taxes.

With the understanding of general goals, issues of change, and the criteria to be used, a strategy with specific elements is outlined. The intention throughout is to identify ways to enhance equality, increase mobility, and mitigate poverty.

The proposed changes focus on shifting patterns in the United States that inhibit fairness, opportunity, merit, and personal responsibility. Income and wealth concentration are major drivers of IMP. Ascribed status (i.e., discrimination) and education/skill-level differentials are also significant. Finally, individuals often fail to take responsibility and are not always supported or encouraged to be responsible.

In brief, the general strategies are:

- Decrease concentration of income and wealth
- Decrease discrimination
- Equalize skill/education levels
- Increase individual responsibility

Specified changes are proposed in these areas to make merit, fairness, and opportunity greater realities. They are recommended with a special attention to changes of the social-order patterns that have emerged in the 1960s and have continued since then. These specific patterns have been especially important in fostering increased inequality, a lack of mobility, and the current status of poverty.

I. DECREASE WEALTH AND INCOME CONCENTRATION

"People now see the negative ramifications of great wealth, and they're starting to push back and demand more equitable policies." —Darrell West, Brookings Institution

Wealth is a predominant power shaping the current patterns of the US social order. Those who possess large amounts of wealth have a disproportionate impact in directing the ideological, economic, political/ governmental, military/police, and voluntary/religious sectors. Concentrated wealth is a primary driving force in the United States.

Wealth's power in the United States extends beyond the economic realm. While wealth has always been important in politics, its influence has grown, increasingly impacting the political realm. Those with wealth expend vast sums on representative elections and lobbying activities to assure the passage of laws that will be of benefit to them, such as tax policies and environmental laws and regulations. Wealth is also a considerable driver of the voluntary sector, providing funds to those efforts that large donors deem most appropriate and useful, and the media sector, up to and including purchasing media outlets to promote their products and, equally important, their ideas and ideology.

Those with wealth have a vested interest in maintaining the current social patterns. Changes in wealth distribution that increase equality and mobility and decrease poverty by increasing fairness, opportunity, and merit are required. The current holders of wealth, however, will oppose changes to patterns that could cause this.

The goal is not to completely eliminate the influence of wealth—an impossible task—but to reduce the disproportionate influence of concentrated wealth. If wealth is diffused, wealth's influence will diminish, and other factors can have greater influence and power. Also, the goal is not to reduce the overall US wealth. Change in wealth concentration can occur along with an overall increase in the nation's total wealth and a continually growing and more fully shared economy.

Before discussing the options proposed here, three commonly discussed options not considered here will be briefly reviewed:

1. Tax wealth
2. Other new forms of taxation, such as the value-added tax (VAT)
3. Provision of wealth (money) directly to all or certain subgroups, such as seed money and reparations

Wealth taxation is often proposed today and has some academic, political, and popular support. It was, however, eliminated from further analysis here. Addressing wealth inequality by decreasing a future amassing of wealth by those with wealth and increasing wealth development opportunities for those without wealth seems more consistent with the overall US ideology. Wealth, as labor, earns income. Taxing wealth's earnings appears to be more appropriate than simply taxing wealth, which can too easily be seen as a confiscation of one's property. Also, wealth taxation has significant practical problems, including how to determine the wealth calculation, the timing of the wealth calculation, and the constitutionality of wealth taxation. Finally, individuals have the ability to move their wealth to other countries and even change citizenship to escape wealth taxes.

To put in place a completely new form of taxation, such as the aforementioned VAT, is extremely difficult. Support for new forms of taxation in the United States has been met with resistance. In addition, developing a completely new tax system that would be consistent with the goals outlined here would be a challenge, and any implementation would lead to protracted debate and, most probably, inaction.

Various options have been offered to directly provide wealth to subgroups, such as low-income households and racial minorities. The direct provision of wealth independent of their effort presents a major departure from some basic American ideological elements—like, for instance, merit and personal responsibility. And, alas, there are multiple practical problems, such as who specifically should receive the wealth, how much should be received, and how distribution should occur.

Wealth taxation, new forms of taxation, and the direct provision of capital have flaws and have little possibility of being enacted. Other possibilities, however, are available to reach the intended goals outlined here. While accepting the difficulty in implementing the proposed alternatives, they have real potential of being put into place.

SUMMARY AND CONCLUSION: SPECIFIC CHANGES

The five options to decrease wealth concentration that will be considered here are:

a Increase taxes on corporations and/or individuals
b. Decrease tax expenditures, both deductions and tax credits
c. Slow mergers and acquisitions
d. Increase the minimum wage
e. Promote worker organizations

These options were selected using the goals and criteria for implementation, and they will incrementally reduce the concentration and power of wealth and result in additional public funds. Later recommendations in the areas of status-barrier removals and education/skill enhancements will suggest ways in which some public funding, as a result of these changes, might be used. The primary purpose and value of the recommendations in this section are, however, to reduce wealth concentration.

A. INCREASE TAXES

At the federal level, the distribution of tax collections is as follows:[2]

TABLE 1. US tax collections, 2018, in millions

Type of tax	Tax collected, in millions ($)
Corporate income taxes	204,733
Individual income taxes	1,683,538
Social Security taxes	1,170,701
Excise taxes	94,986
Other	175,949
Total	3,329,907

Source: "Table 2.1—Receipts by Source: 1934–2024," Office of Management and Budget, White House.

The larger elements of the "Other" category include gift and estate taxes ($22.9 billion) and custom and duty fees ($41.9 billion).[3] Changes can be made in each of the major taxation areas to impact IMP patterns. Each of these sources of tax income will be discussed separately, beginning with corporate taxation.

CHANGES TO CORPORATE TAXATION

In 2017, the IRS collected over $338.5 billion in income taxes (before refunds) from businesses. That number dropped by 22 percent to about $262.7 billion for the fiscal year 2018. In 2016, income taxes collected from corporations was on par with 2017, at $345.6 billion.[4] An Institute on Taxation and Economic Policy analysis shows that, in 2018, sixty of the *Fortune* 500 companies paid no taxes, despite earning income in the United States. These corporations used a variety of legal tax breaks to avoid taxation, such as accelerated depreciation, stock-options cost, fossil-fuel subsidies, alternative-energy subsidies, and tax credit (primarily in research and development).[6] They were not evading taxes since they were simply taking advantage of entirely legal ways to reduce or avoid taxation.

The positions on corporate taxation range from those who believe that corporate taxation should be totally eliminated to those who want higher corporate rates. Corporate tax rates of 1 percent were first imposed during the Taft administration in 1909. Rates grew to 12.5 percent in 1922 and remained in the range of 12.5 percent and 19 percent until 1939. In 1942, the corporate tax rate was raised to 40 percent and grew to 52.8 percent in 1968. From this point in time, corporate tax rates declined to 34 percent in the 1980s. A 35 percent corporate tax rate was put into place in 1993 and remained in place until the enactment of the Tax Cuts and Jobs Act (TCJA) of 2017, which reduced the corporate tax rate to 21 percent.[6]

However, most corporations pay much less than the stated corporate tax rates. The Congressional Budget Office, for example, finds that the "effective" (i.e., actually paid) tax rate of corporations in 2012 was 18.6 percent.[7] Because of an extensive number of exemptions and deductions (often called loopholes) usually obtained through lobbying efforts, most corporations pay far less than the established corporate rate. The recent TCJA legislation did not address many of these exclusions.[8]

The level of taxation and taxation avoidance has allowed already large corporations to grow in size. A review of the use of recent corporate tax deductions shows that the bulk of the funds not expended for tax were used for mergers and acquisitions and for buying back stocks in their own company. For instance, in a survey of 157 larger corporations, $7.1 billion, or approximately 9 percent of their total $79.3 billion in tax cuts, was used for worker wage increases or bonuses. The remainder (i.e., 91 percent) was used for other purposes—in particular, mergers and acquisitions and stock buybacks. These activities added to the growth in size and further concentration of power in large corporations.[9] The year 2018 was a record year for stock buybacks, with estimates ranging from $800 billion to $1.1 trillion.[10] The previous record was in 2017, with $806.4 billion. The 2017 figure was 36.9 percent higher than the previous record of $589.1 billion set in 2007.

The imposition of supplemental corporate taxes would fall primarily on those with wealth. The bulk of corporate profits go to those who are already wealthy: the top 10 percent of Americans. While slightly over 51 percent of Americans own some stocks, the top 10 percent own 84 percent of stocks, and the richest 1 percent own 50 percent of stocks.[11]

Corporate profits in the fourth quarter of 2018 were $1.972 billion.[12] A slightly higher corporate rate, such as that in 2016, applied to the profits of all corporations would have a significant impact on wealth concentration. Along with this corporate-tax increase, financial-corporation profits should be taxed at a slightly higher rate. In the earlier discussion of the US economic order, it was pointed out that financial corporations' profits were disproportionate to their contribution to the employment economy provided by this sector.[13]

A moderate increase of corporate taxes can occur without destructing the US social order. Alas, such increases have occurred in the past without the dismantling of the US economy. The increase in corporate taxes would primarily impact those who are wealthy and result in limiting the growth of wealth concentration. While there may be a small impact on others who hold stocks, such an impact would not be great. Needless to say, it will be difficult to increase corporate and individual taxes (more on individual taxes later), but these changes in taxation are realistic options that can be implemented within the current US social order, which will decrease, in an orderly fashion, the concentration of wealth.

CHANGES TO INDIVIDUAL TAXATION

Elements of an American individual's income are taxed at different rates or not taxed at all. For the majority of Americans, the bulk of their income is taxed at what is called an "ordinary" rate. Investopedia offers a basic overview of the difference between "ordinary" and other forms of income. According to the article, "Ordinary income is any type of income earned by an organization or individual that is taxable at ordinary rates, such as wages, salaries, tips, interest income from bonds and commissions. … Long-term capital gains, the rise in the value of investments owned for more than a year, and qualified dividends are taxed differently and are therefore not considered to be ordinary income."[14] For a variety of reason, sources of personal income are taxed at different and lower rates.[15] Certain forms of income that are not taxed as ordinary income will be discussed in a bit.

The 2020 tax rates for ordinary-wage income were:[16]

TABLE 2. Married individuals filing joint returns, tax brackets and rates, 2020

Rate (%)	Taxable income over ($)
10	0
12	19,750
22	80,250
24	171,050
32	326,600
35	414,700
37	622,050

Source: El-Sibaie (2019).

The current tax rates of ordinary income are generally progressive (i.e., those with higher incomes pay a higher rate). However, a modest change in rates seems reasonable and possible when maximum tax rates are viewed historically. A 1 percent rate increase for households making more than $171,050, a 2 percent rate increase for those making more than $326,600, a 3 percent rate increase for those making $414,700, and a 4 percent rate increase for those making more than $622,050 would retain the progressive nature of ordinary tax rates and result in a small increase in payments for those in the various income brackets. Such an increase would bring rates to 9 percent below the mid-1980s' rate increase, nearly 30 percent below 1970s' rates, and approximately 50 percent below the tax rates of the 1950s. (16a)

SUMMARY AND CONCLUSION: SPECIFIC CHANGES

SOCIAL SECURITY TAXES

Ordinary wage income is subject to Social Security and Medicare taxes. All wage income is taxed for Medicare purposes. A cutoff of wages taxed for Social Security purposes is established annually. For 2020, Social Security taxes were capped at $137,700.[17] Income above this amount was not subject to Social Security taxes.[18] The removal of a cap on income taxed for Social Security purposes would have some impact on decreasing income and wealth concentration and would also contribute significantly to assuring the solvency of Social Security for all Americans.[19]

CARRIED INTEREST, DIVIDEND INCOME, CAPITAL GAINS, AND INHERITANCE TAXATION

Carried interest, dividend income, capital gains, and inheritance are considerable forms of income not taxed at the ordinary-income rate. To a large extent, these forms of income are received by those with a great deal of income and wealth. Instead of personal labor, fiscal capital is used to obtain additional income and wealth.

Lower tax rates on these forms of income contribute to wealth inequality. In the following paragraphs, each of these forms of income will be briefly discussed in the context of how taxing them at the ordinary rate—or even a higher rate—would contribute to the long-term reduction of wealth inequality. In this discussion, the term "ordinary"-income rate will be used in contrast to the rate currently in place for these forms of income.

Carried-interest income, dividend income, and capital-gains income share a common element in how they generate income: a group or individual's financial capital is deployed to make money. Wages are basically the deploying of human capital (i.e., labor) to make money. Money earned from money is treated differently for tax purposes than money earned from labor, and it is taxed at a lower rate. All income could be taxed at the same rate as regular income, but such an extreme position need not be taken. Incremental tax increases on income obtained from capital will be suggested here. Since each is somewhat different, each will be reviewed separately.

CARRIED-INTEREST INCOME

Carried interest refers to a longstanding Wall Street tax break that lets many private equity and hedge-fund financiers pay the lower tax rate on much of their income instead of the higher ordinary income tax rate. Portfolio managers receive a performance fee from the investment profits in the excess of funds that the manager contributes to the partnerships— for example, a private-equity firm or a hedge fund.[20] These managers typically take a fee, 2 percent, from investors and claim a share of whatever profits they generate, generally 20 percent. Under the current tax code, the 20 percent in profits—or carried interest—these managers receive is treated as a long-term capital gain and is taxed at a rate of 23.8 percent. That is well below the 39.6 percent rate they could otherwise be required to pay if the money were treated as ordinary income.[21]

Those who support this special treatment of income to fund managers stress that it is an important incentive—or even the sole incentive—that encourages venture capitalists to invest in startups and create jobs.[22] However, there is a long history of individuals questioning this special tax treatment.[23] While President Trump promised to eliminate carried interest, it remained in the 2017 TCJA with some small changes.[24] The Trump administration once indicated that they were still seeking to remove the special taxation of carried interest.[25] The primary rationale to eliminate the carried-interest special tax treatment was fairness. Fund managers are employed in managing the funds, yet income received from these efforts is not taxed as ordinary-wage income.

The estimates of the amount of taxes collected by taxing the current "carried interest" at the ordinary tax rate vary significantly. In 2018, the Congressional Budget Office estimated the amount of taxes to be approximately $1.4 billion a year, or $14 billion over ten years if carried interest is taxed as ordinary income.[26] An earlier report places the estimate of additional revenue at $17.4 million.[27] One early proponent of the special-tax-treatment elimination of carried interests estimates increased taxes at $180 billion over a ten-year period.[28] Regardless of the amount raised, taxing carried interest as ordinary income would decrease wealth concentration and embody fairness in the tax code.

SUMMARY AND CONCLUSION: SPECIFIC CHANGES

DIVIDEND INCOME

Dividend income is, to quote Jason Hall of the financial-advisory site Motley Fool, "any distribution of a company's earnings to shareholders from stocks or mutual funds" that are owned by an individual. (29) From a taxing perspective, there are two basic forms of dividend income: qualified and nonqualified. Nonqualified dividends are taxed at the same rate as an individual's ordinary income. Qualified dividends are taxed at a lower rate than ordinary income. To be a qualified dividend, the dividend must come from a US corporation and be held for sixty days.

There are basically three tiers of taxation for qualified dividends. For those whose tax rate for ordinary income is between 10 percent and 15 percent, qualified dividends are not taxed; for those whose tax rate is between 25 percent and 35 percent, qualified dividends are taxed at 15 percent; and for those whose ordinary income is taxed at 36.9 percent, dividends are taxed at 20 percent.[30] Dividends in pretax retirement accounts are not taxed—the tax being paid when funds are withdrawn from the account. It should be noted that interest income, the most common earning from capital, is taxed as ordinary income. According to Motley Fool, "All interest that you earn on a savings or checking account is taxable as ordinary income, making it equivalent to money that you earn working at your day job. Thus, the tax rate can be as low as 10% to as high as 39.6% for high-income earners in the 2016 tax year." [31]

In 2010, about 77 percent of dividend income was earned by the top 10 percent of households, with 54 percent going to the top 1 percent.[32]. Data from the Federal Reserve Bank of St. Louis indicate that slightly over $1.3 trillion in dividends were issued in 2018.[33]

Raising the tax on qualified dividends by 2 percent would raise about $7.1 billion per year, or $69.6 billion over ten years. (34) Those with the largest incomes benefit disproportionately from the lower tax rates on dividends earned from capital. Taxing dividends as ordinary income would eliminate this benefit.

CAPITAL GAINS

Per James Chen of Investopedia, "Capital gain is a rise in the value of a capital asset (investment or real estate) that gives it a higher worth than the purchase price."[35] Capital gain is not realized until the asset is sold. Capital gains are taxed as ordinary income for assets that are held for less than one year prior to their sale. If assets are held for more than a year, the income from their increased value at the time of sale, identified as long-term capital gains, is not taxed as ordinary income. If household income is $39,375 or less, there is no tax on long-term gains. If ordinary income is between $80,000 and $496,600, the tax rate on long-term gains is 15 percent; if income is $496,600 or more, the tax rate is 20 percent.[36]

Capital gains go primarily to large investors with wealth. The Tax Policy Center estimates that, in 2017, of the $660 billion in capital gains realized, 85 percent of these capital gains went to those in the top 10 percent of income, with 70 percent going to those with the top 1 percent of income.[37] The Tax Foundation views reduced rates of capital gains as partial compensation for "double taxation" (i.e., taxation of capital gains, as well as taxation of corporate profits).[38] It adds that a reduction in this tax would increase the cost of capital and increase taxation on savings and investments. Sungki Hong and Terry S. Moon, in a paper for the Federal Reserve Bank of St. Louis, signify that "reducing capital gains tax rates would substantially increase investment in the short run, and accounting for dynamic and general equilibrium responses is important for understanding the aggregate effects of capital gains taxes."[39]

The double-taxation label is somewhat misleading. Putting one's money to work to gain more money is, in effect, using one's money versus using one's labor to gain additional income. One generates additional income investing their money. The increases to the original investment are taxed, not the initial investment. The overall impact on investment and tax revenue is also questionable. Joseph Minarik, of the Committee for Economic Development, notes that the historical evidence of this negative impact is highly questionable since the evidence of this occurring is based on data that were, due to prior enactment, gathered in an overall recessionary period. He says that conclusions like Hong and Moon's are tentative and based on theoretical constructs.[40]

It is obvious that a lower taxation of capital gains contributes to the wealth of those who have wealth. An exact estimate is not available of the amounts that would be obtained by taxing all long-term capital gains as ordinary income. Currently, President Joe Biden, Elizabeth Warren, and Bernie Sanders are proposing to tax capital gains at ordinary-income tax rates for those with higher incomes, but they do not provide exact figures on the amount of revenue that would be generated[41] The negative impacts of higher tax rates on capital gains are highly questionable.

ESTATE TAX

Estate tax and inheritance tax are commonly used interchangeably. Here, the discussion will focus on estate taxes, "a tax imposed by a state or the federal government based on the right to transfer a person's assets to their heirs," as defined by the financial website The Balance.[42] Estate taxation has been an element of US taxation since 1916.[43] Since its enactment, a variety of changes have been made to increase and decrease the taxation rate of estates and the amount to be excluded from taxation.[44] Estate tax rates, with differing exclusions, have ranged from 10 percent to 77 percent.[45]

Between 1976 and 1986, a number of major changes occurred in the taxation of inheritance. Economist Patrick Fleenor of the Tax Institute summarizes it thusly:

> A series of legislation passed in 1976, 1981, and 1986 overhauled and modified the federal transfer tax system. Portions of the separate estate and gift tax systems were unified, and levies were imposed on generation-skipping transfers. These Acts also lowered marginal transfer tax rates and significantly reduced the number of transfer tax returns filed each year by raising the filing requirements.

> Prior to the 1976 Act, estate taxes were paid by approximately seven percent of estates in any given year. After 1987, the estate tax was paid by no more than three-tenths of one percent in a given year. [46]

Further changes occurred between 1987 and now. Per-person exemptions were increased from $675,000 in 2001 to $3.5 million in 2009, with double the exemption amounts available to couples. In 2010, the inheritance tax was eliminated, ostensibly as part of the effort to emerge from the 2009–10 recession. The inheritance tax returned in 2011 with a $5 million-per-person exemption and a rate of 35 percent. The exemption was indexed to inflation and reached $5.49 million in 2017, and in 2013 the rate was increased to 40 percent. The 2017 TCJA doubled the individual-exemption level to $11.2 million and the couple-exemption level to $22.4 million and indexed this amount to inflation. The tax rate of 40 percent was maintained.[47]

For the period between 1916 and 2004, the number of taxable estate tax returns represented less than 2 percent of all adult deaths—at least for most of the years during this era. "For deaths after 1954," reports Darien B. Jacobson, Brian G. Raub, and Barry W. Johnson for the IRS, "a growing percentage of estates were taxed, hitting a peak of nearly 8 percent in 1976, when more than 139,000 taxable returns were filed. "[48]

The intended impact of the TCJA law was to reduce the application of inheritance taxation from 2 in 1,000 households to 1 in 1,000 households (.1 percent). While the official tax rate is 40 percent, the applicable rate is, in effect, 16.5 percent because that estate tax is paid only on the amount in excess of $11.2 million for an individual and $22.4 million per couple. Inheritance taxes were paid by only twenty "small" farms in 2017. That same year, only 6,460 of 2.7 million estates were taxed, .24 percent of all estates.[49]

Inheritance tax has historically been a relatively small percentage of overall US tax revenue, for the exception of the Great Depression in the 1930s and the World War II years. From 1916 to 1935 (the middle of the Great Depression), the inheritance tax ranged from 1 percent to 3 percent of federal revenue. From 1935 to 1947, the percentage of federal revenue from inheritance taxes ranged from 2 percent to 10 percent, the highest percentage being 10 percent of federal tax revenue. From 1947 to the present, the estate or inheritance tax has been 2 percent or less that of the total federal revenue.[50]

As currently structured, the estate tax will provide approximately $25 billion a year in taxes for the next ten years. Lower estate taxation primarily benefits the heirs of those with significant assets. Economists Laura Feiveson and John Sabelhaus of the Federal Reserve state that the intergenerational transfer of wealth likely increases wealth concentration. (51) Increasing the estate tax rates and/or lowering the amount that is not taxed would reduce wealth concentration and add to the tax revenue. At the same time, it would further foster the importance of merit so that individuals do not receive large amounts of money that are not earned by them.

B. DECREASE TAX EXPENDITURES

Tax deductions and tax credits (i.e., tax expenditures) are common elements of the US tax system. In simpler terms, a tax expenditure lowers an individual's or household's tax by providing special treatment to some of one's income based on a wide range of considerations. Common tax expenditures are 1) deductions that one can take on income and 2) credits that can be used against tax owed. The US tax system is replete with tax expenditures, departures from the ordinary/normal taxation of income that "lowers a taxpayer's burden, such as an exemption, deduction, or credit," as defined by Robert Bellafiore of the Tax Foundation.[51a]

Deductions provide a reduction in the amount of income that is taxed. Credits are applied to reduce the amount of tax owed. The essential difference between deduction and credit is that a credit directly decreases the amount of tax you owe while a deduction lowers your overall amount of taxable income.[51b] Here's an example that will help clarify this: If one has a tax deduction, such as a charitable contribution, a deduction is taken to reduce the amount of income to be taxed. A charitable contribution of, say, $2,000 can reduce the income that is taxed, decreasing taxable income from $30,000 to $28,000 because of the charitable contribution (i.e., a deduction). If one has a tax credit, such as the child and dependent care credit, the credit's amount is subtracted from the tax owed. If, after all calculations, $4,000 is owed in taxes, a child-care credit of $2,500 would reduce the tax bill to $1,500. In addition, taking a credit can actually result in a payment to the taxpayer. If the tax owed before applying the credit is $1,500 and a child-care tax of $2,500 is applied, the government would pay the taxpayer $1,000. Because of this, in general, tax credits are more beneficial than deductions.

Congress's Joint Committee on Taxation predicted that the 2018 tax expenditures would amount to $1.5 trillion. To individuals, $1.3 trillion would be provided, and to corporations, $200 billion would be provided.[51c] At the individual level, there are multiple tax expenditures, totaling 173 after the enactment of the TCJA.[51d] The three largest tax expenditures for individuals, which provide nearly a third of the tax expenditures, are reduced taxation rates for interest and long-term capital gains, employer-paid health-insurance exclusions, and pension contributions.[51e] With the exception of interest and capital-gains deductions, efforts to change the individual tax expenditures would be disruptive of many current aspects of individual and household life and would not provide benefits proportionate to negative effects.

At the corporate level, a wide range of tax credits and deductions exist. "Together, the reduced tax rate on active income of controlled foreign corporations, depreciation of equipment in excess of the alternative depreciation system, and deduction for foreign-derived intangible income derived from trade or business within the U.S. make up approximately 65 percent of all corporate tax expenditures," says Bellafiore. "In total, corporate tax expenditures are projected to cost $201.8 billion in 2018."[51f]These corporate credits, along with energy-research and energy-exploration credits could be reduced and/or eliminated. A reduction of 10 percent could result in approximately $20 billion in additional taxes that mainly impact corporations and large investors.[52]

C. SLOW MERGERS AND ACQUISITIONS

Mergers and acquisitions (M&A) are common ways for corporations to become larger, increase profits, and further concentrate wealth. While there is a great deal of legal complexity, Christina Majaski of Investopedia provides a basic definition: "A merger occurs when two separate entities combine forces to create a new, joint organization. Meanwhile, an acquisition refers to the takeover of one entity by another. Mergers and acquisitions may be completed to expand a company's reach or gain market share in an attempt to create shareholder value." She goes on to say: "Due to the negative connotation, many acquiring companies refer to an acquisition as a merger even when it is clearly not."[52a]

There are five general types of mergers:

1. Horizontal merger: A merger between companies that are in direct competition with each other in terms of product lines and markets.
2. Vertical merger: A merger between companies that are along the same supply chain.
3. Market-extension merger: A merger between companies in different markets that sell similar products or services.
4. Product-extension merger: A merger between companies in the same markets that sell different, but related, products or services.
5. Conglomerate merger: A merger between companies in unrelated business activities.[52b]

Mergers can have benefits, but most horizontal mergers of large corporations have negative impacts that outweigh any benefits. At the present time, horizontal M&A are proceeding at a high rate, with larger and larger amounts of capital used for these purposes. A review of the fifteen biggest

M&A from 2010 to 2019 finds that all were horizontal.[52c] Increased market share and profits are the most frequently offered reasons for M&A. Indeed, market share and profits may increase. Most often, however, it appears that these profits result not from increased efficiency and productivity or reduced management and administrative costs. Instead, it appears to derive from the ability to charge higher prices due to less competition. Concentration of market power by the new entity increases. Productivity or efficiency gains are not often obtained but increased profits are. It appears that the increased profits are due to a concentration of market power, which allows for increased profits and the ability to raise prices due to less competition.[52d] A domination of a business in the market can result in higher prices, excessive profits (economic rents), a reduction in efficiency, and the exploitation of customers and suppliers due to higher prices.[52e] As pointed out earlier, large corporations currently use a significant amount of benefits from the TCJA tax legislation for M&A.

While generating additional profits, M&A also create larger and more powerful concentrations of wealth both for the merged/acquired corporation and for the shareholders of the new corporation. It appears that these outcomes occur with little overall benefit to customers and without any significant contribution to the economy's productivity.

The Federal Trade Commission (FTC) has responsibility for determining whether M&A will occur. Its mission is in "protecting consumers and competition by preventing anticompetitive, deceptive, and unfair business practices through law enforcement, advocacy, and education without unduly burdening legitimate business activity."[52f]

With this mission, the FTC has the following goals:

1. Protect consumers from unfair and deceptive practices in the marketplace
2. Maintain competition to promote a marketplace free from anticompetitive mergers, business practices, or public-policy outcomes
3. Advance the FTC's performance through excellence in managing resources, human capital, and information technology[52g]

Using its powers, the FTC should take a much more aggressive stance, setting more stringent requirements on horizontal M&A both for the benefit of consumers and to reduce wealth concentration.

D. INCREASE THE MINIMUM WAGE

While addressing taxation issues, it is important to consider the need to provide workers, especially lower-income workers, with additional income so that they may have the ability to develop wealth. The only way to assist most individuals and families is to provide supplemental income, which can be used for purposes over and above addressing essential needs, so that resources can be made available for wealth creation (e.g., additional education for themselves or their children, retirement, etc.). A minimum wage for all Americans has been in place since 1938.[53] In terms of inflation-adjusted dollars, the 1968 minimum wage in current dollars would be $11.55 per hour.[54] The last adjustment to the federal minimum level was in 2009, when the minimum wage was set at $7.25.

In recent years, a number of states have established higher minimum-wage levels for their individual state.[55] However, an increase in the federal minimum wage to $15.00, or at least progressively reaching this amount, would broaden the number of individuals who receive incomes that could support their families and possibly provide such families with opportunities to invest in their futures and that of their children. To have its greatest effect, the minimum wage should be indexed to inflation so that the minimum floor could keep pace with inflation.

E. FOSTER WORKER ORGANIZATION

While addressing the issue of wealth/capital's decreased power, increasing the power of labor will contribute to reducing the concentration of wealth. The unionization of the US workforce is now at its lowest level since the 1930s. Nearly two-thirds of Americans support unions, yet only 10.7 percent of the US workforce is unionized.[56] Union membership decreased from 20.7 percent in 1980 to 10.7 percent in 2017. Nearly 33 percent of wage and salaried workers were unionized in 1960.[57] There is strong evidence that corporations and governments have taken action to reduce union membership and influence and actively oppose the elimination of "right-to-work" laws.[58]

Organized workers have the negotiating power to reduce the influence of the wealth and power held by corporations, and they are able to influence their compensation, among other working conditions. Organized workers can serve as a countervailing force to corporations that are influencing the distribution of income and wealth.

SUMMARY AND CONCLUSION

In the paragraphs above, a number of strategies were presented to reduce wealth concentration through changes in:

- Corporate taxes
- Taxes on an individual's wages and Social Security
- Taxes on income that is not considered "ordinary," such as
  - ✓ Carried interest
  - ✓ Dividends and interest
  - ✓ Capital gains
  - ✓ Inheritance

Changes to corporate and individual taxation offer a more feasible approach to address wealth concentration than a wealth tax, other new forms of taxation, or various forms of restitution. Changes in current taxation rates can be made to decrease wealth concentration over time. These changes will have an impact and can be easily understood by the majority of Americans.

The recent 2017 TCJA reduced corporate tax rates to a percentage higher than most corporations now actually pay. The benefits of corporate-tax reduction were used primarily for M&A and stock buybacks, without any negligible impact on wages, increased productivity, or job creation. A slight increase in corporate taxation would have little negative impact on the economy and would further decentralize wealth. There is also a potential to impose even higher taxes on financial-corporation profits, taking into consideration their profitability and their overall contribution to the economy.

Since wealth concentration occurs among those with the highest incomes, a higher tax on persons with incomes in excess of $1 million seems feasible. A special surcharge for those whose incomes exceed $5 million a year could also be used. This increase could be coupled with lower taxes for those in the lower two quintiles of income distribution (i.e., the 40 percent with the lowest incomes).

To guarantee the solvency of Social Security, and a contribution to a decreased wealth concentration, the Social Security tax could be applied to all wage incomes. This increase would also result in businesses paying additional taxes since the employer is responsible for 50 percent of the Social Security taxes of their employees.

Variations in taxation by income type can be eliminated or reduced. The carried-interest category should be eliminated, and all income gained through this category should be taxed as ordinary income. Interest and dividends should also be taxed at the rate of wage income, as should capital-gains income. All of these forms of income are the result of money being put to work to make income and create wealth. The income from these investments is "working" for the individual, and there are not cogent reasons why this income should not be taxed as wage income, as ordinary income.

Increased estate taxes will reduce the transfer of wealth to individuals in a fashion that is not based on merit. With some allowance for the surviving dependents, a larger tax could be levied and reduce or eliminate wealth inequality through income not earned by the recipient.

A more strenuous review process of M&A can limit wealth concentration by halting growth in corporation size. Adjusting the minimum wage so that the labor's share of income is increased will reduce the percentages of earnings based solely on capital. Since power will be required to change the existing patterns of power, exertion of power by worker organizations will be required.

2. REDUCTION OF ASCRIBED STATUS AND DISCRIMINATION

In the section on inequality, it was pointed out that ascribed status plays an important role in the US social order. Women, minorities, and immigrants are disproportionately those earning lower incomes, evidencing less mobility, and finding themselves in poverty. Through the socialization process, biases based on gender, race, immigration status, and sometimes religion are inculcated in Americans and operate consciously and unconsciously to militate against equalized opportunity for all.

While some progress has been made in the aforementioned areas, deep-seated biases are still operative. These biases maintain and foster attitudes and behaviors that are barriers to opportunity and a more merit-based society. Ascribed status is usually defined as any position that is not chosen nor earned, but rather assigned, and which comes with either positive or negative stereotypes, and which cannot be assumed, discarded, or otherwise changed through the efforts of the individual to whom the status has been described.[59]

Ascribed characteristics are commonly described as those characteristics assigned by others that are present at birth and over which an individual has little or no control, this can include gender, race, skin color, hair color and texture, eye shape, place of birth, parentage, and other various social status markers of an individual's parents.[60]

Women, minorities, and immigrants are often perceived to be "less than" compared to those who are male, non-Hispanic white, native born, and middle income. Individuals have no control over their sex, race, ethnicity, or economic situation at birth. These ascribed perceptions occur without consideration of the individual's other attributes. Due to their ascribed status, women, minorities, foreign-born individuals, the LGBTQIA+ community, and the poor are often considered "less than."

Addressing negative ascribed status in effect means addressing discrimination, a form of negative ascription. Discrimination, as used here and defined by the *Lexico* English dictionary, is "the unjust or prejudicial treatment of different categories of people or things, especially on the grounds of race, age, or sex," to which we could add very-low-income status.[60] Until the impact of these ascribed factors is further reduced or eliminated, inequality, mobility, and poverty will remain as major patterns in American society. All forms of inequality, upward-mobility deterrents, and poverty are strongly related to ascribed status. Women are found to earn less than men, their ability to advance being negatively influenced by sex and race, and poverty is disproportionately found among racial minorities and women.

Laws have been enacted to protect individuals from unjust treatments based on age, sex, race, sexual orientation, age, and a number of other factors. A few examples illustrate important legal changes. The Civil Rights Act of 1964 was enacted almost a hundred years after the 13th, 14th, and 15th amendments to the US Constitution were ratified. This act outlaws discrimination based on race, color, religion, sex, or national origin and extends civil-rights protection to the private, as well as the public, sector. It also offers protections to assure voting rights. Major changes have occurred in the acceptance of LGBTQIA+ relationships and same-sex marriages. Changes have occurred from the "Lavender" Scare of the 1950s (where LGBTQIA+ employees were deemed a security risk) to the Stonewall riots in 1969 to the full legalization of same-sex marriage with the Obergefell v. Hodges decision in June 2015.

Yet the legal changes did not completely remove negative ascriptions. As author Ibram X. Kendi states, "Racism did not end—it progressed. Racism progressed when legislators did not repair past discrimination.

Racism progressed when Americans refused to identify discrimination by outcome (Intent needs to be proven). Racism progressed when new racist ideas blamed black inferiority for persisting racial disparities. Racism progressed when Americans chose the law and order of inequality over the civil right of equality."[62]

While necessary, passing laws and enforcing them (alas, enforcement has not always been the case) is not sufficient.[62]Legal changes by themselves do not remove negative-status ascription. Ascribed statuses are rooted in the identities of most Americans, even though many Americans are not conscious of their biases. The primary image of an American, the standard and norm, is still the non-Hispanic white, urban, and middle-class male.[64]

In effect, there is a culture of ascribed status. As used here, culture, per the authors of "Theorizing Social Context: Rethinking Behavioral Theory," is "the patterned process of people making sense of their world and the (conscious and unconscious) assumptions, expectations, knowledges, and practices they call upon to do so. The term patterned indicates that culture is not random. Instead there are consistencies within culture that are at the same time flexible and situationally responsive; the term process indicates that culture is not bounded or static but rather dynamic, fluid, constantly being shaped and reshaped."[65] Culture is not distinct from or equivalent to religion, politics, or any other social institution, such as economics or kinship. Rather, it is an integral part of all of them—forming them and being formed by them according to situation and circumstance.

Behaviors simultaneously constitute, and are constituted by, the rules, relationships, expectations, and resources of social structures in which individuals live. Much of behavior is formed by what French anthropologist Pierre Bourdieu calls "habitus," influences that are most frequently outside the realm of conscious awareness.[66] These inculcated ways shape and inform attitudes and behaviors and reflect the social and historical context in which a person was raised. The current patterns of a society are instilled in and passed on to the individual.

People have been socialized, some not intentionally, to discriminate. Along with changes in law, efforts must be made to change the socialization processes that contribute to ascribed statuses. Previously, the agents of socialization were identified. Parents, peers, neighborhoods, schools, and churches are especially important socialization agents for children. Each of these socialization agents plays a part in maintaining or changing the social patterns of the United

States. Eliminating or reducing the transmission of biases emerging from this complex network of socialization is a long-term process.

Setting requirements for parents is against the American belief and practice of allowing parents to raise their child(ren) as they see fit (unless there is proven neglect or abuse). It would be practically impossible to establish and implement policies or programs for peers and neighborhoods. In the United States, requiring religions to change their beliefs and practices cannot occur given the "separation" of church and state (i.e., the Establishment Clause). While all of these agents of socialization can be encouraged to act in ways that decrease ascribed status, no policies or practices can be systematically put in place.

Elementary and secondary schools (K-12) offer the best policy and practice option to reducing and moving toward elimination of ascribed-status biases. For the most part, K-12 schools are public institutions, and many of the K-12 schools that are not public still receive public funding. Certainly, an informed curriculum is important, but increased school integration is required. The interaction process of all young people at an early age is a critical element of reducing bias. In fact, actual interaction is more important than any simple didactic approach. To have the maximum impact, schools have to become more socially and economically integrated. Schools have the ability to provide an environment in which all children are able to interact with each other and thus lessen ascribed perceptions and biases through such interaction.

More integrated public schools will require major restructuring. We live in a world that is segregated by race and income. The current alignment of school districts reflects this social order segregated by race and income.

Integration of schools will require legal action and presents a number of personal and practical hindrances. First, major federal, legislative action would be required. The Milliken v. Bradley Supreme Court decision effectively eliminates the requirement to address racial and economic integration across legally constituted and existing school-district boundaries.[67] School districts, administrators, and teachers will oppose this policy due to its impact on their current positions and the need for busing (and the costs associated with it). In addition to busing opposition, many parents will oppose it for a wide range of reasons, including a preference for neighborhood schools. For the most part, local-, state-, and federal-elected officials will not want to pursue this approach, citing many of these same reasons, including local control and responsiveness to their constituents.

With all these obstacles it may seem fruitless to pursue this policy of broader school integration, but its importance warrants consideration. The K-12 public-school population is a large one. Public elementary- and secondary-school enrollment rose from 46.6 million in 2000 to 47.3 million in 2015, an increase of nearly 2 percent. Public elementary enrollment (prekindergarten through eighth grade) increased 1 percent between 2000 and 2015 (from 30.4 million to 30.6 million), while public secondary enrollment (ninth grade through twelfth grade) increased 2 percent (from 15.0 million to 15.3 million).[68]

The proposed school integration would begin at the fourth-grade level. The logistical, developmental, and safety issues related to those in third grade or lower m-ake inclusion of these young children in this proposed integration problematic. If those in third grade and below are not included, the total fourth-grade-to-high-school public-school population is approximately 38 million (20.7 million fourth-through-eighth graders plus 16.5 million high schoolers).[68a]

The approximately 4.9 million students who attend private K-12 schools are about 10 percent of the total K-12 population.[69] Of the total K-12 school population in private education, over 75 percent of K-12 private-school students attend religious schools. (Although private schools account for 10 percent of student enrollment, they account for approximately 25 percent of the number of schools.)[70] To even seek implementing the proposal in private schools, it would likely be seen as infringing on parental and religious rights.

The process of integration would play a part in addressing the problem of differential school resources based on the residents' and school district's abilities to finance schools. If all schools include racial, economic, and sexual diversity, then the provisions of resources would be the same for all. The parents of all students would more likely seek to improve the school, and the parents would also more likely be engaged in seeking resources for all children. Those parents with more resources and power would then be engaged in working for all students.

There are multiple objections to this integration approach for K-12 education. Many favor neighborhood schools. One cannot deny the value and mystique of the neighborhood school. These schools are based on geography, which, in turn, is often based on ethnic and racial groupings. However, this form of education has led to promoting bias toward a wide variety of individuals based on race, sex, and income.

The required busing will also be objected by many, as already stated. Moving children to other areas presents a number of logistical issues and entails some new costs—and, in certain cases, extreme costs.[71] The long-term value of the integrated education being proposed would have benefits that outweigh costs, though. The integration of schools would be a massive element in equalizing educational resources. Such resource equalization is highly unlikely if there are "poor" and "rich" districts or minority and majority non-Hispanic districts. Integration will be a major impulse to equitable funding.

Some seek to establish schools specifically for minority groups. Although there are those who value minority-only schools, the preponderance of data do not support this contention.[72] Still, others propose same-sex schools, especially at the high-school level. The preponderance of data, again, do not support this preference.[73] While the value of these minority-only and gender-specific educational efforts cannot be completely rejected, their benefit in the overall US policy and practice are not equivalent to those of the proposed integration.

The proposed K-12-integration approach will encourage the reduction of ascribed status and will result in a more equitable distribution of public resources for public education. This restructuring of schools would have a positive impact on bias reduction and assure that all children have a solid education (more on this later). The ability to provide quality education is dependent upon resources. School districts made up of those with lower incomes and/or minorities do not usually have the resources, or the power, to provide a quality education. An arrangement where all children are part of the same "system" would result in all children having equal, or at least more equal, educational opportunities. The integration of education would result in furthering a system that ensures equal opportunity, promotes fairness, and fosters an environment of merit.

3. SKILL DEVELOPMENT AND EDUCATION

The integration of schools is critical. The effectiveness of these schools in enhancing the skills of all is of paramount importance for the intended outcome. Currently the public-policy discussion has placed an emphasis on preschool and postsecondary issues such as free college or forgiving student debt. However, basic changes need to occur in the entire education process.

The vast majority of over 50 million young Americans from age three to high school attend public schools. This represents 90 percent of all young people in this age group attending public schools. (As previously noted, we cannot address the issue of the 10 percent of children attending private schools.) At this point in US history, states primarily have responsibility for K-12 education. The data from a variety of sources that rank schools nationally on a state-by-state basis, as well as rank school districts within states, evidence unequal results—with many schools failing to achieve acceptable levels.

The unequal funding provided to schools is the fundamental factor related to success. At a minimum, steps can be taken to assure that schools have at least the same resources to work with their student body. Generally speaking, children who live in areas or neighborhoods with more money and political power are attending schools that have better educational outcomes.

Equality of education cannot occur if the education process is not equally funded. States have the responsibility to education according to the Constitution.[74] As Paul Hill, the founder of the Center on Reinventing Public Education, says, "The state's responsibility in education is a heavy one. Though state constitutions differ in detail, all require states to fund and organize an effective education system. In order to fulfill these responsibilities, states have important, even coercive, powers. They tax citizens and compel parents to send children to school. They create local school districts to ensure that there is a school for every child."[75] There is a wide divergence among states on the total amount of funding provided for education and the formulae used to distribute these funds within a given state. Within states, local communities have widely different levels of resources. To a large extent, local funding comes from property taxes so that more affluent communities with high tax revenue have and provide more funding for their education.

There is little question that equitable funding for education from preschool to college and postcollege is critical. The lack of equalized funding results in many Americans not receiving the quality K-12 education needed for entry into and success in the postsecondary-education sphere, which is required to fully participate in the current US economy.[76]

States can take steps to reduce the unequal funding of schools. Putting formulae in place that will result in the equalization of funding for the children in a state can be accomplished. These formulae would assure that state money, when combined with local funding, results in equalized funding in schools for all children. In some cases where communities have a disproportionate number of low-income residents, the federal government may be required to step in to address shortfalls. Admittedly this would be a complex process, but if there is agreement, it can be accomplished.

Equivalency in K-12 education is critical but needs to be complemented with supplemental opportunities for skill development after high school. As pointed out in the discussion on education and occupation (see the section on inequality), it is clear that postsecondary education is required to obtain a "middle-class" life. A myriad of proposals have been offered up to and including free tuition or complete loan forgiveness. These deserve serious consideration.

Another critical issue is retraining those whose previous employment was lost through changes in the economy. Such retraining programs have been put in place on a temporary basis to "adjust for trade" or to respond to recessions. Retraining programs are needed now, not only for temporary crises but as an ongoing resource for adult American workers so that they can fully participate in today's economy.

4. PROMOTE AND FOSTER INCREASED PERSONAL RESPONSIBILITY

Many propose that an individual's life situation is almost solely a result of an individual's numerous good or bad decisions. Those without "success" don't prioritize, don't act appropriately, don't plan for the future, and thus fail to take actions to achieve this better future for themselves and their families. If they had prioritized, acted appropriately, planned for the future, and taken actions to implement this plan, they would not find themselves as poor, with low incomes, and stuck in their current position.

A massive problem with this position is its failure to recognize that individuals operate in a nexus of social patterns.[77] An individual must take responsibility for their decisions, and thus their consequences, but these decisions are affected by the social situations in which one may find themselves. In life, an interplay of individual decisions with one's social environment is continually occurring. The social environment can help or hinder in making appropriate decisions.

Sendhil Mullainathan. and Eldar Shafir in their book, *Scarcity: Why Having Too Little Means So Much* (2013), provide insight as to how economic stress operates to affect the thinking process of individuals in poverty. They propose that it is difficult to overcome poverty, and poverty itself is a cause of poverty.[78] As they state, "Our data suggest causality runs at least as strongly in the other direction: that poverty—the scarcity mind set—causes failure." In other words, "the experience of poverty reduces anyone's bandwidth," which can be broadly described as one's ability to function and cope.[79]

To more fully understand their theory, it is necessary to understand a few of their basic concepts:

- Scarcity: It is "having less than you feel you need." [80]
- Bandwidth: It is one's "mental capacity." "It is not a person's inherent mental capacity of the mind but how much of that capacity is currently available for use."[81] It consists of two broad and related components of mental function:
    - o Cognitive capacity: The "psychological mechanisms that underlie our ability to solve problems, retain information, engage in logical reasoning and so on."[82]
    - o Executive control: It is "our ability to manage our cognitive activities, including planning, attention, initiating and inhibiting action, and controlling impulses."[83]

Executive functioning is extremely important. The executive functions are "processes that have to do with managing oneself and one's resources to achieve a goal," per clinical psychologists Joyce Cooper-Kahn, PhD, and Laurie Dietzel, PhD. They include such activities as stopping and/or controlling one's behavior, controlling one's emotions, starting and following through on required actions, planning, organizing, and finally assessing one's own performance.[84]

Mullainathan and Shafir posit that almost all of the psychic energy of low-income individuals is consumed with immediate needs. As a result, they are not able to clearly solve problems (i.e., cognitive capacity), nor are they easily able to plan, control impulses, and focus on the future (i.e., executive control). The continuous and ongoing struggle to make ends meet completely engrosses the mind and blocks other considerations. Other areas of life are not adequately addressed; immediate concerns for basic essentials overwhelm any possibility to address future needs. Concern with basic essentials also negatively impacts parenting impulses and requirements. Bad decisions with long-term effects are evidenced in areas such as child rearing and medication and/or alcohol abuse, among others. Scarcity leads to numerous bad decisions.[85]

In a similar vein, Charles Karelis, in his book, *The Persistence of Poverty: Why the Economics of the Well-Off Can't Help the Poor* (2007), argues that the behavior of the poor is not irrational. He classifies goods into three categories: relievers, pleasers, and goods that serve as relievers at low levels of consumption but as pleasers at high levels of consumption. The goods in this third category include basic things such as food, shelter, and transportation. At the insufficient level, goods in the third category simply relieve up to a point. Additional consumption provides relief until a sufficient level is reached. Once above-sufficient levels are reached, positive enjoyment or pleasure is found.[86]

According to Karelis, the poor most frequently act to reach the sufficient level (i.e., to provide relief). Given their situation, it is completely rational for them to continually act to reach the sufficient level. The way to address this situation is to make the poor less poor since as long as they are at insufficient levels, they will continue to act for relief. In his view, being poor causes poverty. Karelis further hypothesizes that providing more money will lead individuals to take the next step in obtaining additional misery-relieving dollars.[87]

A good illustration of how poverty contributes to poverty is found Heather Seggel's personal account. As she recollects in an essay, "What's hardest to work with is that my instincts and reactions are bodily things. My head may know it's foolish to eat rotten food, or even too much good food, but a life spent waiting for the other shoe to drop, the power to be cut off, the next unwanted groping from the guy I'm paying rent to, is not a life that has room for plans beyond the present moment." Seggel, who is accustomed to the struggles of securing a reliable place to stay, also describes the voice in her head, the "low burble," that provides a constant commentary and says, "Do what you like, but you'll end up in a place like the last one. And if it's not like the last one you'll MAKE it like the last one. That's what we do! We ruin things. Stop trying to live above your pay grade."[88]

In a more reflective way, professor of psychology Ramani Durvasula, PhD, states, "Poverty makes it less likely that a person can 'recover' from a mistake. A vicious cycle sets in whereby more scarcity begets fewer cognitive resources (less bandwidth), and decreased ability to attend to all aspects of life—children, work, self-care."[89]

The scarcity mentality and the absorption of the immediate are also true of those with lower incomes and who experience less mobility, as well as those in poverty. All must take responsibility for their actions, but the social context in which they live can contribute to or retard taking responsibility. Failure to take responsibility cannot be accepted, yet it should be recognized that individuals act in a social context.

Ongoing support and encouragement of responsible actions are essential, including offering supports that enable responsible action. While implementing changes in social patterns that will increase opportunity and merit, efforts to support personal responsibility without blame are absolutely critical.

SUMMARY AND CONCLUSION

Addressing IMP requires prominent changes to how wealth is accumulated and retained. These changes must take place in the context of the United States and how it works. Gradual economic changes can occur through the current tax system. Such changes will have an impact but will, recognizably, take time.

Simply changing economic conditions, while necessary, will not be completely effective if other changes are not also put into place. Ascribed status is a major obstacle to more equality and mobility and less poverty. Integration efforts need to be supported, and the creation of spaces where all children can meet and live with each other on an ongoing basis is essential. Drastic changes in how public K-12 schools are structured would be an important element of this process.

An element of this integration can be a more widely distributed and effective primary education. A reallocation of educational resources to benefit all is required. Due to the ongoing change in the US economy, permanent and affordable educational opportunities must be available to those who complete high school, as well as to adults who require new or increased skills to participate in the US economy.

While all these listed actions are occurring, continued emphasis on individual responsibility is vital. Regardless of structure, individuals ultimately must act responsibly if inequality and poverty is to be reduced and mobility increased.

And Americans support such changes. A significant majority agree that taxes on the rich should be increased. A majority also seek a more equitable distribution of income.[90] Americans support upward mobility, and a large majority wish to decrease poverty.[91] Individually, and especially together, the changes proposed can help attain these aspirations.

Notes

(1) Earlier while describing the presence of power to maintain the social order, it was noted that these powers are significant. But this power is not absolute, and change is ever present.

(2) "Table 2.1—Receipts by Source: 1934–2024," Office of Management and Budget, White House, https://www.whitehouse.gov/omb/historical-tables/.

(3) "Table 2.5—Composition of 'Other Receipts': 1940–2024," Office of Management and Budget, White House, https://www.whitehouse.gov/omb/historical-tables/.

(4) Kristin Myers, "Corporations Paid $91 Billion Less in Taxes in 2018 under Trump's Tax Law," Yahoo! Finance, May 30, 2019, https://finance.yahoo.com/news/corporations-paid-91-billion-less-in-taxes-in-2018-under-trumps-tax-law-160745447.html.

(5) Matthew Gardner et al., "Corporate Tax Avoidance Remains Rampant under New Law," ITEP, April 2019, https://itep.org/wp-content/uploads/04119-Corporate-Tax-Avoidance-Remains-Rampant-Under-New-Tax-Law_ITEP.pdf.

(6) Kimberly Amadeo, "U.S. Corporate Income Tax: Its Effective Rate and History," Balance, https://www.thebalance.com/corporate-income-tax-definition-history-effective-rate-3306024.

(7) Molly Saunders-Scott and Jennifer Gravelle, *International Comparisons of Corporate Income Tax Rates* (Washington, DC: CBO, March 2017), 2, https://www.cbo.gov/system/files?file=115th-congress-2017-2018/reports/52419-internationaltaxratecomp.pdf.

(8) These exclusions will be reviewed as part of the discussion on tax expenditures.

(9) "Key Facts: How Corporations Are Spending Their Trump Tax Cuts," Americans for Tax Fairness, https://americansfortaxfairness.org/key-facts-american-corporations-really-trump-tax-cuts/.

(10) Bob Pisani, "Stock Buybacks Hit a Record $1.1. Trillion, and the Year's Not Over," CNBC, December 18,2018, https://www.cnbc.com/2018/12/18/stock-buybacks-hit-a-record-1point1-trillion-and-the-years-not-over.html.

(11) Louis Jacobson, "What Percentage of Americans Own Stocks?," PolitiFact, Poynter Institute, September 18, 2018, https://www.politifact.com/california/statements/2018/sep/18/ro-khanna/what-percentage-americans-own-stocks/; Rob Wile, "The Richest 10% of Americans Now Own 84% of All Stocks," Money, December 19, 2017, http://money.com/money/5054009/stock-ownership-10-percent-richest/; Heidi Chung, "The Richest 1% Own 50% of Stocks Held by American Households," Yahoo! Finance, January 17, 2019, https://finance.yahoo.com/news/the-richest-1-own-50-of-stocks-held-by-american-households-150758595.html; see also B. Ravikumar and Evan Karson, "How Has Stock Ownership Trended in the Past Few Decades?," *St. Louis Fed On the Economy* (blog), Federal Reserve Bank of St. Louis, April 9, 2018, https://www.stlouisfed.org/on-the-economy/2018/april/stock-ownership-trended-past-few-decades.

(12) "Corporate Profits after Tax with Inventory Valuation Adjustment (IVA) and Capital Consumption Adjustment (CCAdj) (CPATAX)," line chart, FRED Economic Data, Federal Reserve Bank of St. Louis, https://fred.stlouisfed.org/series/CPATAX. While it will be difficult to increase corporate and individual taxes (more on individual taxes later), this is a more realistic option that can be implanted within the current US social order and, at the same time, decrease wealth concentration in an orderly fashion.

(13) See Michael Cooper et al., "Business in the United States: Who Owns It and How Much Tax Do They Pay?" (working paper no. 21651, NBER, October 2015), doi: 10.3386/w21651. It should be noted that more and more corporations are organized as "pass-through corporations" that do not pay corporate taxes but pass through profits to individuals who are owners of these corporations. The taxation of this income is addressed in the discussion on individual taxation.

(14) Daniel Liberto, "Ordinary Income," Investopedia, https://www.investopedia.com/terms/o/ordinaryincome.asp.

(15) See Eric Toder, "1986 RIP: Different Tax Rates for Different Income Sources,"TaxVox (blog), Tax Policy Center, May 26, 2018, https://www.taxpolicycenter.org/taxvox/1986-rip-different-tax-rates-different-income-sources. Mr. Toder notes, "The 2017 Tax Cuts and Jobs Act (TCJA) was the most far-reaching tax legislation since the Tax Reform Act of 1986 (TRA86). It also put the final nail in the coffin of a tax reform movement whose major goal was to tax all forms of income equally."

(16) Amir El-Sibaie, "2020 Tax Brackets," Tax Foundation, November 14, 2019, https://taxfoundation.org/2020-tax-brackets/.

(16a) "Historical Highest Marginal Income Tax Rates: 1913 to 2020," Tax Policy Center, https://www.taxpolicycenter.org/statistics/historical-highest-marginal-income-tax-rates; see also "History of Federal Income Tax Rates: 1913–2020," Bradford Tax Institute, https://bradfordtaxinstitute.com/Free_Resources/Federal-Income-Tax-Rates.aspx.

(17) "Maximum Taxable Earning," Social Security, https://www.ssa.gov/planners/maxtax.html.

(18) "Contribution and Benefit Base," Social Security, https://www.ssa.gov/oact/cola/cbb.html; see also "Topic No. 751 Social Security and Medicare Withholding Rates," https://www.irs.gov/taxtopics/tc751.

(19) This change would require recognition that Social Security is not solely an insurance program, but it would have elements of a social program.

(20) *Wikipedia*, s.v. "Carried Interest," https://en.wikipedia.org/wiki/Carried_interest.

(21) Renae Merle, "What Is 'Carried Interest' and Why It Matters in the New GOP Tax Bill," *Washington Post,* November 7, 2017, https://www.washingtonpost.com/news/business/wp/2017/11/07/what-is-carried-interest-and-why-it-matters-in-the-new-gop-tax-bill/?utm_term=.5e089785d168.

(22) Ibid.; see comments of Ben Veghte, spokesman for the National Venture Capital Association.

(23) See for example, Victor Fleischer, "Two and Twenty: Taxing Partnership Profits in Private Equity Funds" (legal studies research paper series, working paper no. 06-27, NYU Law Review, August 2, 2007), https://www.researchgate.net/publication/228213316_Two_and_Twenty_Taxing_Partnership_Profits_in_Private_Equity_Funds.

(24) Hazel Bradford, "Carried Interest Lives on Despite Tax Reform," *Pensions and Investments*, March 19, 2018, https://www.pionline.com/article/20180319/PRINT/180319865/carried-interest-lives-on-despite-tax-reform.

(25) David Morgan, "U.S. Treasury to Close 'Carried Interest' Loophole in New Tax Law," Reuters, March 1, 2018, https://www.reuters.com/article/us-usa-tax-carriedinterest/u-s-treasury-to-close-carried-interest-loophole-in-new-tax-law-idUSKCN1GD5YE; see also Adam Lewis, "Donald Trump Pledges to Finally Address Carried Interest Loophole," PitchBook, May 21, 2019, https://pitchbook.com/news/articles/donald-trump-pledges-to-finally-address-carried-interest-loophole.

(26) "Tax Carried Interest as Ordinary Income," Congressional Budget Office, December 13, 2018, https://www.cbo.gov/budget-options/2018/54795.

(27) "Tax Carried Interest as Ordinary Income," Congressional Budget Office, November 13, 2013, https://www.cbo.gov/budget-options/2013/44804.

(28) Victor Fleischer, "How a Carried Interest Tax Could Raise $180 Billion," DealBook (blog), New York Times, June 5, 2015, https://www.nytimes.com/2015/06/06/business/dealbook/how-a-carried-interest-tax-could-raise-180-billion.html
.

(29) Jason Hall, "What Is Dividend Income?," Motley Fool, https://www.fool.com/knowledge-center/what-is-dividend-income.aspx.

(30) Ibid.

(31) Motley Fool Staff, "Home Much Taxes Do You Have to Pay on Money in a Savings Account?," Motley Fool, last modified October 24, 2016, https://www.fool.com/knowledge-center/how-much-taxes-do-you-have-to-pay-on-money-in-a-sa.aspx.

(32) Josh Bivens, "The Top 1 Percent's Share of Income from Wealth Has Been Rising for Decades," Economic Policy Institute, April 23, 2014, https://www.epi.org/publication/top-1-percents-share-income-wealth-rising/.

(33) "Net Corporate Dividend Payments," line chart, FRED Economic Data, Federal Reserve Bank of St. Louis, https://fred.stlouisfed.org/series/B056RC1A027NBEA; see also "Table 1.12. National Income by Type of Income: Annual," FRED Economic Data, Federal Reserve Bank of St. Louis, 2018, https://fred.stlouisfed.org/release/tables?rid=53&eid=42133; "Table 1.16. Sources and Uses of Private Enterprise Income: Annual," FRED Economic Data, Federal Reserve Bank of St. Louis, 2018, https://fred.stlouisfed.org/release/tables?eid=42395&rid=53.

(34) "Raise the Tax Rates on Long-Term Capital Gains and Qualified Dividends by 2 Percentage Points and Adjust Tax Brackets," table, Congressional Budget Office, https://www.cbo.gov/budget-options/2018/54788.

(35) James Chen, "Capital Gain," Investopedia, last modified July 30, 2019, https://www.investopedia.com/terms/c/capitalgain.asp.

(36) "Topic No. 409 Capital Gains and Losses," IRS, https://www.irs.gov/taxtopics/tc409.

(37) Robert McClelland, "Raise the 15 Percent Tax Rate on Capital Gains to Boost Revenue in a Progressive Way," TaxVox (blog), Tax Policy Center, October 11, 2017, https://www.taxpolicycenter.org/taxvox/raise-15-percent-tax-rate-capital-gains-boost-revenue-progressive-way; see also, "T13-0243—Distribution of Individual Income Tax on Long-Term Capital Gains and Qualified Dividends by Expanded Cash Income Level, 2012," table, Tax Policy Center, October 2, 2013, https://www.taxpolicycenter.org/model-estimates/distribution-individual-income-tax-long-term-capital-gains-and-qualified-dividends.

(38) https://taxfoundation.org/capital-gains-taxes/

(39) Sungki Hong and Terry S. Moon, "Capital Gains Taxation and Investment Dynamics" (working

paper series no. 2018-031F, Federal Reserve Bank of St. Louis, October 2018), 23, https://doi.org/10.20955/wp.2018.031.

(40) Joseph Minarik, "Do Capital Gains Tax Increases Reduce Revenue?," CED, https://www.ced.org/blog/entry/do-capital-gains-tax-increases-reduce-revenue.

(41) Taylor LaJoie, "Comparing Capital Gains Tax Proposals by 2020 Presidential Candidates," Tax Foundation, December 4, 2019, https://taxfoundation.org/2020-capital-gains-proposals/.

(42) Julie Garber, "What Is an Inheritance Tax?," Balance, last modified October 4, 2019, https://www.thebalance.com/definition-of-inheritance-tax-3505560; see also "Inheritance Tax vs. Estate Tax," Protective, https://www.protective.com/learning-center/wills-and-estate-planning/what-is-the-difference-between-inheritance-tax-and-estate-tax/. As mentioned in the latter article, "The main difference between an inheritance and estate taxes is the person who pays the tax. Unlike an inheritance tax, estate taxes are charged against the estate regardless of who inherits the deceased's assets. The executor is responsible for filing a single estate tax return and pays the tax out of the estate's funds. An estate tax is calculated on the total value of a deceased's assets, and is to be paid before any distribution is made to the beneficiaries."

(43) See *Wikipedia*, s.v. "Estate Tax in the United States," https://en.wikipedia.org/wiki/Estate_tax_in_the_United_States. In 1862, a death tax was imposed to assist with Civil War funding, and another death tax was imposed to help fund the Spanish-American War. Both were repealed soon after their enactment.

(44) See "Frequently Asked Questions on Gift Taxes," IRS, https://www.irs.gov/businesses/small-businesses-self-employed/frequently-asked-questions-on-gift-taxes. Related to the discussion of estate tax is the topic of gift tax.

(45) "A Historical Look at Estate and Gift Tax Rates," CCH, https://www.cch.com/press/news/historicalestategifttaxrates.pdf; *Wikipedia*, s.v. "Estate Tax in the United States," https://en.wikipedia.org/wiki/Estate_tax_in_the_United_States.

(46) Patrick Fleenor, "A History and Overview of Estate Taxes in the United States," Tax Foundation, January 1994, 1, https://files.taxfoundation.org/legacy/docs/f7c34848582a114133f90711b50b9a3a.pdf.

(47) "Policy Basics: The Federal Estate Tax," Center on Budget and Policy Priorities, last modified November 7, 2018, https://www.cbpp.org/research/federal-tax/policy-basics-the-federal-estate-tax.

(48) Darien B. Jacobson, Brian G. Raub, and Barry W. Johnson, "The Estate Tax: Ninety Years and Counting," IRS, 124–25, https://www.irs.gov/pub/irs-soi/ninetyestate.pdf.

(49) "Policy Basics."

(50) Jacobson, Raub, and Johnson, "The Estate Tax"; see also "Fact Sheet: The Estate (Inheritance) Tax," Americans for Tax Fairness, https://americansfortaxfairness.org/tax-fairness-briefing-booklet/fact-sheet-the-estate-inheritance-tax/.

(51) Laura Feiveson and John Sabelhaus, "How Does Intergenerational Wealth Transmission Affect Wealth Concentration?," *FEDS Notes*, Federal Reserve, June 1, 2018, https://www.federalreserve.gov/econres/notes/feds-notes/how-does-intergenerational-wealth-transmission-affect-wealth-concentration-20180601.htm.

(51a) Robert Bellafiore, "Tax Expenditures Before and After the Tax Cuts and Jobs Act," Tax Foundation, December 2018, 2, https://taxfoundation.org/tax-expenditures-pre-post-tcja/.

(51b)"What Is the Difference between a Tax Deduction and a Tax Credit?," H&R Block, https://www.hrblock.com/tax-center/filing/credits/difference-between-tax-deduction-and-tax-credit/.

(51c) Bellafiore, "Tax Expenditures Before and After," 4.
(51d) Ibid., 9.
(51e) Ibid., 7.

(51f) Ibid., 11.

(52) For a breakdown of credits by economic sector and industry, see "Tax Expenditures," Office of Tax Analysis, US Department of the Treasury, October 19, 2018, https://home.treasury.gov/system/files/131/Tax-Expenditures-FY2020.pdf. These corporate credits and deductions in the TCJA are in addition to the overall reductions of corporate tax rates. This overview does not detail with the multiple credits to specific industries. For example, large credits are provided to the energy industry for exploration. Each of the corporate deductions contributes to corporate profits and wealth concentration.

(52a) Christina Majaski, "What Are the Differences between Mergers and Acquisitions?," Investopedia, https://www.investopedia.com/ask/answers/021815/what-difference-between-merger-and-acquisition.asp.

(52b) "Types of Mergers," CFI, https://corporatefinanceinstitute.com/resources/knowledge/deals/types-of-mergers/.

(52c) "15 Biggest Mergers and Acquisitions of the Decade (2010–2019)," Mirror Review https://www.mirrorreview.com/15-biggest-mergers-and-acquisitions-of-the-decade-2010-2019/.

(52d) Bruce A. Blonigen and Justin R. Pierce, "Mergers May Be Profitable, but Are They Good for the Economy?," *Harvard Business Review*, November 15, 2016, https://hbr.org/2016/11/mergers-may-be-profitable-but-are-they-good-for-the-economy.

(52e) abiggs27, "The Reasons Why the Government Might Support or Intervene in Takeovers or Mergers," *BUSS 4* (blog), May 10, 2012, http://aston-buss4.blogspot.com/2012/05/6-reasons-why-government-might-support.html.

(52f) "About the FTC," Federal Trade Commission, https://www.ftc.gov/about-ftc.

(52g) Ibid.

(53) "History of Federal Minimum Wage Rates under the Fair Labor Standards Act, 1938–2009," Wage and Hour Division, US Department of Labor, https://www.dol.gov/agencies/whd/minimum-wage/history/chart.

(54) Annalyn Kurtz, Tal Yellin, and Will Houp, "The US Minimum Wage through the Years," line chart, CNN, April 9, 2019, https://www.cnn.com/interactive/2019/business/us-minimum-wage-by-year/index.html.

(55) Ernie Tedeschi, "Americans Are Seeing Highest Minimum Wage in History (Without Federal Help)," Upshot, *New York Times*, April 24, 2019, https://www.nytimes.com/2019/04/24/upshot/why-america-may-already-have-its-highest-minimum-wage.html.

(56) Jeffrey M. Jones, "As Labor Day Turns 125, Union Approval near 50-Year High," Gallup, August 28, 2019, https://news.gallup.com/poll/265916/labor-day-turns-125-union-approval-near-year-high.aspx; Drew DeSilver, "Most Americans View Unions Favorably, Though Few Workers Belong

to One," *Fact Tank*, Pew Research Center, August 30, 2018, https://www.pewresearch.org/fact-tank/2018/08/30/union-membership-2/
.

(57) *Wikipedia*, s.v. "Labor Unions in the United States," https://en.wikipedia.org/wiki/Labor_unions_in_the_United_States; see also Quoctrung Bui, "50 Years of Shrinking Union Membership, In One Map," interactive map, NPR, February 23, 2015, https://www.npr.org/sections/money/2015/02/23/385843576/50-years-of-shrinking-union-membership-in-one-map.

(58) See, for example, William E. Fulmer, "Step by Step through a Union Campaign," *Harvard Business Review*, July 1981, https://hbr.org/1981/07/step-by-step-through-a-union-campaign.

(59) Weeks, John Robert (2015-01-01). Population : an introduction to concepts and issues (Twelfth ed.). Boston, MA: Cenage

(60) Ibid.

(61) *Lexico*, s.v. "Discrimination," https://www.lexico.com/en/definition/discrimination.

(62) Ibram X. Kendi, The Civil Rights Act Was a Victory Against Racism. But Racists Also Won," *Washington Post*, July 2, 2017, https://www.washingtonpost.com/news/made-by-history/wp/2017/07/02/the-civil-rights-act-was-a-victory-against-racism-but-racists-also-won/?utm_term=.2cab574ffcaf.

(63) See for example, Wendy Sawyer and Peter Wagner, "Mass Incarceration: The Whole Pie 2019," Prison Policy Initiative, March 19, 2019, https://www.prisonpolicy.org/reports/pie2019.html; Vincent Schiraldi, "Parole and Probation Have Grown Far Beyond the Resources Allocated to Support Them," *Conversation*, August 16,2018, http://theconversation.com/parole-and-probation-have-grown-far-beyond-resources-allocated-to-support-them-98372; Erinn J. Herberman, PhD, and Thomas P. Bonczar, "Probation and Parole in the United States, 2013," Bureau of Justice Statistics, US Department of Justice, last modified January 21, 2015, https://www.bjs.gov/content/pub/pdf/ppus13.pdf. There are numerous laws in place, but are these laws enforced? Are there laws that are not enforced? Are there laws enforced that result in discriminatory practices?

(64) See Nancy J. Burke, PhD, et al., "Theorizing Social Context: Rethinking Behavioral Theory," *Health, Education, and Behavior* 36, no. 5 (October 2009), https://www.ncbi.nlm.nih.gov/pubmed/19805791.

(65) Ibid., 6.

(66) Pierre Bourdieu, *Outline of a Theory of Practice* (Cambridge: Cambridge University Press, 1977).

(67) Milliken v. Bradley, 418 U.S. 717 (1974), https://www.law.cornell.edu/supremecourt/text/418/717.

(68) "Public and Private School Comparison," National Center for Education Statistics, https://nces.ed.gov/fastfacts/display.asp?id=55; see also "CPS Historical Time Series Tables on School Enrollment,"

(68a) US Census Bureau, https://www.census.gov/data/tables/time-series/demo/school-enrollment/cps-historical-time-series.html.

(69) "Public and Private School Comparison"; see also Stephen B. Broughman, Adam Rettig, and Jennifer Peterson, *Characteristics of Private Schools in the United States: Results From the 2015–16 Private School Universe Survey* (Washington, DC: US Department of Education, August 2017), https://nces.ed.gov/pubs2017/2017073.pdf. Private schools are not administered by the government but by another organization. With the many changes in education, funding for private schools comes from a variety of sources, including governmental funds.

SUMMARY AND CONCLUSION: SPECIFIC CHANGES

(70) "FAQ About Private Schools," Council for American Private Education, https://www.capenet.org/facts.html.

(71) Some might raise the issue of facilities cost, but since the number of students would be roughly the same, additional facilities would probably not be required.

(72) See, for example, Laura Hoxworth, "Understanding the Benefits of School Diversity in the Majority-Minority Age," *UVA Today,* University of Virginia, September 6, 2018, https://news.virginia.edu/content/understanding-benefits-school-diversity-majority-minority-age.

(73) Melinda D. Anderson, "The Resurgence of Single-Sex Education: The Benefits and Limitations of Schools That Segregate Based on Gender, *Atlantic,* December 22, 2015, https://www.theatlantic.com/education/archive/2015/12/the-resurgence-of-single-sex-education/421560/.

(74) "The Federal Role in Education," US Department of Education, https://www2.ed.gov/about/overview/fed/role.html.

(75) Paul Hill, "Rethinking the State Role in Education," CRPE, February 13, 2014, https://www.crpe.org/thelens/rethinking-state-role-education.

(76) See, for example, Kimberly Amadeo, "Income Inequality in America," Balance, https://www.thebalance.com/income-inequality-in-america-3306190.

(77) Michael D. Tanner, "The Success Sequence—and What It Leaves Out," CATO Unbound, May 9, 2018, https://www.cato-unbound.org/2018/05/09/michael-d-tanner/success-sequence-what-it-leaves-out.

(78) Sendhil Mullainathan and Eldar Shafir, *Scarcity: Why Having Too Little Means So Much* (New York: Times Books, 2013).

(79) Ibid., 155.

(80) Ibid., 4.

(81) Ibid., 47.

(82) Ibid.

(83) Ibid. In another section of the book, they identify cognitive capacity as "how we process information and make decisions" and executive control as "a key resource that affects how impulsively we behave" (13).

(84) Joyce Cooper-Kahn, PhD, and Laurie Dietzel, PhD, "What Is Executive Functioning?," LD Online, http://www.ldonline.org/article/29122/. Originally published in *Late, Lost, and Unprepared: A Parents' Guide to Helping Children with Executive Functioning* (Bethesda: Woodbine House, 2008), 9–14.

(85) See also Abhijit V. Banerjee and Esther Duflo, *Poor Economics: A Radical Rethinking of the Way to Fight Global Poverty* (New York: Public Affairs, 2011). See especially the "Foreword" and the section "In Place of a Sweeping Conclusion." Banerjee and Duflo offer a theory similar and related to that of Mullainathan and Shafir based to a large degree on behavioral economics.

(86) Charles Karelis, *The Persistence of Poverty: Why the Economics of the Well-Off Can't Help the Poor* (New Haven: Yale University Press, 2007).

(87) Ibid.

(88) Heather Seggel, "Money on My Mind: On Poverty," Toast, January 15, 2015, http://the-toast. net/2015/01/15/money-on-my-mind-poverty/.

(89) Ramani Durvasula, PhD, "What Can Behavioral Economics Tell Us About Depletion and Decision Making?," *SES Indicator,* American Psychological Association, November 2014, http:// www.apa.org/pi/ses/resources/indicator/2014/11/behavioral-economics.aspx; see also Lucy Barnes, Peter Hall, and Rosemary C.R. Taylor, "The Social Sources of the Health Gradient: A Cross-National Analysis," July 20, 2010, http://www.people.fas.harvard.edu/~phall/Gradient.pdf. The authors of the latter piece put it another way: "Those who confront more difficult life challenges or bring fewer capabilities to them will experience higher levels of stress, anxiety, anger and frustration" (6). They also say that these levels are acerbated by a lower social status.

(90) "Taxes," line chart and tables, Gallup, https://news.gallup.com/poll/1714/taxes.aspx.

(91) Neil Gilbert, "Prosperity, Not Upward Mobility, Is What Matters," *Atlantic,* January 5, 2017, https://www.theatlantic.com/business/archive/2017/01/prosperity-upward-mobility/511925/; see also the "Perceptions of Poverty" section in this book.

PART IV: SUMMARY AND CONCLUSIONS

SUMMARY AND CONCLUSION

The goals of this book were 1) to provide an understanding of inequality, mobility, and poverty (IMP) in the United States, viewed as part of the US social order, and 2) to suggest changes that would decrease inequality, increase mobility, and decrease poverty. The US social order is the result of patterns of powers operating together in the ideological, economic, political/governmental, military/police, and voluntary/religious realms. Major elements of this order were identified as causing current IMP patterns. With this understanding, a number of actions, which would result in changes to this order, were proposed. At the same time, increased individual responsibility was also called for.

While the changes offered here are modest, they will be difficult to implement, and they will take time to have their intended effects. They are not designed to change the capitalistic, mixed-economy system of the United States. If implemented, though, the changes will improve the overall US social order. While wealth concentration will decrease, more wealth will be created and more broadly shared. More Americans will be able to contribute to economic growth, as well as participate in this growth.

These changes are consistent with the core US ideology, yes, but they will be challenging to enact because they call for adjustments in the way powers operate in the United States—adjustments that those who currently hold power will oppose.

The argument in support of the importance and value of changes to social patterns begins with a basic position that societies exist to meet human needs. To meet these needs, societies require order. This order is created and maintained by powers operating throughout society. Through the society's socialization processes and its use of power, a society transmits order to its members and inculcates this order into individual identities.

The United States, like other societies, has clear patterns of ideological, economic, political/governmental, military/police, and voluntary/religious order, yet US social patterns are unique. Powers operating in multiple sectors establish stable patterns of behavior that are consistent with and supporting of the patterns of other sectors. They act together to develop the American way of life.

US ideology exerts overarching powers, identifying what is desired and what ideals should be pursued. It provides a variety of critical influences that direct Americans' behavior—influences that establish societal and personal goals and identify acceptable and unacceptable behaviors.

The US economic system consists of powers that affect not only physical survival but a wide array of other criteria used in assessing one's societal position. The US economy is clearly enmeshed in the global economy. In the United States, the influence of private property is a basic foundation, and money is the common vehicle used to transfer property. Property exercises influence through the US system of capitalism, a "mixed economy" in which the general principals of capitalism are implemented but with government playing a strong role. Corporations, too, play an important role in the US mixed economy. Major corporations continue to grow and exert ever-increasing power. Among corporations, financial corporations wield an increasing influence by controlling the flow of money. Banks and shadow banks, along with insurance companies, are the major financial institutions.

While strongly influencing the direction of the economy, the government's influence, and power, extends beyond the economic realm. Based in the US Constitution, US laws draw their legitimacy and authority from the fact that those who enact laws are chosen by the citizens. Laws are then enacted at the federal, state, and local levels of government. These laws and regulations then influence the behavior of Americans in almost all aspects of their daily lives.

From the power provided by the US Constitution and state constitutions, the federal government, states, and local jurisdictions establish laws and deploy police and military to enforce these laws.

SUMMARY AND CONCLUSION

Although law-enforcement personnel are circumscribed by law, they have great discretion in exercising their power in concrete situations, using coercion up to and including death. A major component of military and police powers is deterrence (i.e., the awareness that action will be taken if laws are violated). A force of 4.5 million individuals in the military and law enforcement influences and maintains social order, supported in their efforts by courts, jails and prisons, and private security.

The voluntary sector also employs a significant influence in the United States. Employees and volunteers in nonprofit organizations total over 80 million Americans. The voluntary sector is large in terms of size, finances, and employed individuals. Americans voluntarily join with others and provide their money and time to address needs or achieve goals. Most voluntary organizations that continue to exist obtain federal and state tax-exempt status. These organizations must meet purposes that are designated in the tax code (and the laws of the state and country) so that most contributions to them are tax exempt. Voluntary associations have a special place in the minds and hearts of their members and other supporters, especially religious organizations.

Ideological, economic, political/governmental, military/police, and voluntary/religious institutions exercise their powers. While separately identifiable, their powers most often work in conjunction. For example, in the United States, an individual who makes a lot of money and/or is wealthy, has a high social status, hires security guards, influences elections, gives large amounts to charity, and serves as a deacon of a church will be regarded differently than a lower-income person who makes little income, has no wealth, depends on the public police force, just has time to vote, gives little to charity, volunteers with a group that feeds the hungry, and occasionally attends church.

Within this broad US social order are patterns of inequality, lack of mobility, and poverty. Current patterns in these areas can be traced back at least fifty years. Although there is some debate regarding income inequality, the concentration of wealth and its pattern of uneven distribution are generally accepted. In addition to income, differentiations are found in education and employment, as well as in certain types of ascribed status, such as sex, race, birthplace, and sexual orientation.

Five major causes of inequality, or sources of power, that are part of the US order's patterns directly impacting IMP were identified:

- Concentration of wealth
- Status, social, and spatial segregations
- Skill gaps and low quality of education
- Individual responsibility
- Luck

While nothing can be done about luck, steps can be taken to change the other patterns. Change is possible and can be implemented in ways that are consistent with US ideology. In fact, increased emphasis can be placed on elements within US ideology currently not receiving great attention, such as fairness, opportunity, merit, and personal responsibility.

Using these values, actions can be taken to change IMP:

- Reduce wealth concentration
- Reduce ascribed status and discrimination
- Enhance the educational and skill development of all
- Increase personal responsibility

Based on the data, there is a high confidence in the effectiveness of changes in these areas. Americans seek changes to prominent causes of IMP patterns rooted in the powers of the US social order.

In each of the four areas, specific changes are proposed. These specific changes, however, are offered with less confidence. Their selection is based on analysis of current information, but other options are possible.

In the preface, some guiding principles were put forth:

- Don't be seduced by the obvious
- Be skeptical of promised miracles, the simplistic "silver bullet"
- Accept the complexity of major issues
- Be honest about what is known, what is still unknown, and what may never be known

This analysis does not propose miracles. Rather, it accepts the complexity of IMP and tries to lay out what is known, even when there is much that is still unknown.

It is with this recognition that these specific changes are offered:

- Reduce wealth inequality
  - Slightly raise corporate taxes with some additional increases to financial corporations
  - Tax all individual income as ordinary income
  - Extend Social Security tax to all income levels
  - Increase the inheritance tax by lowering the amount that can be taxed and the amount that is exempted
  - Increase the minimum wage
  - Support worker organizations
- Reduce ascribed status
  - Increase integration of K-12 schools
- Enhance educational and skill development
  - Provide equalization of funding for K-12 schooling
  - Put in place postsecondary training options
- Increase personal responsibility
  - Promote nonblaming, ongoing encouragement of personal responsibility
  - Recognize and eliminate the barriers to taking responsible actions

All these recommendations are difficult. They're not simple but not impossible. Each will require concerted effort and time, and each will be opposed by those with power who wish to maintain the status quo. They are proposed with the belief that these changes can go a long way in creating a more equal society, a more mobile society, and a society with less poverty.

It would be satisfying to conclude that, with absolute certainty, the proposals offered are the best and only path. However, if one is to be true to the principles of this analysis, such a conclusion is not possible. Even so, the solutions are based on what is known and present a feasible path.

SELECTED BIBLIOGRAPHY

Abiggs27. "The Reasons Why the Government Might Support or Intervene in Takeovers or Mergers." *BUSS 4* (blog), May 10, 2012. http://aston-buss4.blogspot.com/2012/05/6-reasons-why-government-might-support.html.

Amadeo, Kimberly. "Income Inequality in America." Balance. https://www.thebalance.com/income-inequality-in-america-3306190.

Amaral, Pedro. "Monetary Policy and Inequality." *Economic Commentary,* January 10, 2017. https://www.clevelandfed.org/newsroom-and-events/publications/economic-commentary/2017-economic-commentaries/ec-201701-monetary-policy-and-inequality.aspx.

ASPE. "U.S. Federal Poverty Guidelines Used to Determine Financial Eligibility for Certain Federal Programs." Last modified January 11, 2019. https://aspe.hhs.gov/poverty-guidelines.

Auten, Gerald, and David Splinter. "Income Inequality in the United States: Using Tax Data to Measure Long-term Trends." Working paper, on David Splinter's personal website, December 20, 2019. http://davidsplinter.com/AutenSplinter-Tax_Data_and_Inequality.pdf.

Balestra, Carlotta, and Richard Tonkin. "Inequalities in Household Wealth across OECD Countries: Evidence from the OECD Wealth Distribution

Database." Working paper no. 88, OECD, June 20, 2018. https://www.oecd.org/officialdocuments/publicdisplaydocumentpdf/?cote=SDD/DOC(2018)1&docLanguage=En.

Bellafiore, Robert. "Tax Expenditures Before and After the Tax Cuts and Jobs Act." Tax Foundation, December 2018. https://taxfoundation.org/tax-expenditures-pre-post-tcja/.

Banerjee, Abhijit V., and Esther Duflo. *Good Economics for Hard Times.* New York: Public Affairs, 2019.
———. *Poor Economics: A Radical Rethinking of the Way to Fight Global Poverty.* New York: Public Affairs, 2011.

Bénabou, Roland, and Efe A. Ok. "Social Mobility and the Demand for Redistribution: The POUM Hypothesis." *Quarterly Journal of Economics* (May 2001): 447–87. https://www.princeton.edu/~rbenabou/papers/d8zkmee3.pdf.

Berger, James. "This Is the Media's Real Bias—Pro-business, Pro-corporate, Pro-CEO." Salon, October 30, 2015. https://www.salon.com/2015/10/30/this_is_the_medias_real_bias_pro_business_pro_corporate_pro_ceo/.

Bivens, Josh. "The Top 1 Percent's Share of Income from Wealth Has Been Rising for Decades." Economic Policy Institute, April 23, 2014. https://www.epi.org/publication/top-1-percents-share-income-wealth-rising/.

Bourdieu, Pierre. *Outline of a Theory of Practice.* Cambridge: Cambridge University Press, 1977.

Brenner, Philip S., Richard T. Serpe, and Sheldon Stryker. "The Causal Ordering of Prominence and Salience in Identity Theory: An Empirical Examination." *Social Psychology Quarterly* 77, no. 3 (September 2014): 231–52. https://www.ncbi.nlm.nih.gov/pmc/articles/PMC4896744/.

Brink, Lindsey, and Steven M. Teles. *The Captured Economy: How the Powerful Enrich Themselves, Slow Down Growth, and Increase Income Inequality.* New York: Oxford University Press, 2017.

Bui, Quoctrung. "50 Years of Shrinking Union Membership, In One Map." Interactive map. NPR, February 23, 2015. https://www.npr.org/sections/money/2015/02/23/385843576/50-years-of-shrinking-union-membership-in-one-map.

Burke, Nancy J., Galen Joseph, Rena J. Pasick, and Judith C. Barker. "Theorizing Social Context: Rethinking Behavioral Theory." *Health, Education,*

and Behavior 36, no. 5 (October 2009). https://www.ncbi.nlm.nih.gov/
pubmed/19805791.

Carter, Prudence L., and Sean F. Reardon. "Inequality Matters." William T.
Grant Foundation. Stanford University, September 2014. https://ed.stanford.edu/
sites/default/files/inequalitymatters.pdf.

Center on Budget and Policy Priorities. "Policy Basics: The Federal Estate Tax."
Last modified November 7, 2018. https://www.cbpp.org/research/federal-tax/
policy-basics-the-federal-estate-tax.

Chalfin, Aaron, and Justin McCrary. "Criminal Deterrence: A Review of the
Literature." *Journal of Economic Literature* 55, no. 1 (March 2017): 5–48. https://
www.aeaweb.org/articles?id=10.1257/jel.20141147.

**Chaudry, Ajay, Christopher Wimer, Suzanne Macartney, Lauren Frohlich,
Colin Campbell, Kendall Swenson, Don Oellerich, and Susan Hauan.** *Poverty in
the United States: 50-Year Trends and Safety Net Impacts.* Washington, DC: ASPE,
March 2016. https://aspe.hhs.gov/system/files/pdf/154286/50YearTrends.pdf.

Chung, Heidi. "The Richest 1% Own 50% of Stocks Held by American
Households." Yahoo! Finance, January 17, 2019. https://finance.yahoo.com/news/
the-richest-1-own-50-of-stocks-held-by-american-households-150758595.html.

Cole, Nicki Lisa. "What Is Social Order in Sociology?" ThoughtCo., last
modified September 30, 2019. https://www.thoughtco.com/social-order-
definition-4138213.

Columbus, Louis. "The Future of Manufacturing Technologies." *Forbes*, April
15, 2018. https://www.forbes.com/sites/louiscolumbus/2018/04/15/the-future-of-
manufacturing-technologies-2018/#187ca5d72995.

Conger, Rand D., and Shannon J. Dogan. "Social Class and Socialization in
Families." *In Handbook of Socialization: Theory and Research*, edited by Joan
E. Grusec and Paul D. Hastings, 433–60. New York: Guilford Press, 2015.

Congressional Budget Office. "The Distribution of Household Income and
Federal Taxes, 2013." June 2016. https://www.cbo.gov/publication/51361.
———. "Raise the Tax Rates on Long-Term Capital Gains and Qualified
Dividends by 2 Percentage Points and Adjust Tax Brackets." Table. https://www.
cbo.gov/budget-options/2018/54788.
———. "Tax Carried Interest as Ordinary Income." December 13, 2018. https://
www.cbo.gov/budget-options/2018/54795.

Cooper, Michael, John McClelland, James Pearce, Richard Prisinzano, Joseph Sullivan, Danny Yagan, Owen Zidar, and Eric Zwick. "Business in the United States: Who Owns It and How Much Tax Do They Pay?" Working paper series no. 104, Office of Tax Analysis, October 2015. https://www.treasury.gov/resource-center/tax-policy/tax-analysis/Documents/WP-104.pdf.

Corak, Miles. "Income Inequality, Equality of Opportunity, and Intergenerational Mobility." Discussion paper series no. 7520, IZA, July 2013. http://ftp.iza.org/dp7520.pdf.
———. "Social Mobility and Social Institutions in Comparison: Australia, Canada, the United Kingdom, the United States." PowerPoint. Sutton Trust/Carnegie Foundation seminar on social mobility, London, May 21/22, 2012. On Miles Corak's personal website. https://milescorak.files.wordpress.com/2012/05/social_mobility_summit_v3.pdf.

Cranston, Maurice. "Ideology." In *Encyclopedia Britannica Online*. https://www.britannica.com/topic/ideology-society#ref12154.

Davidai, Shai, and Thomas Gilovich. "How Should We Think About Americans' Beliefs About Economic Mobility?" *Judgment and Decision Making* 13, no. 3 (May 2018): 297–304. http://journal.sjdm.org/17/17911b/jdm17911b.pdf.

Davis, Jonathan, and Bhash Mazumder. "The Decline in Intergenerational Mobility after 1980." Working paper no. 2017-05, Federal Reserve Bank of Chicago, last modified January 19, 2019. https://www.chicagofed.org/publications/working-papers/2017/wp2017-05.

Deaux, Kay. "Social Identity." In *Encyclopedia of Women and Gender*, edited by Judith Worell. Cambridge: Academic Press, 2001.

DeSilver, Drew. "The Many Ways to Measure Income Inequality." *Fact Tank*. Pew Research Center, September 22, 2015. http://www.pewresearch.org/fact-tank/2015/09/22/the-many-ways-to-measure-economic-inequality/.
Dungan, Adrian. "Individual Income Tax Shares, 2015." *IRS Statistics of Income Bulletin*. IRS, 2018. https://www.irs.gov/pub/irs-soi/soi-a-ints-id1801.pdf.

Elwell, Craig K. "The Distribution of Household Income and the Middle Class." Congressional Research Service, March 10, 2014. https://fas.org/sgp/crs/misc/RS20811.pdf.

Fallatah, Rodwan Hashim Mohammed, and Jawad Syed. "A Critical Review of Maslow's Hierarchy of Needs." In *Employee Motivation in Saudi Arabia*, 19–59. London: Palgrave Macmillan, 2018. https://link.springer.com/book/10.1007/978-3-319-67741-5#about.

Federal Reserve. "Changes in U.S. Family Finances from 2013 to 2016: Evidence from the Survey of Consumer Finances." *Federal Reserve Bulletin* 103, no. 3 (September 2017). https://www.federalreserve.gov/publications/files/scf17.pdf.

Federal Reserve Bank of St. Louis. "Corporate Profits after Tax with Inventory Valuation Adjustment (IVA) and Capital Consumption Adjustment (CCAdj) (CPATAX)." Line chart. FRED Economic Data. https://fred.stlouisfed.org/series/CPATAX.
―――. "Net Corporate Dividend Payments." Line chart. FRED Economic Data. https://fred.stlouisfed.org/series/B056RC1A027NBEA.
―――. "Table 1.12. National Income by Type of Income: Annual." FRED Economic Data. 2018. https://fred.stlouisfed.org/release/tables?rid=53&eid=42133.
―――. "Table 1.16. Sources and Uses of Private Enterprise Income: Annual." FRED Economic Data. 2018. https://fred.stlouisfed.org/release/tables?eid=42395&rid=53.
―――. "Total Assets, All Commercial Banks." Line chart. FRED Economic Data. https://fred.stlouisfed.org/series/TLAACBW027SBOG.

Feiveson, Laura, and John Sabelhaus. "How Does Intergenerational Wealth Transmission Affect Wealth Concentration?" FEDS Notes. Federal Reserve, June 1, 2018. https://www.federalreserve.gov/econres/notes/feds-notes/how-does-intergenerational-wealth-transmission-affect-wealth-concentration-20180601.htm.

Financial Stability Board. *Global Shadow Banking Monitoring Report* 2016. Basel, Switzerland: May 10, 2017. https://www.fsb.org/wp-content/uploads/global-shadow-banking-monitoring-report-2016.pdf.
Fleenor, Patrick. "A History and Overview of Estate Taxes in the United States." Tax Foundation, January 1994. https://files.taxfoundation.org/legacy/docs/f7c34848582a114133f90711b50b9a3a.pdf.

Fleischer, Victor. "Two and Twenty: Taxing Partnership Profits in Private Equity Funds." Legal studies research paper series, working paper no. 06-27, NYU Law Review, August 2, 2007. https://www.researchgate.net/publication/228213316_Two_and_Twenty_Taxing_Partnership_Profits_in_Private_Equity_Funds.
―――. "How a Carried Interest Tax Could Raise $180 Billion." *DealBook* (blog). New York Times, June 5, 2015. https://www.nytimes.com/2015/06/06/business/dealbook/how-a-carried-interest-tax-could-raise-180-billion.html.

Flowers, Andrew. "Big Business Is Getting Bigger." FiveThirtyEight, May 18, 2015. https://fivethirtyeight.com/features/big-business-is-getting-bigger/.

Fox, Liana, Christopher Wimer, Irwin Garfinkel, Neeraj Kaushal, JaeHyun Nam, and Jane Waldfogel. "Trends in Deep Poverty from 1968 to 2011: The Influence of Family Structure, Employment Patterns, and the Safety Net." *Russell Sage Foundation Journal of the Social Sciences* 1, no. 1 (November 2015): 14–34. https://muse.jhu.edu/article/603797/pdf.

Gale, Thomas. "Constrained Choice." In Encyclopedia.com. Last modified 2008. https://www.encyclopedia.com/social-./applied-and-social-sciences-magazines/constrained-choice.

Garber, Julie. "What Is an Inheritance Tax?" Balance, last modified October 4, 2019. https://www.thebalance.com/definition-of-inheritance-tax-3505560.

Geloso, Vincent, Phillip Magness, John Moore, and Philip Schlosser. "How Pronounced Is the U-Curve? Revisiting Income Inequality in the United States, 1917–1945." SSRN, February 4, 2018. http://dx.doi.org/10.2139/ssrn.2985234.

Gerharz, George. *Show Me the Cash: Engaging Families to Help Very Poor Children Succeed.* Caritas Communications, 2018.

Gilbert, Neil. "Prosperity, Not Upward Mobility, Is What Matters." *Atlantic,* January 5, 2017. https://www.theatlantic.com/business/archive/2017/01/prosperity-upward-mobility/511925/.

Giridharadas, Anand. *Winners Take All: The Elite Charade of Changing the World.* New York: Alfred A. Knopf, 2018.
Gordon, Robert J. "Misperceptions About the Magnitude and Timing of Changes in American Income Inequality." Working paper series no. 15351, NBER, September 2009. https://www.nber.org/papers/w15351.pdf.

Gordon, Robert J., and Ian Dew-Becker. "Controversies about the Rise of American Inequality: A Survey." Working paper series no. 13982, NBER, May 2008. http://www.nber.org/papers/w13982.pdf.

Greenwood, Robin, and David Scharfstein. "The Growth of Finance." *Journal of Economic Perspectives* 27, no. 2 (Spring 2013): 3–28. https://www.aeaweb.org/issues/303.

Grusky, David B. "The Past, Present, and Future of Social Inequality." In *Social Stratification: Class, Race, and Gender in Sociological Perspective,* 2nd ed., 3–51. Boulder: Westview Press, 2001. http://homepage.ntu.edu.tw/~khsu/mobile/sup2.pdf.

Guidetti, Giovanni, and Boike Rehbein. "Theoretical Approaches to Inequality in Economics and Sociology: A Preliminary Assessment." *Transcience* 5, no. 1 (2014). https://www2.hu-berlin.de/transcience/Vol5_No1_2014_1_15.pdf.

Harding, Jennifer, and E. Deidre Pribram. "The Power of feeling: Locating Emotions in Culture." *European Journal of Culture Studies* 5, no. 4 (November 2002): 407–26. https://journals.sagepub.com/doi/10.1177/1364942002005004294.

Haskins, Ron. *Testimony of Ron Haskins, Brookings Institution and Annie E. Casey Foundation, Before the Subcommittee on Human Resources, Committee on Ways and Means, US House of Representatives, Hearing on Challenges Facing Low-Income Individuals and Families.* Washington, DC, February 11, 2015. https://www.brookings.edu/wp-content/uploads/2016/06/2-11-15-lowincome-families-haskins-testimony.pdf.

Hauser, Oliver P., and Michael I. Norton "(Mis)perceptions of Inequality." Special issue on inequality and social class. *Current Opinion in Psychology* 18 (December 2017): 21–25. https://www.hbs.edu/ris/Publication%20Files/Hauser%20%20Norton%20(2017)_5b0d07bb-f8d6-4edc-bddc-434ef6cd930e.pdf.

Herberman, Erinn J., and Thomas P. Bonczar. "Probation and Parole in the United States, 2013." Bureau of Justice Statistics. US Department of Justice, last modified January 21, 2015. https://www.bjs.gov/content/pub/pdf/ppus13.pdf.
Hong, Sungki, and Terry S. Moon. "Capital Gains Taxation and Investment Dynamics." Working paper series no. 2018-031F, Federal Reserve Bank of St. Louis, October 2018. https://doi.org/10.20955/wp.2018.031.

Hoxworth, Laura. "Understanding the Benefits of School Diversity in the Majority-Minority Age." *UVA Today.* University of Virginia, September 6, 2018. https://news.virginia.edu/content/understanding-benefits-school-diversity-majority-minority-age.

International Monetary Fund. "Globalization: A Brief Overview." May 2008. https://www.imf.org/external/np/exr/ib/2008/053008.htm.

Irani, Rustom M., Rajkamal Iyer, Ralf R. Meisenzahl, and José-Luis Peydró. "The Rise of Shadow Banking: Evidence from Capital Regulation." Finance and Economics Discussion Series (FEDS). Federal Reserve, April 2018. https://www.federalreserve.gov/econres/feds/files/2018039pap.pdf.

IRS. "Sourcing of Income." PowerPoint. Last modified April 12, 2017. https://www.irs.gov/pub/int_practice_units/ftc_c_10_02_05.pdf.

Jones, Jeffrey M. "As Labor Day Turns 125, Union Approval near 50-Year High." Gallup, August 28, 2019. https://news.gallup.com/poll/265916/labor-day-turns-125-union-approval-near-year-high.aspx.

Jullieflavia. "How the School Performs the Function of Socialization." Blog post via Kenyaplex, November 3, 2012. https://www.kenyaplex.com/resources/5742-how-the-school-performs-the-function-of-socialization.aspx.

Karelis, Charles. The Persistence of Poverty: Why the Economics of the Well-Off Can't Help the Poor. New Haven: Yale University Press, 2007.

Kochhar, Rakesh, and Anthony Cilluffo. "How Wealth Inequality Has Changed in the U.S. Since the Great Recession, by Race, Ethnicity and Income." *Fact Tank.* Pew Research Center, November 1, 2107. http://www.pewresearch.org/fact-tank/2017/11/01/how-wealth-inequality-has-changed-in-the-u-s-since-the-great-recession-by-race-ethnicity-and-income/.

Kreps, David M., and Evan L. Porteus. "Temporal Resolution of Uncertainty and Dynamic Choice Theory." *Econometrica* 46, no. 1 (January 1978): 185–200. https://www.jstor.org/stable/1913656?seq=1.

Levine, Linda. "An Analysis of the Distribution of Wealth Across Households, 1989–2010." Congressional Research Service, July 17, 2012. https://fas.org/sgp/crs/misc/RL33433.pdf.

Levine, Martin. "The Deserving and Undeserving Poor: A Persistent Frame with Consequences." *Nonprofit Quarterly,* June 23, 2018. https://nonprofitquarterly.org/the-deserving-and-undeserving-poor-a-persistent-frame-with-consequences/.

Lewis, Adam. "Donald Trump Pledges to Finally Address Carried Interest Loophole." PitchBook, May 21, 2019. https://pitchbook.com/news/articles/donald-trump-pledges-to-finally-address-carried-interest-loophole.

Lundeen, Andrew, and Kyle Pomerleau. "Corporations Make Up 5 Percent of Businesses but Earn 62 Percent of Revenues." Bar chart. Tax Foundation, November25, 2014. https://taxfoundation.org/corporations-make-5-percent-businesses-earn-62-percent-revenues/.

MacKechnie, Chris. "What Are the Duties of an Insurance Commissioner?" Career Trend, last modified September 26, 2017. https://bizfluent.com/list-6742445-duties-insurance-commissioner-.html.

Mann, Michael. *Sources of Social Power.* Vol. 1, *A History of Power from the Beginning to A.D. 1760.* New York: Cambridge University Press, 1986. https://uniteyouthdublin.files.wordpress.com/2015/01/the-sources-of-social-power-michael-mann.pdf.

Mathur, Aparna. "The U.S. Does Poorly on Yet Another Metric of

Economic Mobility." Forbes, July 16, 2018. https://www.forbes.com/sites/
aparnamathur/2018/07/16/the-u-s-does-poorly-on-yet-another-metric-of-
economic-mobility/?sh=3a1960766a7b.

McCarthy, Justin. "Six in Seven Americans Satisfied with Their Personal Lives."
Line charts. Gallup, February 5, 2019. https://news.gallup.com/poll/246326/six-
seven-americans-satisfied-personal-lives.aspx.

Merle, Renae. "What Is 'Carried Interest' and Why It Matters in the New GOP
Tax Bill." *Washington Post,* November 7, 2017. https://www.washingtonpost.com/
news/business/wp/2017/11/07/what-is-carried-interest-and-why-it-matters-in-
the-new-gop-tax-bill/?utm_term=.5e089785d168.

Meyer, Bruce D., and James X. Sullivan. "Annual Report on US Consumption
Poverty: 2016." AEI, September 13, 2017. https://www.aei.org/research-products/
report/annual-report-on-us-consumption-poverty-2016/.

Mirror Review. "15 Biggest Mergers and Acquisitions of the Decade (2010–
2019)." https://www.mirrorreview.com/15-biggest-mergers-and-acquisitions-of-
the-decade-2010-2019/.

Mullainathan, Sendhil, and Eldar Shafir. *Scarcity: Why Having Too Little Means
So Much.* New York: Times Books, 2013.

National Association of Insurance Commissioners. "2017 Report Card."
https://www.naic.org/state_report_cards/report_card_fl.pdf.

Newport, Frank. "Majority in U.S. Satisfied with Opportunity to Get Ahead."
Gallup, March 7, 2018. https://news.gallup.com/poll/228914/majority-satisfied-
opportunity-ahead.aspx.

Niehues, Judith. "Subjective Perceptions and Redistributive
Preferences: An International Comparison." Cologne Institute for
Economic Research, August 14, 2014. https://pdfs.semanticscholar.
org/1fa2/10b6340448329be06aca72950e7ad1105dcc.pdf.

OECD. "OECD Income Distribution Database (IDD): Gini, Poverty, Income,
Methods and Concepts." http://www.oecd.org/social/income-distribution-
database.htm.
———. "An Overview of Growing Income Inequalities in OECD Countries:
Main Findings." 2011. https://www.oecd.org/els/soc/49499779.pdf.
Pew Research Center. "Most Americans Point to Circumstances, Not Work Ethic,
for Why People Are Rich or Poor." March 2, 2020. https://www.pewresearch.org/
politics/2020/03/02/most-americans-point-to-circumstances-not-work-ethic-as-

reasons-people-are-rich-or-poor/.

———. "The Partisan Divide on Political Values Grows Even Wider." October 5, 2017. https://www.pewresearch.org/politics/2017/10/05/the-partisan-divide-on-political-values-grows-even-wider/.

———. "What Americans Say They Believe in God, What Do They Mean?" April 25, 2018. http://www.pewforum.org/2018/04/25/when-americans-say-they-believe-in-god-what-do-they-mean/.

Piketty, Thomas. *Capital in the Twenty-First Century.* Translated by Arthur Goldhammer. Cambridge: Belknap Press of Harvard University Press, 2014.

Rao, Venkatesh. "A Brief History of the Corporation: 1600 to 2100." *Ribbonfarm* (blog), June 8, 2011. https://www.ribbonfarm.com/2011/06/08/a-brief-history-of-the-corporation-1600-to-2100/.

Raven, Bertram H. "Bases of Power and the Power/Interaction Model of Interpersonal Influence." *Analyses of Social Issues and Public Policy* 8, no. 1 (2008): 1–22. http://psyc604.stasson.org/Raven.pdf.

Reich, Rob. *Just Giving: Why Philanthropy Is Failing Democracy and How It Can Do Better.* Princeton: Princeton University Press, 2018.

Reynolds, Alan. "Has US Income Inequality Really Increased?" Cato Institute, January 8, 2007. https://www.cato.org/publications/policy-analysis/has-us-income-inequality-really-increased.

Ridgeway, Cecilia L. "Why Status Matters for Inequality." *American Sociological Review* 79, no. 1 (2014): 1–16. https://www.asanet.org/sites/default/files/savvy/journals/ASR/Feb14ASRFeature.pdf.

Roberts, James. "Cronyism: Undermining Economic Freedom and Prosperity Around the World." Heritage Foundation, August 9, 2010. https://www.heritage.org/international-economies/report/cronyism-undermining-economic-freedom-and-prosperity-around-the.

Ross, Sean. "Financial Services: Sizing the Sector in the Global Economy." Investopedia. https://www.investopedia.com/ask/answers/030515/what-percentage-global-economy-comprised-financial-services-sector.asp.

Rudden, Jennifer. "Number of Merger and Acquisition Transactions in the United States in 2019 and 2020, by Deal Value." Bar Chart. Statista, October 15, 2020. https://www.statista.com/statistics/245977/number-of-munda-deals-in-the-united-states/.

SELECTED BIBLIOGRAPHY

Rummel, R. J. "The Fundamental Nature of Power." In *Understanding Conflict and War*. Vol. 2, The Conflict Helix. Beverly Hills: Sage Publications, 1976. https://www.hawaii.edu/powerkills/TCH.CHAP19.HTM.

Ryan, Camille L., and Kurt Bauman. "Educational Attainment in the United States: 2015." US Census Bureau, May 2016. https://www.census.gov/content/dam/Census/library/publications/2016/demo/p20-578.pdf.

Saez, Emmanuel, and Gabriel Zucman. "Wealth Inequality in the United States Since 1913." PowerPoint. University of Michigan, April 2015. http://fordschool.umich.edu/files/zucman-4-24-15.pdf.

Saunders-Scott, Molly, and Jennifer Gravelle. *International Comparisons of Corporate Income Tax Rates*. Washington, DC: CBO, March 2017. https://www.cbo.gov/system/files?file=115th-congress-2017-2018/reports/52419-internationaltaxratecomp.pdf.

Sawyer, Malcolm. "What Is Financialisation?" *International Journal of Political Economy* 42, no. 4 (2014). http://eprints.whiterose.ac.uk/82350/3/Sawyer.pdf.

Shokri, Mehdi. "What is Political Power? (Theory of Political Consciousness and Integrated Concept of Power)." *Arts and Social Sciences Journal* 8, no. 3 (May 2017). https://www.omicsonline.org/open-access/what-is-political-power-theory-of-political-consciousness-and-integrated-concept-of-power-2151-6200-1000269.php?aid=88804.

Shorrocks, Anthony, Jim Davies, and Rodrigo Lluberas. Research Institute: Global Wealth Report 2018. Zurich, Switzerland: Credit Suisse AG, October 2018. https://www.credit-suisse.com/corporate/en/research/research-institute/global-wealth-report.html.

Smeeding, Timothy, Robert Erickson, and Markus Jäntti, ed. *Persistence, Privilege, and Parenting: The Comparative Study of Intergenerational Mobility*. New York: Russel Sage Foundation, 2011.

Snyder, Glenn H. "Deterrence and Power." *Journal of Conflict Resolution* 4, no. 2 (June 1960): 163–78. https://journals.sagepub.com/doi/abs/10.1177/002200276000400201?journalCode=jcrb.

Stiglitz, Joseph E. *The Price of Inequality*. New York: W. W. Norton and Company, Inc., 2012.

Stone, Chad, Danilo Trisi, Arloc Sherman, and Jennifer Beltrán. "A Guide to Statistics on Historical Trends in Income Inequality." Center on Budget and Policy

Priorities, last modified August 21, 2019. http://www.cbpp.org/research/poverty-and-inequality/a-guide-to-statistics-on-historical-trends-in-income-inequality.

Tanner, Michael D. "The Success Sequence—and What It Leaves Out." *Cato Unbound,* May 9, 2018. https://www.cato-unbound.org/print-issue/2355.

Tedeschi, Ernie. "Americans Are Seeing Highest Minimum Wage in History (Without Federal Help)." Upshot. *New York Times,* April 24, 2019. https://www.nytimes.com/2019/04/24/upshot/why-america-may-already-have-its-highest-minimum-wage.html.

Toder, Eric. "1986 RIP: Different Tax Rates for Different Income Sources." *TaxVox* (blog). Tax Policy Center, May 26, 2018. https://www.taxpolicycenter.org/taxvox/1986-rip-different-tax-rates-different-income-sources.

Tomlinson, Kelli D. "An Examination of Deterrence Theory: Where Do We Stand?" *Federal Probation* 80, no. 3 (December 2016): 33–38. https://www.uscourts.gov/federal-probation-journal/2016/12/examination-deterrence-theory-where-do-we-stand.

Turak, August. "Is the American Dream Dead? The Four Inconvenient Truths Behind Income Inequality." *Forbes,* June 2, 2012. https://www.forbes.com/sites/augustturak/2012/07/02/is-the-american-dream-dead-the-four-inconvenient-truths-behind-income-inequality/?sh=6fc8b24d27e8.

US Bureau of Labor Statistics. "Annual Mean Wages by Typical Entry-Level Educational Requirement, May 2017." Table. Last modified March 30, 2018. https://www.bls.gov/oes/2017/may/education3.htm.
———. "Consumer Spending and U.S. Employment from the 2007–2009 Recession through 2022." Monthly Labor Review. October 2014. https://www.bls.gov/opub/mlr/2014/article/consumer-spending-and-us-employment-from-the-recession-through-2022.htm.
———. Standard Occupational Classification Structure. https://www.bls.gov/soc/2018/soc_structure_2018.pdf.

US Census Bureau. "American Indian and Alaska Native Heritage Month: November 2017." October 6, 2017. https://www.census.gov/content/dam/Census/newsroom/facts-for-features/2017/cb17-ff20.pdf.
———. "Educational Attainment in the United States: 2016." Tables. March 2017. https://www.census.gov/data/tables/2016/demo/education-attainment/cps-detailed-tables.html.
———. "HINC-02. Age of Householder-Households, by Total Money Income, Type of Household, Race and Hispanic Origin of Householder." https://www.

census.gov/data/tables/time-series/demo/income-poverty/cps-hinc/hinc-02.2016.html#par_textimage_10.

———. "Table 2. Poverty Status of People by Family Relationship, Race, and Hispanic Origin: 1959 to 2019." https://www.census.gov/data/tables/time-series/demo/income-poverty/historical-poverty-people.html.

US Department of the Treasury. "Tax Expenditures." Office of Tax Analysis, October 19, 2018. https://home.treasury.gov/system/files/131/Tax-Expenditures-FY2020.pdf.

Watson, Audrey L. "Employment Trends by Typical Entry-level Education Requirement." *Monthly Labor Review.* US Bureau of Labor Statistics, September 2017. https://doi.org/10.21916/mlr.2017.22.

Weber, Max. From Max Weber: *Essays in Sociology.* New York: Oxford University Press, 1958.

Weigand, Max. "Why Change Is So Hard: The Chemistry of Habits." Personal blog via Medium, November 4, 2017. https://medium.com/@MaxWeigand/why-change-is-so-hard-the-chemistry-of-habits-f0c226f00bff.

White House. "Table 2.1—Receipts by Source: 1934–2024." Office of Management and Budget. https://www.whitehouse.gov/omb/historical-tables/.

Wile, Rob. "The Richest 10% of Americans Now Own 84% of All Stocks." Money, December 19, 2017. http://money.com/money/5054009/stock-ownership-10-percent-richest/.

Winship, Scott. "Assessing Income Inequality, Mobility and Opportunity." Brookings, February 9, 2012. https://www.brookings.edu/testimonies/assessing-income-inequality-mobility-and-opportunity/.

———. "Making Sense of Inequality." Brookings, August 3, 2012. https://www.brookings.edu/opinions/making-sense-of-inequality/.

Wolff, Edward N. "Household Wealth Trends in the United States, 1962 to 2016: Has Middle Class Wealth Recovered?" Working paper no. 24085, NBER, November 2017. http://www.nber